George Phillips

A Letter by Mar Jacob, Bishop of Edessa, on Syriac Orthography

George Phillips

A Letter by Mar Jacob, Bishop of Edessa, on Syriac Orthography

ISBN/EAN: 9783337018962

Printed in Europe, USA, Canada, Australia, Japan

Cover: Foto ©ninafisch / pixelio.de

A LETTER

BY

MĀR JACOB, BISHOP OF EDESSA,

ON

SYRIAC ORTHOGRAPHY;

ALSO

A TRACT BY THE SAME AUTHOR,

AND

A DISCOURSE BY GREGORY BAR HEBRÆUS ON SYRIAC ACCENTS.

NOW EDITED, IN THE ORIGINAL SYRIAC, FROM MSS. IN THE BRITISH MUSEUM, WITH AN ENGLISH TRANSLATION AND NOTES,

BY

GEORGE PHILLIPS, D.D.,
PRESIDENT OF QUEENS' COLLEGE, CAMBRIDGE.

To which are added Appendices.

WILLIAMS AND NORGATE,
14, HENRIETTA STREET, COVENT GARDEN, LONDON;
AND 20, SOUTH FREDERICK STREET, EDINBURGH.

1869.

W. M. WATTS, 80, GRAY'S INN ROAD.

PREFACE.

The two MSS. of Mār Jacob, Bishop of Edessa, on Grammar, which are edited and translated in the following pages, form part of a Volume of the Nitrian Collection in the British Museum, marked Additional 12,178, and are said to be of the 10th century.

The first is a Letter on Syriac Orthography, addressed to Mār George, Bishop of Sarug. More than thirty years ago, a Latin Translation, with the Syriac Text, of a considerable part of this Letter, and that the most important part, comprising in fact all of it, which really treats of Orthography, was published in Rosen and Forshall's Catalogue of the Syriac MSS. in the British Museum. The remainder of the Letter is almost entirely taken up with scolding copyists.

The next is a Tract, which in the beginning speaks very briefly of genders, persons, tenses and sounds. It then proceeds with the consideration of Syriac Accents, the subject about which the rest, nearly the whole of the Tract, is occupied. Jacob must have been a very early writer on the Accents, for it is supposed, that they were not introduced till the end of the fifth, or the beginning of the sixth century. If so, the system had not been originated more than a hundred and thirty or forty years before Jacob's time. But although an early, he was certainly not the earliest writer on the subject, for the accentuation system seems in his day to have been pretty well matured. There is also, following this Tract, a Letter on this subject, the beginning of which seems to be wanting, and which I believe is of more ancient date than that of the Tract of Jacob. This Letter I have given, as it is in the MS., with a Translation, in Appendix I. The name of the Author is not mentioned, but I have in the Appendix brought forward reasons, satisfactory to my mind, to show that the Letter must have been, if not the earliest, certainly one of the earliest treatises on the Accents, and that it was written as early as and probably before, the time of Thomas the Deacon, i.e. in the 6th century. The system must then have been in an early stage of development, for the number of Accents mentioned therein, is smaller than that found in the Tract of Jacob, and further, compound ones are designedly not treated of, because the Author says, their system up to that period was unsettled, and there existed no writing on the subject. Compound Accents, however, are treated of by Jacob, and I have no doubt that in his time, the system was tolerably settled and complete, for six hundred years after Jacob, precisely the same compound Accents in number and in name are treated of by Bar Hebræus in his larger Grammar. This remark indeed is applicable to the simple Accents; except that two or three additional ones are named by Bar Hebræus, as having been introduced by the Eastern Syrians, and used only by them. We may hence infer that the system of Accents continued substantially unaltered from the time of Jacob to that of Bar Hebræus; indeed, that it never afterwards underwent any material change. Some of them are used, as are some of the Hebrew accents, for pausal purposes; but by far the greater part of them are employed to indicate, whether a syllable be long or short, to mark the rise and fall of the voice, and in fact to perform strictly the office of Accents.

Ewald has stated as his opinion, that these Accents are more ancient than the Hebrew, and that the former suggested the introduction of the latter. His words are, "Dass diese (die hebräische Accentuation) aus der ältern und einfachen syrischen Accentuation sich hervor gebildet hat, schien mir schon längst, so bald ich jenes syrische system kennen gelernt hatte, sehr wahrscheinlich, und wird sich bei näherer Ansicht immer mehr bestätigen. So sehr auch die hebräische noch viel feiner und genauer ausgebildet ist: in ihrem Wesen und Geist, in ihrem Zweck und Ziel, ja auch in der Stellung und Gestalt der wichtigsten und sichtbar ältesten Zeichen hat sie doch die grösste Aehnlichkeit mit der syrischen." Abhandlungen, Erster Theil, S. 130. Assuming his view to be correct, the Syriac accents may serve to throw light on the theory of Hebrew Accentuation.

Viewed historically, these Accents are interesting. They were introduced at a time, when the vowel punctuation, if indeed it had then any existence, was certainly in a very imperfect state of development, and were designed for a two-fold purpose. First, they were used to regulate the voice in the reading of the Scriptures in churches and in chaunting, and hence we find them sometimes called by Bar Hebræus ܢܩܕ̈ܐ ܡܫܘܚܝܐ, *metrical signs*. The second purpose of these points was to serve as a Commentary on the Scriptures, in passages where the sense would be otherwise doubtful. Bar Hebræus says, that they are often *necessary* for determining the sense of a passage. In the first section of the chapter of the larger Grammar, which is edited in this work, he quotes two examples in confirmation of his statement, for which see p. 34 of the translation.

My original intention was not to edit more on the Accents than the Tract of Jacob; but when I examined the MS., I found that it was of itself perfectly useless to the student for the purpose of teaching him the Theory of Syriac Accents. For first there is a list of Accents given; following it, is a repetition of the list, but to the name of each Accent there is a passage of Scripture appended, containing its mark. Now as this mark consists of one or two points, and as points perform many and diverse offices in Syriac MSS. and printed books, it is impossible for the student to distinguish the mark of the Accent from the other points, which are found in the word or the expression. Besides, the marks of the Accents themselves are often not rightly placed, and sometimes are not placed at all, through the blundering of the copyist. In the Vatican MS., of which some lithographs have been just issued at Paris, in respect to the position of the forty-one marks that are named, I have counted not fewer than seventeen errors. In the British Museum MS., which I have edited, there are five. I therefore repeat, that Jacob's Tract is thoroughly useless, unless it be accompanied by a Commentary. I am happy to say that I am able to present to the student, two Commentaries in this work, which have never before been printed, viz. the Discourse of Bar Hebræus, and the Letter in Appendix I., already spoken of. In each of these Commentaries, is mentioned in *words*, in every instance, where the Accent should be put.[a] I have on the authority of these, stated in the foot notes to the Translation of Jacob's Tract, where each Accent should be, so as to remove all doubt that might otherwise exist in the mind of the student. Indeed in the Translations of these documents with the Notes, he will, I trust, find a distinct, consistent and complete theory.

There has been no European writer, so far as I know, who has ever written on Syriac Accents except Ewald. The pausal accents, indeed, are mentioned in Syriac Grammars, and in that of Dr. Adelbert Merx, which is now in the course of publication, the names of some of the others are given, occupying about half a page, but the accents themselves are not treated of. The three Treatises, which I have translated in the following pages, and which are the first Translations that have ever been made of them in a Western language, comprise the earliest and latest productions extant on the system of the accents by native writers.

The copy of Bar Hebræus's larger Grammar, from which I have transcribed the Discourse edited in

---

[a] I beg to say here to the reader, that he must look to the letter-press for learning the system of Accents, and not to the points of the Syriac Text, which through the carelessness of copyists are sometimes inaccurate. I considered the right and honest thing to be to present to him the Syriac Text, as it is in the MSS., with its imperfections.

the following pages, is a MS. in the British Museum, numbered in Rosen and Forshall's Catalogue 720 *l*. This copy I have compared with the two more ancient ones in the Bodleian Library at Oxford.

There is in the British Museum, another copy of the Letter and Tract of Jacob marked in the same Catalogue 7183. It is said to be of the 12th century, and is probably taken from the Nitrian MS. here edited. I have noticed the principal various readings, and have placed them at the foot of each page of the Syriac Text, as the readings of Codex *b*.

I cannot close this Preface without thanking my friend Dr. W. Wright, of the British Museum, which I do now most sincerely, for his kind and valuable help in correcting the proof-sheets.

MĀR JACOB ON SYRIAC ORTHOGRAPHY.

THE Epistle of the holy and wise in divine things, Mār Jacob, bishop of Edessa, to the pious and holy Mār George, bishop of Sarug, and through him to all the scribes, who may meet with this book.

Jacob, poor in the Lord, to the pious and honoured of God, our spiritual brother, one in mind and in the office of the ministry, Mār George, greeting.

I have seen that this is no little reproach, O thou lover of God—for I judge that I may intimate to thee that which I have seen, and through thee also to many others, who may meet with this writing—that in all those arts, which are for the use of men in this life, the artists, *i.e.* the makers and teachers of them, understand them much better than those, who only use them, when they are finished. But this great and primary art (*of writing*), and, as I think, high above all arts, that which, contrary to these, unfortunately befalls it *is*, that they who become acquainted *with it*, when it is completed, know it accurately and fully, its faults and the corrections of them and all the methods, which are useful for its construction, more than its artists, those who perform and make it, more, I say, than such as those I am about to speak of.

Understand, all ye who read these things, that with respect to the art of carpentry, those carpenters, who perform *the work*, understand it, and are versed in the faults and in those blemishes, which are in it, and are sagacious in correcting them, more than those who make use *of it* when *its parts* are finished. I am speaking of a waggon, or a table, or a chest, or a seat, or of other useful things of those, which are constructed by it (*the art*).[a] So also it will appear with respect to workmanship in gold, silver, iron, &c., and also with respect to pottery. I say, that they, the workmen, skilful in making vessels of iron, the rudder of a ploughshare, the mallet, the axe and the hook, *know* more than those, who make use of them. Similarly it is seen that makers of vessels, viz. potters, know how to construct conveniently and very usefully the jar, and the bucket, and the pot, and other earthen vessels, better than the rest of men, who only buy and make use of them. Also with respect to all arts, *these remarks apply*. The makers of bows *understand them* better than the archers; architects more than the dwellers *in the buildings;* those who fix[b] ships more than the navigators; shoemakers more than those who wear the shoes, and tailors more than those who wear the clothes.

But with respect to the great and high art of constructing books, that is called writing, they who make use of *the writing*, when it is finished, i. e. the readers, they who read these books, which are constructed by it (*the art*), know it accurately, both those things, which are useful in it, and the blemishes, which are in it, and their corrections, more than the writers themselves, who made it (*the book*). It is not a reproach, which all arts share with this art. I judge, that it is not a

---

[a] The argument is that a carpenter is a better judge of a waggon, table, &c., than those who only make use of them, after they are made.

[b] Adjust the parts of a ship, build it.

little one, and that it doeth not a little detriment. It is right that, as the art is great, and honoured and the first of all arts, the performance of it should also be the most honoured of all useful *arts ;* so also they who learn it, and labour at it, should be of those who are skilful, and penetrating and excelling in mind above many, and not of those who are *so* in any degree whatever.[c] But I perceive that here also it (the art) is greatly discredited. There are those who, much inferior to others, *being only* as the multitude in mind and natural penetration, enter upon and learn it (*the art*), and work at it and make books, but they know not what they see, nor what they write, concerning those matters they, the scribes, read. It is not for the purpose of their erring more, that these remarks have been brought forward; but that they may receive *them* readily and learn and be corrected. Let them hasten to come wisely and discreetly to understand that we know many things in this art of copying (writing) ; we, who read, more than they who copy (write). For they, indeed, anxious to complete the number of quaternions of leaves according to distances,[d] either diminish the lines or expand the letters of the writing. They either lengthen or shorten ; or they compress because of the red.[e] They either add letters and

---

[c] Dr. Payne Smith in his *Thesaurus Syriacus* p. 149 under ܐܝܟܢ says that ܐܝܟܢ ܕܗܘ means *ἐν μορίῳ τινί*, or *quocunque modo*, and he quotes several passages from different authors in which this expression occurs.

[d] *According to distances*, i.e. the distances of the lines from each other, so that a certain number of lines may fill the page.

[e] *They compress because of the red.* The red refers to the expression which is added to the end of a book or a chapter, and is

take away *letters;* or they expand a member into two, and divide it where it is not suitable; or they blend inconveniently two into one. But we who read, ardently desire that the reason and sense of those things, which are written, should be preserved, and be carefully kept free for those who may meet with the writings; although the red at the end of the lines may have to be assigned *to a place* beyond the intention of the scribes. This they are instructed of; but they do it not.[f] But that the design of those things which we have mentioned may be known to them, behold, I lay before them a few cautions, in order that they may be very careful of our purpose, although it may be that they will despise it, learning that it is more expedient that a line redundant or deficient be brought forth, although there be something to disturb the reason and injure the sense.

1st. I prohibit all those, who may copy the books, which I have translated or composed, from changing of their own accord anything of those which they have undertaken to copy, either in the writings, or in the points, whatsoever they may find; if even a manifest error be found, for every man is liable to error, ourselves, the scribe, who hath received *the book* from us, those who compare *copy with copy*, the eye of the reader which errs and deviates from correct vision. Let them not

---

usually found in MSS. written with red ink. The engagement of the copyist having been to copy a book or a chapter for a certain sum of money, his object was, to get to the red as soon as possible, and with that purpose in view he was reckless as to the accuracy of his copy, and cared not as to what liberties he took with the text.

[f] They do not put the red farther off, although they know that it is required for the preservation of the sense, &c.

afterwards introduce again those letters which we have cut off from nouns and verbs, and from other parts of speech; not, if the nouns be from the Hebrews, nor if they be from the Greeks and Romans. They shall not write ܫܠܡܘܢ according to their custom for my ܫܠܝܡܘܢ, *Solomon.* I well know what I have written. They shall not put for me ܒܪܫܝܬ without a yūd, for ܒܪܝܫܝܬ, which I put. Neither the noun ܪܫܐ, nor ܪܫܢܘܬܐ, nor any words which are derived from this noun ܪܫܐ, shall they write without a yūd. They shall not introduce for us ܗ in the noun ܪܘܡܝܐ, *the Romans*; nor in that of ܪܘܡܝ, *Rome,* their city: nor in that of ܣܘܢܗܕܘܣ, *Synod;* nor in that of ܦܪܪܗܣܝܐ Παρρησία, *freedom* or *confidence,* nor in other nouns such as these, because of ancient custom. They shall not write ܗ̇ܝ ܕܝܢ, which are separate, and are significant of something, together in the form ܗܝܕܝܢ, which, blended, signify a particle of time. Let them also understand that, when they are separate, ܗ̇ܝ requires a point above it, but when blended and made significant of time, *it does not require* any *point* whatever. Let them not in any place confound the particle ܐܝܟܢܐ. But let them understand where we have written ܐܝܟܢܐ together, and where we have written ܐܝܟ ܗܢܐ separate. Let them know where we have written ܐܦܠܐ blended, and where we have written ܐܦ and have not blended it with that which is adduced after it. They shall not write ܠ in ܐܬܬܦܝܣܬ, nor in those *words* which *are derived* from this same verb; because I have been entreated by a man and I have received his request and ܐܬܛܦܝܣܬ, *I have acquiesced* to make a distinction, as to that which signifies *request*,[g] viz. *obedience*, and in it ܝ is not placed. They shall not write yūd in the noun, viz. the word for the day, which we call ܐܬܡܠ, *yesterday*, or ܩܕܡܬܡܠ, *three days ago*. But they shall understand that in the passive verb ܐܬܡܠܝ the yūd is required; also in that which we call ܐܬܡܠܝ or ܐܬܬܡܠܝ. They shall understand with respect to these matters, where we write ܒܪܝܬܐ, *creatures*, and not ܒܪܝܬܐ, *streets*. They shall understand where it is needful for them to put the points *to these words*, that they may distinguish between ܒܪܝܬܐ, *streets*, and those ܒܪܝܬܐ, which are created, and also ܒܪܝܬܐ, *exterior*.[h] They will also understand why with these we mention ܒܪܝܘܬܐ, *exterior part*. They shall not write ܪܕܝܢ ܚܢܢ together, nor ܩܝܡܝܢ ܚܢܢ, nor ܒܥܝܢ ܚܢܢ, nor ܒܢܝܢ ܚܢܢ, nor ܩܢܝܢ ܚܢܢ, nor others such as these; so that they may be distinguished from those nouns, which we enunciate; ܪܕܝܢܢ, ܩܝܡܝܢܢ, ܒܥܝܢܢ, ܒܢܝܢܢ, ܩܢܝܢܢ, and from the verbs of the præterite tense. The noun

---

[g] There must be some word or words omitted in the MS. here; for ܒܥܘܬܐ means *request*, and not *obedience*. Ebdokus, however who has adopted Jacob's distinction, makes the matter quite clear, He says that ܐܬܛܦܝܣ signifies ܐܫܬܡܥ, *he obeyed*, and ܐܬܦܝܣ, ܩܒܠ ܒܥܘܬܐ, *receiving a request*.

[h] In the MS. we have the words ܠܘܩܒܠ ܗܘ ܓܘܝܬܐ, denoting that the sense of ܒܪܝܬܐ is the opposite of that of ܓܘܝܬܐ, *interior*.

ܡܬܟܬܫܢܐ, *a fighter*, must be distinguished, in writing it,from the verb ܡܬܟܬܫ ܐܢܐ, *I am fighting*, and from others which are like it in sound. ܝܕܥܢ, ܡܫܚܢ, ܕܚܠܢ, ܡܕܚܠܢ, ܡܘܬܢ.[i] They shall not take away any of those letters, which are written by us in those nouns, which are Greek or Hebrew, and they shall not add to them; viz. ܩܐܛܐܣܛܐܣܝܣ κατάστασις, ܦܐܢܛܐܣܝܐ φαντασία, ܬܐܘܠܘܓܝܐ θεολογία, ܦܠܐܪܘܦܘܪܝܐ πληροφορία, ܦܝܠܘܣܘܦܝܐ φιλοσοφία, and many others. ܩܘܣܛܢܛܝܢܘܣ *Constantine*, ܐܬܢܐܣܝܘܣ *Athanasius*, ܐܡܦܝܠܘܟܝܘܣ *Amphilochius*,[i] ܐܘܢܓܠܝܐ Εὐαγγέλια, ܐܘܢܓܠܣܛܐ Εὐαγγελισταί or ܕܝܐܬܩܐ διαθήκη, or others such as these, which I am not able now to remember.

Let them not reject the noun ܗܘܒܗܘܬܐ, by changing it, because they do not know what it is, *viz.* that it denotes ܗܘ ܒܗ ܗܘ, *identity* of something. Neither let them reject ܐܬܪܬܐ, which signifies *the second time*. Neither ܕܝܠܬܐ, *a property*, nor ܕܝܠܝܘܬܐ, *a property*, was known a hundred years ago to the Syriac language, and is certainly not found among the Syrian Doctors, viz. Mār Ephraim,

---

[i] These words which are singular nouns with the pronominal affix of the 1st. pers. plur. should evidently follow the word *enunciate* above; then should follow "and from the verbs of the præterite tense," and then should come the examples ܝܕܥܢ, etc.

[i] Amphilochius was Bishop of Iconium in the fourth century. He attended the first general council at Constantinople A.D. 381, and also the councils held A.D. 385 and 394. He was the friend of Gregory Nazianzen and Basil.

Mār Jacob, Mār Isaac, or Mār Xenaja, nor in any of those *books*, which in those times were translated from the Greek; neither was ܐܝܟܢܝܘܬܐ, *quality*, known, nor the noun ܐܘܣܝܐ, οὐσία. But instead of ܕ̈ܠܝܠܬܐ, they said ܫ̈ܢܝܫܝܬܐ; instead of ܐܝܟܢܝܘܬܐ, *quality* or *species*, ܙܢܐ; instead of ܐܘܣܝܐ, they put either ܟܝܢܐ or ܐܝܬܘܬܐ, or, as the multitude, they said ܐܝܬܝܐ. Let them not blend with ܠܥܠܡܝܢ, the word ܐܡܝܢ, which is at the end of discourses. With these I should have had many other things to have taken notice of in this my writing, if they had kept in my memory, for admonition to the Scribes, to those who by custom write, of their own accord, whatsoever is agreeable to them, thinking that they are not to blame for this.

What have I to say concerning those marks, which they make as they please in the beginning of books or discourses, and similarly at the end of them; also concerning the changes, additions and abbreviations? With respect to the position of the points also, every man takes authority to himself to place them as he pleases. A very few words I judge I may add here, if they would acquiesce to receive and attend to *them*. Before these, however, I will mention a certain example from nature, which is nothing but deformity, odiousness, and ugliness, that a natural and living body should be deprived of those members which have been given to it by nature. For example, that it (the body) should have one eye, or one ear, or one horn, or a hand or foot of four digits only. Again there is something absurd and ugly, when the face or the head of a man or beast is found to have three ears, or three eyes, or any other redundant *member*, besides those which nature in general has granted. For a hand or foot in which are six digits is not pleasing; nor a mouth in which are superfluous teeth, and dog teeth, which move and go forth beyond it; nor lips, which are long and pouting. This also is ugly, that members should be changed and put out of those places, which have been fixed by nature. It is not becoming to have the eye in the chin, nor the ear in the region of the eyes of a man; nor the fingers in the knees or the elbows; nor the nails in the legs, nor in the backs of the middle part of the arms or in the shoulders. But this is the beauty of nature, that there be in it neither superfluity nor defect. Every one of the members should be made fit for the place, which has been prepared and rendered convenient for it by nature, the workman, which God the creator has created.

Similarly it may be seen with respect to the placing of the points, which are distinguishing and explanatory of the various things which are placed in this Mesopotamian, or Edessene, or, to speak more distinctly, Syriac Book; not in abundance or superfluity, nor where a member has no need to be distinguished from another which is similar to it in the letters, is it right that points should be placed; nor that they should be thick, and like to hands and feet in each of which there are six digits. Neither should they be deficient or fewer than the portion by which a member may, if possible, be distinguished from the others, which are like it; because that as superfluity, it has been observed, is not becoming, so also deficiency *is not becoming.*

It is right that they be also put in places, which are convenient for them, and not where there is a vacant place, whether it be suitable or unsuitable. For the sake of argument, I attempt to suppose something, which is not significant of that which I wish to teach. A lady works occasionally[1] and then she commands the men servants and maid servants to work very hard.[2] [k] I know that the noun ܝܕܥܬܐ does not require Olaph at the beginning of it; because that this my ܠܝܕܥܬܐ would be judged *to be* ܠܐ ܝܕܥܬܐ *not knowledge* or *ignorance*. Because that I am not a child; but I consider myself to be a producer of inventions, for that nature hath brought to me all those things which are needful to instruct and confirm me; I must, therefore, know against what letter, and whether above it, or below it, I may make the places of the points. These are sufficient at present, for the information of the scribes, lovers of God, who are right minded, acquiescing, and receiving correction, and for thee, my pious brother.

This *thing* I request, I say. With respect to this my writing, which *is intended* for thy piety;

---

[1] Lit. She does one or two works.

[2] Lit. To do many works.

[k] The meaning of this sentence is probably something like the following. A mistress wants to inculcate industry in her servants. The mode by which she endeavours to effect this purpose is this: she works occasionally herself, and then she commands her servants to work very hard, as if her own example were an argument for supporting her command. This, to use Jacob's language, would not be significant of what she proposed to inculcate, and would be like a copyist placing a point in a vacant place whether suitable or not.

command the scribes copying it *to place it* before the middle book of the work of the Epithronian[l] discourses. Concerning those points which are bound[m] in the book which has been mentioned,—most of which I myself have collated, and have bound, first, because of love to you, and second in order that my design may be known,—leave them in it as they are, and erase not one of them from it; so that a copy is written by which the scribe sees both those points which are bound, and those which are put in the place of them. Let them (*the scribes*) understand my design, concerning those points, in this my letter to thee.[n] Afterwards I request thee, my brother, to seal it with thy ring, and with my letter *before it;* when thou writest to the Abbot Mār Julian, and salutest him from my humble self, send to him the letter and the middle book; so that he first may copy it, and also consider the disposition of those points, both those which are bound, and those which are in the place of them, also those illustrations, that were composed by me, which the scribe has not well placed, nor are they in suitable places. I require that you also intimate to him *my* love, for the pious, the elect one spoken of, and that also he

[l] The *Logoi Epithronii* of Severus of Antioch, which were translated into Syriac by Jacob.

[m] Points which are bound, are, according to Assemani, those, about which he (Jacob) has placed with the pen a diacritic circle. His words are the following: "Colligata vocat puncta, queis circulum diacriticum calamo apposuerat:" Bibliotheca Orientalis. Tom. i., p. 478.

[n] Those points, which Jacob had substituted in the place of those that were bound, and also the bound ones.

may learn of my will, that I wish to undertake to write for his tranquillity. Lastly, he is there who knows what he sees more than others who may meet with those things which have been mentioned. Mayst thou be preserved sound in our Lord, O pious brother, praying for my humble self and seeking for me mercies from God. Amen.

The end of the Epistle of Mār Jacob to the Scribes.

MĀR JACOB ON PERSONS AND TENSES.[a]

These things then, it is right for a man to keep in contemplation, respecting persons, genders, tenses, sounds, and names of accents; for the Syrians give names to points, when they are placed on words. They are simple and compound. There are forty seven variations of accents. There are three persons; first, second and third. There are two genders; masculine and feminine. There are three tenses, præterite, present and future. There are sounds, which are thick and pure. Every word or member, where the sound is thick or broad, takes a point above. Where *the sound* is narrow or pure, *it takes the point* below. If it be intermediate, between narrow and broad, and there are two other *words*, which are like it in the writing, it takes two points, one above and the other below, and this is called ܡܦܓܕܢܐ, *bridling;* ܒܪ݁ܐ, ܒܘܪܐ. Also the names of accents; there is a proper name to each one of the points, and they have measure.

CHAPTER I.

PERSONS.

There are three persons: e.g. first, ܐܘܕܐ, *I will confess;* second, ܐܘܕܐ, *confess thou;* and third,

[a] This Tract is said here to be on Persons and Tenses; but the greater part of it treats of ܢ̈ܒܪܐ accents.

ܐܘܕܐ ܕܢܘܪܐ, *a firebrand.*[b] But this ܐܘܕܐ has ܚܒܨܐ for the vowel.

CHAPTER II.

GENDERS.

THERE are two genders, masculine and feminine. Masc. ܥܒܕܬ, *I have made,* ܓܒܠܬ, *I have formed,* ܐܟܠܬ, *I have eaten.*[c] Fem. ܥܒܕܬ, *she has made,* ܓܒܠܬ, *she has formed,* ܐܟܠܬ, *she has eaten.* Genders and persons being united in consequence of the equality of the writings (i.e. the consonants of each word being the same), they are distinguished from each other by the points; thus: ܩܪܒܬ, *I have approached,* ܩܪܒܬ, *I have caused to approach,* ܩܪܒܬ, *thou hast approached,* masc. ܩܪܒܬ, *thou hast caused to approach,* masc. ܩܪܒܬ, *she has approached,* ܩܪܒܬ, *she has caused to approach.* Again, I know also of another distinction between the masc. and fem. genders, when they are equal in the consonants or the sounds. In like consonants, the points distinguish; as when we write in the masc. ܥܒܕܝܢ, *doing* ܥܒܕܝܢ

---

[b] Jacob brings forward this example of a third person. *A firebrand,* when referred to by a pronoun, would be *it.* It seems to have been his object to fix on a word having the same letters for each person, and the person to be distinguished only by the pointing.

[c] We should have called the first person common. But as there are only two genders in Syriac, and as the masc. is more worthy than the fem., Jacob calls these examples *masc.*

writing, ܐܳܡܪ̈ܺܝܢ *saying*, *without* the placing of the two points, which are called ܣܽܘܓܳܐܐ, *many;* or when we write in the fem. ܥܒܶܕ̈ܝܢ, *do ye*, ܟܬܘܒ̈ܝܢ, *write ye*, ܐܡܰܪ̈ܝܢ, *say ye*, *with* the placing of ܣܽܘܓܳܐܐ. Again, there are others, which are equal and similar (to the foregoing) and signify a certain person, singular or plural; as, ܥܒܳܕ̈ܝܢ, *our works;* ܟܬܳܒ̈ܝܢ, *our books*, ܐܡܪ̈ܝܢ, *our lambs*, the same as saying ܥܒܳܕ̈ܐ ܕܝܠܢ, *our works*, ܟܬܳܒ̈ܐ ܕܝܠܢ, *our books*, ܐܡܪ̈ܐ ܕܝܠܢ, *our lambs.* These are equal (to the preceding participial and imperative forms) in the writing; but distinguished in the sound, by the points which are upon them. There are also those distinguished in the consonants; but equal in the sound; i.e. he who hears, distinguishes them by the sense, or he who reads, by the sight. They are such as these: ܩܘܡ ܐܢܗܪ, *arise, shine* (imper. sing. masc.) ܩܘܡܝ ܐܢܗܪܝ, *arise, shine* (imper. sing. fem.), ܩܘܡܘ ܐܢܗܪܘ, *arise, shine* (imper. plu. masc.), ܙܠ ܥܡ ܦܠܢ, *go with so and so*, (imper. sing. masc.), ܙܠܝ ܥܡܝ, *go with me* (imper. sing fem.), ܙܠܘ ܠܬܡܢ, *go thither* (imper. plu. masc.), ܙܠܝ ܠܟܝ, *go thou* (imper. sing. fem.).

CHAPTER III.

TENSES.

TENSES are such as: the præterite *with a point below;* as, among a multitude such as, ܥܒܰܕ, *he did*, ܦܩܰܕ, *he commanded*, ܐܡܰܪ, *he said*, and such as these: the present, *with a point* above; as, ܥܳܒܶܕ, *doing*, ܦܳܩܶܕ,

commanding, ܐܡܪ, *saying*, and such as these: the future, as, ܟܬܒ, ܦܩܕ, ܐܡܪ.[d]

CHAPTER IV.

SOUNDS.

Sounds which are broad *are* ܡܬܚܫܠܠ, ܡܬܡܫܬܟܠ, ܐܬܕܪܢ, ܐܫܬܟܠ, ܕܠܠ, and such as these, i.e. those which keep the place of persons, genders and tenses together.[e] With a point above are also, ܢܚܫܐ, ܚܕܪܐ ܚܕܝܪܐ ܚܕܝܪܐ ܚܠܚܐ ܠܓܐ. With a point below are ܠܓܐ ܚܕܝܪܐ ܥܝܢܐ. We have also ܐܡܪ. ܐܡܪ. ܐܡܪ. ܐܡܪ. ܐܬܐ. ܐܬܐ. ܐܬܐ. ܐܬܐ. ܐܟܠ. ܐܟܠ. ܐܟܠ. ܓܢܐ. ܓܢܐ. ܓܢܐ. ܟܐܪܐ. ܟܐܪܐ. ܓܪܒܐ. ܓܪܒܐ. ܓܪܒܐ. ܦܓܪܐ. ܦܓܪܐ. ܦܒܝܐ. ܡܒܝܐ. ܡܒܝܐ.[f] These are also named both in the singular and the plural, being distinguished by the points or the letters; such as, ܐܠܗܐ. ܐܠܗܐ. ܓܢܒܐ ܓܢܒܐ. ܓܢܒܐ. ܓܢܒܐ. ܠܚܕܪܐ. ܠܚܕܪܐ. ܕܝܠܗ. ܕܝܠܗ. ܥܒܕܗ. ܥܒܕܝܗ. ܬܕܒܪܗ. ܬܕܒܝܪܗ, and such as these.

---

[d] The copyist has here through carelessness copied the examples just mentioned of the present tense, as examples also of the future. In the MS., which I have called codex ܒ, the examples of the future are omitted.

[e] Jacob is probably speaking of words, which in themselves indicate the person, gender and tense, respectively belonging to them.

[f] These examples consist of groups of words, each word of the group having the same letters, but with sounds, coarse or fine or intermediate, according to the sense of that word.

CHAPTER V.

METRICAL POINTS, OR ACCENTS.

METRICAL Points are those with which accuracy of meaning is especially sought for; because that they contain the elegance and polish *of measure* in this language, as has been previously mentioned.[h] They are simple and compound. Simple, when they take one point *only* of those that are named, besides the necessary distinctions, which are placed in the passage, that is to say, ܥܠܝܐ only, ܪܗܒܐ only, &c.; compound, when their passages take on them two of the points, which are named, as ܦܩܘܕܐ, or ܬܚܘܬܝܐ, or ܪܗܒܐ and ܣܡܟܐ,[i] &c. It is possible to show that all or many of them may

[h] Here seems to be an allusion to the last words of the introductory remarks of this Tract: viz. ܡܫܘܚܬܐ ܐܝܬ ܠܗܘܢ, *they have measure.*

[i] ܣܡܟܐ is to be here understood as attached to ܦܩܘܕܐ and ܬܚܘܬܝܐ, as well as to ܪܗܒܐ, making three separate examples of compound signs.

be compounded with one another; if not all of them, yet once and twice, and more.[j]

Points with their names* are the following. :ܥܠܝܐ, *above*, .ܬܚܬܝܐ, *beneath*, :ܫܘܝܐ, *equals*, ܫܘܚܠܦ ܫܘܝܐ, *variation of* :ܫܘܝܐ, namely, ܫܪܝܐ ܕܡܫܬܥܝܬܐ *loosening of the discourse*, ..ܪܗܛܐ ܕܦܣܩ, *the* ܪܗܛܐ *which divides*, ܦܣܘܩܐ, *section*, ܡܒܟܝܢܐ, *weeping*, or ܡܟܦܘܦܢܐ, *drooping*, ܫܘܚܠܦ ܥܠܝܐ, *variation of* ܥܠܝܐ, ܫܘܚܠܦ ܬܚܬܝܐ, *variation of* ܬܚܬܝܐ, ܦܩܘܕܐ, *commanding*, ܫܒܝܩܐ, *simple*, ܬܟܫܦܐ, *reproof*, ܡܫܐܠܢܐ, *interrogating*, ܪܗܛܐ ܕܦܣܩ ܘܕܠܐ ܦܣܩ, *the* ܪܗܛܐ, *which divides, and that which does not divide*, ܬܠܬܐ ܪ̈ܗܛܐ, *three* ܪ̈ܗܛܐ, ܡܩܠܣܢܐ *praiser*, viz. that which is called in Greek παροξύτονος, i.e. *the accent on the penultimate;* ܡܗܒ ܛܘܒܐ *giving happiness*, ܩܪܘܝܐ, *calling*, ܡܚܘܝܢܐ, *indicating*, ܡܨܠܝܢܐ, *praying*, ܡܦܝܣܢܐ, *supplicating*, ܡܫܐܠܢܐ,[k] ܡܚܬܝܬܐ, *making to descend*, ܡܬܕܡܪܢܐ, *admiring*, ܡܓܙܠܢܐ, *discontinuing*, ܡܚܝܕܢܐ, *uniting*, ܫܘܚܠܦ ܡܚܝܕܢܐ, *variation of* ܡܚܝܕܢܐ, is as it went forth from the Greek Language;[l] ܥܨܘܪܐ, *tearing away*,

---

[j] The sense of this remark I apprehend to be, that a sign may be compounded with others, once, twice, or more, e.g. ܬܟܫܦܐ is found compounded with ܫܪܝܐ ܕܡܫܬܥܝܬܐ, with ܡܫܐܠܢܐ, ܫܘܝܐ, &c. Other signs are also found in several different combinations.

* The points are frequently not put with their names, the copyist through ignorance or carelessness having omitted them. They will, however, be found in the description which follows.

[k] This sign has already appeared in the list.

[l] I.e. In the sign ܡܚܝܕܢܐ one Greek word is translated by two Syriac words; but in *the variation* there are two words in Greek as well as in Syriac.

or *drawing out*, ܫܘܚܠܦ ܓܪܘܪܐ, *variation of* ܓܪܘܪܐ, ܚܪܝܢܐ, *resistance*, ܙܘܥܐ, *motion*, ܣܡܟܬܐ, *a prop*, ܫܘܚܠܦ ܣܡܟܬܐ, *variation of* ܣܡܟܐ; ܙܘܥܐ ܘܣܡܟܐ, ܙܘܥܐ and ܣܡܟܐ; ܣܡܟܐ ܘܡܟܦܠܢܐ, ܣܡܟܐ and ܡܟܦܠܢܐ; ܡܫܐܠܢܐ ܘܙܘܥܐ, ܡܫܐܠܢܐ and ܙܘܥܐ; ܪܗܛܐ ܕܦܣܘܩ ܙܘܥܐ ܘܪܗܛܐ ܕܠܐ ܦܣܘܩ ܘܦܣܘܩܐ; ܪܗܛܐ ܕܦܣܘܩ, ܙܘܥܐ, ܪܗܛܐ ܕܠܐ ܦܣܘܩ, and ܦܣܘܩܐ; ܩܘܡܐ, *standing*, with the letters, ܡܗܦܟܢܐ, *turning back*, or ܡܚܕܪܢܐ, *circling* (?), a variation of it by letters or by lines;[m] ܬܫܥܐ ܥܡ ܥܣܪ, ܬܫܥܝܬܐ, ܬܫܥܐ with ܥܣܪ, ܬܫܥܝܬܐ.[n]

Variations of *the names of signs* with passages (of Scripture) are the following:

ܟܬܒܐ ܕܝܠܝܕܘܬܗ ܕܝܫܘܥ ܡܫܝܚܐ: ܚܠܝܐ:,[1] *the book of the generation of Jesus Christ.*[o]

ܟܬܒܐ ܩܕܡܝܐ ܟܬܒܬ ܐܘ ܬܐܘܦܝܠܐ . ܬܘܬܐ .,[2] *the former book have I written, O Theophilus.*[p]

---

m Nestorians sometimes put a small line over a letter as a sign. Jacob perhaps calls the sign by this name because it is a line. Bar Hebraeus, however, says he does not know it.

n Jacob says in the beginning of this Chapter, that there are forty-seven *names of signs*; but in this list he has mentioned only forty-one. This may be accounted for in this way. It may be that he has not recorded all the signs which were known in his day. Some of the compound signs may have been omitted. There are indeed two or three of these signs, which are mentioned by Bar Hebraeus, but are not noticed in this tract. The list given by Thomas the Deacon contains only seventeen names. See Appendix II.

1 Matthew i. 1.

o The mark of this sign is ∴ as, ∴ ܡܫܝܚܐ .

2 Acts i. 1.

p The mark of this sign is . as . ܬܐܘܦܝܠܐ .

ܚܙܐ ܡܪܝܐ ܕܣܓܝܐܬ ܒܝܫܘܬܗ ܕܒܪܢܫܐ ܒܐܪܥܐ: ܙܘܥܐ:[3] *the Lord saw that the wickedness of man was great in the earth.*[q]

ܫܘܚܠܦ ܙܘܥܐ, *variation of* ܙܘܥܐ, ܓܢܒܪܐ ܕܡܢ ܥܠܡ:,[4] *giants, who were of old.*[r] This is ܙܥܝܪܐ ܕܬܫܥܝܬܐ.

ܦܣܘܩܐ. Every point, which is at the end of a sentence, its name is ܦܣܘܩܐ, except ܫܘܫܠܐ.

ܠܐ ܠܟܘܢ ܟܠ ܥܒܪܝ ܐܘܪܚܐ .. ※ ܪܗܛܐ ܕܦܣܘܩ ..[5] *not to you all ye passing the way.*[s]

ܐܠܗܐ ܕܐܒܝ ※ ܡܫܡܥܢܝܬܐ ܐܘܚܕܬ ܦܣܘܩܝܢܐ[6] ܐܒܪܗܡ. ܐܠܗܐ ܕܐܒܝ ܐܝܣܚܩ. *the God of my father Abraham, the God of my father Isaac.*[t]

---

[3] Gen. vi. 5.

[q] The mark of this sign is : as : ܒܐܪܥܐ.

[4] Gen. vi. 4.

[r] *The variation of* ܙܘܥܐ does not appear to be distinguished from ܙܘܥܐ by the mark, but according to Bar Hebræus, by the elongation of the sound in pronouncing it, and it is put at the end of the protasis, when the apodosis follows with ܦܣܘܩܐ.

[5] Lam. i 12.

[s] The mark of this sign is put after ܐܘܪܚܐ, and, therefore, we learn that its form is (··). Jacob, however, sometimes puts it thus ⁚. Bar Hebræus says, "its mark is two points in a straight line below." By *below*, I suppose he means, below or under the expression, which bears the name of this sign. In the example he has cited, the two points are not in a straight line, which according to the above rule they ought to be, but in an oblique one. This apparent discrepancy is only a blunder of the copyist, for in a MS. I have seen of the sixth century in the British Museum, the two points are put horizontally, thus ·· ; and so they are in the two copies of the ܟܬܒܐ ܕܨܡܚܐ in the Bodleian Library.

[6] Gen. xxxii. 9.

[t] The mark of this sign is the same as that of ܬܚܝܬܝܐ.

ܟܠ ܚܕܘܬܐ ܢܗܘܐ ܠܟܘܢ ܐܚܝ̈ ※ ܥܣܘܠܐ ܚܠܝܐ܀,[7] *all joy be to you brethren.*[u]

ܫܐܘܠ ܐܚܝ ※ ܥܣܘܠܐ ܬܟܫܬܐ܂,[8] *brother Saul.*[v]

ܢܦܘܩ ܚܬܢܐ ܡܢ ܓܢܘܢܗ܂ ※ ܦܣܘܩܐ,[9] *the bride-groom shall go forth from his chamber.*[w]

ܘܟܠܬܐ ܡܢ ܒܝܬ ܓܢܘܢܗ܂ ※ ܫܡܝܫܐ, *and the bride from her closet.*[x]

ܐܢܝ ܢܬܩܛܠ ܒܡܩܕܫܗ ܕܡܪܝܐ ܟܘܡܪܐ ※ ܬܟܣܐ܂[10]
ܘܢܒܝܐ܂, *Alas, shall the priest and the prophet be slain in the sanctuary of the Lord.*[y]

---

[7] James i. 2.

[u] The mark of ܥܣܘܠܐ ܚܠܝܐ is the same as that of ܚܠܝܐ, but is distinguished from it, according to Bar Hebræus, by the length of its sound, &c.

[8] Acts ix. 17.

[v] The same as ܬܟܫܬܐ in its mark. See Bar Hebræus for the mode by which one sign is distinguished from the other.

[9] Joel. ii. 16.

[w] The mark is a point over the ܢ of ܢܦܘܩ. See Appendix I.

[x] The mark of ܫܡܝܫܐ is the same as that of ܦܣܘܩܐ. It is said of ܦܣܘܩܐ (see p. 20) "that every point which is at the end of a sentence is ܦܣܘܩܐ except ܫܡܝܫܐ." The word ܦܬܓܡܐ used in the Syriac, in the case of ܦܣܘܩܐ means a *sentence*, and in the case of ܫܡܝܫܐ, *a member of a sentence*, or *a clause*. Bar Hebræus says that ܫܡܝܫܐ may be each of the three first radical signs ܚܠܝܐ, ܬܟܫܬܐ, or ܥܨܝܐ, as to its pausal value. It has no ܬܪܝܢܐ, i.e. it has not the second point of any one of these three signs, and therefore it is called ܫܡܝܫܐ, *simple*, or *single*.

[10] Lam. ii. 20.

[y] ܬܟܣܐ has for its mark two points, which are placed obliquely (see Appendix I.) over the last letter of the member of those found placed in the middle, the tenour of the sentence being that of chiding. A further explanation of this sign is given by Bar Hebræus.

ܥܠ ܗܠܝܢ ܠܐ ܐܣܥܘܪ. ܐܡܪ ※ ܡܦܩܕܢܐ ܘܫܐܘܠܐ 11
ܡܪܝܐ: , *shall I not visit for these things, saith the Lord?*[z]

ܠܐ ܐܡܪܬ ܠܟܘܢ ܠܐ ※ ܡܦܩܕܢܐ ܘܡܐܟܠܢܐ 12
ܬܐܙܠܘܢ. , *did I not say to you, go not.*[a]

ܐܠܗܐ, ܗܟܢܐ ܡܠܒܫ. ※ ܡܦܩܕܢܐ ܘܬܘܬܝܬܐ 13
God so clothed.[b] . . . .

---

11 Jer. v. 9.

za ܡܦܩܕܢܐ is here compounded in z with ܫܐܘܠܐ and in a with ܡܐܟܠܢܐ. The ܡܦܩܕܢܐ shows that each expression is admonitory, and hence the sign is useful in defining the sense.

12 2 Kings ii. 18.
13 Matth. vi. 30.

b We have come here to a decayed place in the MS. and the writing is altogether obliterated. Happily the blank may be made good by means of Codex ܒ. I have made the following extract from it to supply the defect in our copy.

ܠܐ ܬܬܬܢܚܘܢ ܚܕ ܥܠ ܚܕ ܐܚܝ̈ ※ ܪܗܛܝܐ ܕܠܐ ܗܘܐ 14
ܕܠܐ ܬܬܕܝܢܘܢ. , *do not groan one against another, brethren, that ye be not condemned.*[c]

ܨܘܬ ܠܝܫ̈ ܘܥܢܝ ※ ܪܗܛܝܐ ܕܠܐ ܗܘܐ ܘܕܗܘܐ 15
ܥܢܬܘܬ.. , *hear, O Laish, and answer, O Anathoth.*[d]

ܡܢ ܒܪܝ̈ ܘܡܢ ܒܪ ܟܪܣܝ̈ ܘܡܢ ܒܪ ܢܕܪܝ̈ ※ ܬܠܝܬܐ ܪܗܛܝܐ 16
O my son, and O son of my womb, and O son of my vows.[e]

ܓܘܪܝܐ. ※ ܡܫܠܡܢܐ ܘܐܡܝܪܬܐ ܡܪܝܡܢܝܬܐ 17
ܕܐܪܝܐ ܝܗܘܕܐ, *Judah is a lion's whelp.*[f]

---

14 James v. 9.

c The mark of this sign is ̈.

15 Isaiah, x. 30.

d It will be observed that the sign ̈ after ܠܝܫ does not divide, for it is followed by ܘܥܢܝ.

16 Prov. xxxi. 2.

e Bar Hebræus calls this sign also ܬܠܝܬܐ ܪܗܛܝܐ, and quotes this example.

17 Gen. xlix. 9.

f This example is given in Appendix I. as that of ܓܘܪܝܐ,

. . . .

. . . . ܗܢܘ ܗܘ ܕܐܡܪܬ ܕܒܬܪܝ، ܐܬܐ

this is he of whom I said that he cometh after me.

ܚܘܣ، ܚܛܗܝܢ ܥܘܠܢ ܫܒܘܩ ܡܪܝܐ. ※ ܡܦܝܣܢܝܬܐ [18]

blot out our sins, forgive our iniquities, O Lord.[g]

ܛܘܒܘܗܝ، ܠܓܒܪܐ ܕܕܚܠ ܡܢ ܡܪܝܐ. ※ ܡܗܝܒ ܛܘܒܐ [19]

blessed is he, who feareth the Lord.[h]

ܩܪܘ، ܠܝ ܠܢܬܢ ※ ܩܪܘܝܐ [20] *call me Nathan;* ܬܘ ܠܘܬܝ، [21] ܟܠܟܘܢ ܠܐܝܢܐ, *come unto me all ye that are wearied ;* ܗܐ، ܐܡܪܗ ܕܐܠܗܐ [22] *behold the lamb of God.*[i]

---

and ܬܫܒܘܚܬܐ is mentioned as another name for the sign ܡܗܝܒ ܛܘܒܐ, because it is said that those beatitudes, which are in the Gospel, were given by the Lord of all, to those doing good, *with praise.* Gen. xlix. 9 is stated to be the only example of this sign, and whether it be called ܦܬܘܪܐ or ܬܫܒܘܚܬܐ, there is no doubt whatever respecting its mark and the position of it. The mark is a point over the penultimate of ܡܗܘܕܐ. The accent is acute, and is called in Greek παροξύτονος, i.e. next to the last syllable, which is called ὀξύτονος.

18 The example is probably from the 51st Psalm, although not exactly the same as what we now have in the Syriac version.

g The mark of this sign is a point over the first letter of ܚܘܣ with ܬܚܬܝܐ at the end of ܡܪܝܐ. See Appendix I. under ܡܦܝܣܢܘܬܐ and ܡܦܝܣܢܝܬܐ.

19 Ps. cxii. 1.

h The mark of this sign is a point over the first letter of the first word; as ܛܘܒܘܗܝ،. See Appendix I., paragraph ܡܗ.

20 1 Kings i. 32. 21 Matth. xi. 28. 22 John i. 29.

i The mark of this sign is a point over the first letter of the *calling* word. For confirmation of this, see also paragraph ܡܗ. The third example, viz. ܗܐ ܐܡܪܗ ܕܐܠܗܐ, is one of ܡܫܐܠܢܐ and not of ܩܪܘܝܐ. The next example of ܡܫܐܠܢܐ is found in our copy, and is that with which the MS. ܐ recommences.

ܒܥܐ ܐܢܐ ܡܢܟ ܡܪܝܐ. ※ ܒܥܘܬܐ[23] *I beseech Thee, o Lord.*[j]

ܐܝܟܘ ܗܒܝܠ ܐܚܘܟ ※ ܡܫܐܠܢܐ[24] *where is Abel thy brother?*[k]

ܐܢ[25] ܐܝܬ ܟܐܒܐ ܐܝܟ ܟܐܒܝ ܕܥܒܕ ※ ܡܟܝܟܘܬܐ ܠܝ ܡܪܝܐ. , *if there be sorrow like unto my sorrow, which the Lord hath done to me.*[l]

ܐܝܟܢܐ[26] ܐܬܒܨܝ ܥܣܘ ܘܐܬܒܥܝ ※ ܡܬܕܡܪܢܐ ܡܛܫܝܬܗ. , *how is Esau searched out, how are his secret things sought up!* ܐܝܟܢܐ[27] ܗܘܘ ܠܬܕܡܘܪܬܐ ܡܢ ܫܠܝ, *how suddenly have they become an astonishment!*[m]

---

23 Luke ix. 38.

j This example is used in Appendix I. for ܡܨܠܝܢܐ, and the example there given for ܒܥܘܬܐ is that which in this tract is employed for the sign ܡܨܠܝܢܐ. The truth is, that both signs are intended to mark prayer. The difference, so far as it can be inferred from what is said of each sign in the Appendix is, that ܡܨܠܝܢܐ marks prayer to God only; while ܒܥܘܬܐ indicates prayer not only to God, but also to man, as that of the prodigal son to his father on his return. The mark according to Bar Hebræus, is the same for both, viz. a point over the beginning of the protasis &c.

24 Gen. iv. 9.

k The mark of this sign is a point over the asking word.

25 Lam. i. 12.

l The mark of this sign is a point below the beginning of the clause, as the point under ܐܢ in the example given above. Bar Hebræus says that ܡܟܝܟܘܬܐ expresses *humility, gentleness,* and *contrition of heart.*

26 Obad. i. 6.

27 This example I cannot find in the Syriac Scriptures.

m The mark of this sign (see Appendix I.) is a point *below* the beginning of the first member, as ܐܝܟܢܐ in the example above; but Bar Hebræus makes the mark one or two points *above.*

ܐܝܬܘܗ̇ܝ,[28] ܓܝܪ ܐܠܗܐ ܫܪܝܪܐ ※ ܡܫܬܐܠܢܐ *for God is true.*[n]

ܫܘܐ̇ ܒܐܘܣܝܐ ※ ܡܫܘܕܥܢܐ *equal in substance;* ܫܠܝܛ ܒܟܠ *omnipotent;* ܠܐ ܡ̇ܝܘܬܐ *immortal.*[o]

ܡܙܕܪܥ ܒܚܒܠܐ. ܩܐܡ ܕܠܐ ܚܒܠܐ ※ ܥܘܠܦ ܡܫܘܕܥܢܐ[29] ܫܚܠܐ, *sown in corruption, raised in incorruption.*[p]

ܒܫܗܪܐ, ܒܨܘܡܐ ܒܠܐܘܬܐ ܒܐܣܘܪ̈ܐ ※ ܟܢܘܪܐ,[30] *in watching, in fasting, in labour, in bonds.*[q]

---

[28] Rom. iii 4.

[n] The mark of this sign is the same as that for ܡܫܐܠܬܐ, according to Appendix I.; but not according to Bar Hebræus. Further on in this tract it is stated that the sign ܡܫܬܐܠܢܐ is the contrary of ܙܘܥܐ *motion* or *progress,* and therefore the mark is required to be put wherever the progress is expected, but not had. The English of this remark I apprehend to be, that wherever there is a sudden change or interruption of the subject, this change or interruption is called by the name ܡܫܬܐܠܢܐ. See ex. above and John iii. 7.

[o] These examples are expressed by one word in Greek. Its mark (see Appendix I.) is a point below the last letter of the first member, and another point below the first letter of the second member. ܕܢܘܩܙܐ ܚܕ ܢܣܝܡܘܢ ܠܬܚܬ ܡܢ ܐܬܘܬܐ ܐܚܪܝܬܐ ܕܗܕܡܐ ܩܕܡܝܐ. ܘܢܘܩܙܐ ܐܚܪܢܐ ܠܬܚܬ ܡܢ ܐܬܘܬܐ ܩܕܡܝܬܐ ܕܗܕܡܐ ܕܬܪ̈ܝܢ. ܕܡܫܚܘܢ ܕܐܝܟ ܠܒܥܝܐ ܗܘܪܫܢܐ ܬܪ̈ܝܢ ܐܢܘܢ ܗ̈ܕܡܐ. ܐܠܐ ܒܡܠܬܐ ܚܕܐ ܗܕܡܐ ܐܝܬܝܗܘܢ. Bar Hebræus says the mark is a point after the first member.

[29] 1 Cor. xv. 42.

[p] The mark of this sign is, according to Bar Hebræus, a point after the first member. He says, ܒܬܪ ܗܕܡܐ ܡܩܕܡܝܐ.

[30] 2 Cor. vi. 5.

[q] The mark of this sign is similar to that of ܦܩܘܕܐ. See Bar Hebræus.

ܝܘ̈ܡܬܐ· ܘܝܪ̈ܚܐ· ܘܙܒ̈ܢܐ. ܘܫ̈ܢܝܐ ※ ܫܘܚܠܦ ܬܪ̈ܘܢܐ 31
ܢܛܪܝܢ ܐܢܬܘܢ ·, *ye observe days, and months, and times, and years.*[r]

ܗܘ ܒܝܘܡܐ ܬܕܥܘܢ ܕܐ̈ܢܐ ܒܐܒܝ· ※ ܡܙܝܚܢܐ 32
ܘܐܢܬܘܢ ܒܝ ܐܢܬܘܢ, *in that day ye shall know that I am in my father, and ye are in me.*[s]

ܕܐܬܐܡܪ ܝܘܡܢܐ ܒܛܘܪܐ ※ ܟܢܘܫܬܐ ܘܡܙܝܚܢܐ 33
ܗܢܐ· ܡܪܝܐ ܢܚܙܐ, *that which was said today in this mountain, the Lord shall appear.*

ܘܒܘܪܠܐ· ܘܣܦܝܠܐ ※ ܝܘܟܐ, *and beryl and sapphire.*[t]

ܙܕܝ̈ܩܐ ܢܥܡܪܘܢ ܒܐܪܥܐ. ܘܥ̈ܘܠܐ ※ ܣܡܟܐ 34
ܢܬܥܩܪܘܢ ܡܢܗ̇, *the righteous shall dwell in the land, but sinners shall be rooted from it.*[u]

ܠܐ ܡܘܬܐ. ܘܠܐ ܚܝ̈ܐ. ※ ܫܘܚܠܦ ܣܡܟܐ, 35
neither death, nor life.[v]

---

31 Gal. iv. 10.

r Here the members are joined by *Vau*. The sign seems to be read with the mark of ܬܚܬܝܐ or ܣܡܟܐ.

32 John xiv. 20.

s The mark of this sign (see Appendix I.) is a point. It seems that this sign is called by Bar Hebræus ܫܘܚܠܦ ܡܙܝܚܢܐ The same example, viz. John xiv. 20, is quoted by him as one of ܫܘܚܠܦ ܡܙܝܚܢܐ. The mark also, he says, is a point like ܬܚܬܝܐ, which corresponds accurately with what is said in the Appendix to which reference has been made in the beginning of this note. In the example cited, the mark is after ܒܐܒܝ, thus ܒܐܒܝ·.

33 Gen. xxii. 14.

t The mark of the sign ܝܘܟܐ is similar to that of ܡܙܝܚܢܐ.

34 Prov. ii. 21, 22.

u The mark of this sign is a point below the final letter of a word, or it may be said to be the same in mark as ܬܚܬܝܬܐ omitting the upper point.

35 Rom. viii. 38.

v The mark of this sign is as that of ܣܡܟܐ.

ܙܪܥܐ ܒܝܫܐ· ܒܢܝܐ ※ ܥܠܝܐ ܘܦܣܘܩܐ 36
ܡܚܒܠܢܐ., *an evil seed, children that are corruptors.*

ܒܪܫܝܬ ܐܝܬܘܗܝ ܗܘܐ ܡܠܬܐ. ※ ܡܩܪܝܢܐ ܘܡܓܪܓܠܢܐ, 37
in the beginning was the word.[w]

ܐܝܟܐ ܗܘ ※ ܡܫܐܠܢܐ ܘܥܠܝܐ ܘܪܗܛܐ ܕܦܣܘܩܐ 38
ܙܟܘܬܟ· ܡܘܬܐ̈, *O death, where is thy victory?*[x]

※ ܦܩܘܕܐ ܘܥܠܝܐ ܘܪܗܛܐ ܕܠܐ ܦܣܩ ܘܦܣܘܩܐ 39
ܐܚܒܘ ܙܕܝܩܘܬܐ· ܕܝܢܝܗ̈ ܕܐܪܥܐ., *love righteousness, ye judges of the earth.*[y]

ܘܚܙܐ. ܘܗܐ ܝܒܫܘ ܐܦ̈ܝ ܐܪܥܐ ※ ܦܩܘܕܐ, 40
and he saw, and behold the face of the earth was dry;

ܘܒܢ̈ܘܗܝ ܕܒܠܗܐ ܐܡܬܗ ܕܪܚܝܠ ܕܢ. ܘܢܦܬܠܝ., 41
and the sons of Bilhah, the handmaid of Rachel, were Dan and Naphtali.[z]

---

36 Is. i. 4. 37 John i. 1.

w We have in this example ܡܩܪܝܢܐ under ܫ of ܒܪܫܝܬ and the mark of ܡܓܪܓܠܢܐ is after ܡܠܬܐ.

38 1 Cor. xv. 55.

x The accent ܡܫܐܠܢܐ is over ܐܝܟܐ; that of ܥܠܝܐ after ܟ of ܙܟܘܬܟ· and the points ܪܗܛܐ ܕܦܣܘܩܐ at the end of ܡܘܬܐ̈.

39 Wisdom i. 4.

y Here we have ܐܚܒܘ for ܦܩܘܕܐ, ܙܕܝܩܘܬܐ· for ܥܠܝܐ, ܕܝܢܝܗ̈ for ܪܗܛܐ ܕܠܐ ܦܣܩ and ܕܐܪܥܐ. for ܦܣܘܩܐ.

40 Gen. viii. 13. 41 Gen. xxxv. 25.

z The mark of this sign is the same as that of ܦܣܘܩܐ. Bar Hebræus says, that it is distinguished from ܦܣܘܩ ܥܐܠܐ in that the clause which comes next, is connected by the letter ܘܐܘ. What constitutes ܦܣܘܩ ܥܐܠܐ is fully explained by him in the discourse here edited.

ܡܦܪܘܣܝܐ or ܡܗܦܟܢܝܐ ※ . ܐܨܬܘ ܫܡܝܐ ܘܐܡܠܠ, 42
give ear, O ye heavens, and I will speak.[a]
A *variation* of it by letters, ܬܫܡܥ ܐܪܥܐ 43
ܡܐܡܪܗ ܕܦܘܡܝ, *the earth shall hear the word of my mouth.*[a]
Another *variation* by lines, ܢܪܣܦ ܐܝܟ ܡܛܪܐ 43
ܝܘܠܦܢܝ, *my doctrine shall drop as the rain.*[a]
With respect to the letters, when *the point* is below, it is that of ܕܠܬ; above, of ܪܝܫ.
ܬܚܘܬܝܬܐ ,ܫܪܝ ܥܡ ܬܫܡܫܐ ※ : ܕܠܡܐ ܐܬܐ 44
ܘܐܡܚܝܘܗ̇ܝ ܠܐܪܥܐ ܠܚܪܡܐ. *lest I come and smite the earth with destruction.*[b]

It is thought that because of the proximity of the place, or because of the suitability of the expressions and the similitude of the points, it is possible for a man to change the order of the reading of the points. But this distinction must be added.[c]

. . . .

. . . .

There may be many ܫܘܝܐ after one another; but ܫܪܝܐ or ܫܘܝܐ ܡܥܠܝܢ, is only one *accent* in the discourse, and ܡܫܚܠܦܐ is after it, and not ܬܚܘܬܝܐ.

---

42 Deut. xxxii. 1.

[a] It is not stated by Jacob, what may be the mark of this accent. Bar Hebræus confesses that he does not know the sign, nor had he ever heard it in his time. See his discourse, where he quotes the authority of a learned Greek.

43 Deut. xxxii. 2. 44 Mal. iv. 6.

[b] In the list of signs in this tract, ܬܚܘܬܝܬܐ ,ܫܪܝ is mentioned as another name for ܫܘܝܐ ܡܥܠܝܢ. In the example we have ܬܫܡܫܐ and ܬܚܘܬܝܬܐ ,ܫܪܝ together after ܐܬܐ.

[c] Here is another decayed place in the MS. The blank thus caused is filled up by the following extract from Codex ܒ.

ܡܫܐܠܢܐ and ܦܩܕܐ differ in that ܡܫܐܠܢܐ is alone in the expression, whilst ܦܩܕܐ is put with ܦܣܘܩܐ.

Again there are points which are similar to one another, ܡܒܟܝܢܐ, ܡܦܝܣܢܐ, ܬܚܘܬܐ.

The ܬܚܘ̈ܬܐ are constantly being brought forth in discourse. ܡܦܝܣܢܐ is said to him who is great; such as, ܒܥܐ ܐܢܐ ܡܢܟ ܡܪܝ ܐܬܪܚܡ ܥܠܝ. *I beseech Thee, O Lord, have mercy on me;* ܒܥܐ ܐܢܐ ܡܢܟܘܢ ܡܪ̈ܝ ܣܛܘ ܠܘܬ ܥܒܕܟܘܢ.[45] *I beseech you, my lords, turn to your servant.*[d]

ܡܒܟܝܢܐ indicates oppression, or causes to weep from fear, as that which is said by Jacob the patriarch; ܐܠܗܗ ܕܐܒܝ ܐܒܪܗܡ. ܐܠܗܗ ܕܐܒܝ[46] ܐܝܣܚܩ. ܡܪܝܐ ܕܐܡܪ ܠܝ. ܗܦܘܟ ܠܐܪܥܐ ܕܡܘܠܕܘܬܟ ܘܐܛܐܒ ܠܟ. *O God of my father Abraham, O God of my father Isaac, the Lord who hath said to me, return to the land of thy birth, and I will deal well with thee.*

It is needful that there be one order of reading of ܥܠܝܐ and ܙܘܓܐ ܥܠܝܐ. But *the reading* is distinguished in two ways. One is, that they put ܙܘܓܐ ܥܠܝܐ in the place of ܪܗܛܐ ܕܠܐ ܦܘܫ. It is put because of the length of the expression on which it is put. The second is, because it is possible that two or three ܥܠܝ̈ܐ, may be placed after one another; this ܙܘܓܐ ܥܠܝܐ has ܦܣܘܩܐ before it and ܦܣܘܩܐ after it. So also ܙܘܓܐ ܬܚܘܬܐ has ܦܣܘܩܐ before it and after it, and it is read interrogatively. Similarly ܬܚ̈ܬܝܐ and ܙܘܓܐ ܬܚ̈ܬܝܐ.

[45] Gen. xix. 2.

[d] ܡܦܝܣܢܐ, like ܡܫܐܠܢܐ, is farther distinguished by a point at the head of the first word.

[46] Gen. xxxii. 9.

Also of ܦܘܩܕܢܐ, ܩܪܘܝܐ, ܡܚܘܝܢܐ, ܡܫܐܠܢܐ, ܡܗܦܟ ܠܬܘܒܐ, ܡܬܟܫܦܢܐ; ܡܫܐܠܢܐ is mentioned in two ways; either he who asks is desirous to learn, or he asks temptingly. He who *asks* to learn; as that which is said by the disciples to our Saviour, ܐܡܬܝ, ܗܠܝܢ ܢܗܘ̈ܝܢ,[47] *when shall these things be?* Isaac to his father, ܗܐ ܢܘܪܐ ܘܩܝ̈ܣܐ. [48] ܐܝܟܘ ܐܡܪܐ ܠܥܠܬܐ, *behold the fire and the wood; where is the lamb for a burnt offering?* He who *asks* to tempt or try; as that which is said by the Lord, ܐܝܟܐ ܐܢܬ ܐܕܡ,[49] *Where art thou Adam?* ܘܐܝܟܘ ܗܒܝܠ ܐܚܘܟ,[50] *and where is Abel thy brother?* ܡܢܘ ܗܢܐ ܕܒܐܝܕܟ,[51] *what is this, which is in thy hand?*

ܡܚܘܝܢܐ, as he who points with the finger, according to that which is said; ܗܐ ܐܡܪܗ ܕܐܠܗܐ[52] ܗܘ ܕܫܩܠ ܚܛܝܬܗ ܕܥܠܡܐ, *behold the lamb of God, which taketh away the sin of the world;* also, ܗܢܘ[53] ܗܘ ܕܐܢܐ ܐܡܪܬ ܕܒܬܪܝ, ܐܬܐ, *this is he of whom I said that he cometh after me.*

ܩܪܘܝܐ ※ . ܩܪܘ ܠܝ ܠܢܬܢ ܢܒܝܐ,[54] *call me Nathan the prophet;* ܬܘ ܟܠܟܘܢ ܠܐܝ̈ܐ,[55] *come all ye wearied;* ܬܘ ܒܪ̈ܝܟܘܗܝ ܕܐܒܝ,[56] *come ye blessed of my father.*

ܦܘܩܕܢܐ ※ . . ܗܪܛ ܠܘܛ ܠܓܐܪ̈ܐ ܕܫܕܐ ܐܢܐ[57] *run, gather the arrows, which I cast.*

ܡܬܟܫܦܢܐ, such as that which is said by the priests to God in prayer, ܫܒܘܩ ܣܟ̈ܠܘܬܢ, *pardon our crimes;*

---

[47] Matt. xxiv. 3. [48] Gen. xxii. 7. [49] Gen. iii. 9.
[50] Gen. iv. 9. [51] Ex. iv. 2. [52] John i. 29.
[53] John i. 30. [54] 1 Kings i. 35. [55] Matth. xi. 28.
[56] Matth. xxv. 14. [57] 1 Sam. xx. 36.

ܥܛܝ ܚܛܗܝܢ, *blot out our sins;* ܫܒܘܩ ܣܟܠܘܬܢ, *forgive our iniquities;* &c.

ܙܘܥ ܛܘܒܐ is in the word by which happiness is conveyed, ܛܘܒܘܗܝ, ܠܓܒܪܐ,[58] *blessed is the man.*

There is also ܬܚܘܡܐ with ܙܥܝܪ, ܬܚܘܡܝܬܐ, thus: ܕܠܐ ܐܬܐ: ܘܐܡܚܝܗ̇ ܠܐܪܥܐ ܠܚܪܡܐ,[59] *lest I come and smite the earth with destruction;* ܘܢܗܘܘܢ[60] ܠܬܗܪܐ: ܠܟܠ ܒܣܪ, *and they shall be a wonder to all flesh.*

ܡܬܕܡܪܢܐ varies from ܡܢܝܚܬܐ and ܡܙܝܥܢܐ. ܡܬܕܡܪܢܐ, looking to the greatness of the thing, admires it, thus: ܐܝܟܢܐ ܗܘܘ ܠܬܡܗܐ ܡܢ ܫܠܝܐ, *how suddenly have they become for an astonishment!* ܐܝܟܢܐ ܐܬܒܨܝ, ܥܣܘ ܘܐܬܒܥܝ ܡܛܫܝܬܗ,[61] *how is Esau searched out, and how are his secret things sought up!*[e]

ܡܢܝܚܬܐ one will read without being suddenly and quickly excited; the word on which ܡܢܝܚܬܐ is placed, will be read slowly.

ܡܙܝܥܢܐ is the contrary of ܢܘܚܐ, and, therefore, ܡܙܝܥܢܐ is put everywhere when motion is thought to be required, (*but is not had.*[f]) It is also put against ܡܫܐܠܢܐ, where the two erect points[g]

---

[58] Ps. i. 1. [59] Mal. iv. 6. [60] Ps. lxvi. 24.

[61] Obad. i. 6.

[e] Jacob in the last two pages has been recapitulating some of the names of ܢܝ̈ܫܐ, arranging them in groups according to the similarity of the marks and their positions, as is done more fully in Appendix I. We have first a group of three signs, then one of six, and here one of three.

[f] ܟܕ ܠܐ ܐܝܬ ܢܫܡܫ. Bar Hebræus.

[g] By the two erect points, ܫܘ̈ܝܐ is to be understood, and not the two points of the accent ܦܩܘܕܐ, for that would not at all

are mentioned. But it is the contrary, ܗܒܟܐ and ܡܒܥܝܢܐ being put, i.e. ܡܒܛܠܠܢܐ will stand by the sign ܬܚܬܝܬܐ, when we mention neither ܗܒܟܐ nor ܡܒܥܝܢܐ in the sentence.

ܦܣܘܩܐ and ܝܚܝܕܝܐ differ in that with respect to every point which is put at the end of a sentence, it is named ܦܣܘܩܐ; but ܝܚܝܕܝܐ, we say of this *sign*, it is private, because that it is in the sentence by itself, without another point, i.e. without ܬܚܬܝܐ, ܥܠܝܐ, &c.

ܪܗܛܐ ܕܫܡܥ ܘܕܠܐ ܫܡܥ. There is ܗܒܟܐ with it constantly, upon the member which is before ܪܗܛܐ, as, ܚܘܪ· ܡܪܝܐ·· ܘܚܙܝ ܫܥܒܘܕܝ, *look, O Lord, and see my subjection;* ܪܚܡ ܥܠܝ· ܡܪܝܐ··, *have mercy on me, O Lord.*

Again, with respect to the sounds, which indicate ܐܝܟ ܐܡܪܬ ܐܠܟܕ, with all others which are similar, and after these ܐܕܘܢ, have points below.[1]

---

agree with the context; also the mark of ܦܩܘܕܐ is not two points, but one, and further on ܙܘܓܐ ܕܬܚܬܝܬܐ is mentioned, the same as ܫܠܝܘܢ ܙܘ̈ܓܐ, which possesses the same mark as ܙܘ̈ܓܐ. The meaning is that ܡܒܛܠܠܢܐ will stand against ܡܫܐܠܢܐ, by ܙܘܓܐ ܕܬܚܬܝܬܐ, when ܗܒܟܐ and ܡܒܥܝܢܐ are not put.

[1] I think that this and the following remarks belong to the introduction or the 1st Chapter of this tract. It is probable that the copyist may have omitted these sentences in their proper place, and so added them at the end of the tract. A similar omission is to be found in the letter. See note h p. 7. Why I consider that these sentences are out of place here is, 1st, that ܡܨܥܝܢܐ occurs in the last of them, and this is the name of the intermediate vowel sound mentioned in the introduction. 2nd,

Those *sounds*, which indicate ܐܟ̇ܠ, ܐܡ̇ܪ, &c., *have points* above.

Those *sounds*, which denote ܐܢܬ, ܐܠܗܐ ܐܕܘܢܝ, *O Lord God*, have two *points* i.e. *have* ܡܦܩܕܢܐ.

---

that these remarks are headed ܠܘܬ ܩ̈ܠܐ *concerning sounds*, as if vowel sounds were the subject of the remarks.

The object of these remarks seems to be to state the punctuation proper for each of the three persons. For the 1st and 3rd persons the author has selected verbs for his examples; but for the 2nd, the noun ܐܕܘܢܝ, which, although the points are omitted by the copyist, should have ܡܦܩܕܢܐ, viz. ܐܕܘܢ̣ܝ̇, i.e. a point above and a point below. I suspect that ܡܢ ܠܬܚܬ, and ܡܢ ܠܥܠ should change places; for the examples of the 1st person should have the point above, as it actually appears in the text, and the examples of the 3rd person should have the point below, according to the received theory; although the copyist has somehow managed to put it above.

THE BOOK OF RAYS,

BY

GREGORY BAR HEBRÆUS.

THE FOURTH DISCOURSE, SIXTH CHAPTER, ON THE GREAT POINTS, FIVE SECTIONS.

THE FIRST SECTION.

ON THE NECESSITY OF METRICAL SIGNS.[a]

BECAUSE in all speech, the hearer is able from the hearing of one real word, without addition to it, by connection of nouns, verbs and conjunctions, to acquire the different senses, but by a vocal variation only, Syrian Scribes have been industrious in composing structures, directing their speech, and have ordained point marks for metrical signs; so that there is an appropriate sign indicating the various sounds of every one of them. After this manner, those who speak barbarously may become at once (lit. at sight) known, from hearing the speaking, or from the reading.

A RAY.

That placing the points of metrical signs is necessary, may be known from this : he who reads, ܠܐ ܗܘܐ ܡܢ ܙܪܥܗ ܕܕܘܝܕ : ܘܡܢ ܒܝܬ ܠܚܡ ܕܢܚ ܡܫܝܚܐ. *did not Christ spring from the seed of David, and from*

---

[a] A summary of these sections is to be found in the 2nd. Vol. of the *Zeitschrift für die Kunde des Morgenlandes*, by Ewald.

*Bethlehem?** if he did not see the mark of ܬܟܫܦܐ with ܠܐ ܗܘܐ, and ܦܩܘܕܐ with :ܕܘܝܕ and ܡܟܠܐ with .ܡܫܝܚܐ, might think that the Messiah was *not* born of the seed of David and of Bethlehem. Revelation also is, not whether He was born, but whether the Scripture required him to be born *of David and at Bethlehem.* So also, he who reads ܐܝܢܐ ܠܐܢܬܬܐ ܕܦܐ ܟܕ ܓܠܐ ܪܫܗ ܬܨܠܐ ܠܐܠܗܐ., *is it comely for a woman to pray unto God with her head uncovered?*† except he saw ܬܟܫܦܐ with ܐܢܬܬܐ, and ܬܚܘܬܐ, with .ܐܠܗܐ, he would not know whether the blessed Apostle requested a woman to pray with her head uncovered, or forbade. The Scriptures abound with many other *such passages.*

A RAY.

THESE vocal marks, composed of great points, are named *metrical signs;* because that as to every logical speech there is an appropriate measure estimated by the sign and indicated by it, so also to every one of these point marks for every logical speech, there is an appropriate measure estimated in regard to the sign and known by it.

Observation. In the invention of the marks of metrical signs, the Greek and our Syriac Literature are especially distinguished. Hence, with respect to other books, which are deprived of them, they lift up the head, as being shorn. Because that these signs are of the kind of musical sounds, it would not indeed be possible for the ear to find their species from rumour and from the tradition of

* John vii. 42. † 1 Cor. xi. 13.

the teacher to the learner not flowing from the tongue; nor to comprehend them.

THE SECOND SECTION.

On the number of the metrical signs and their names with their marks.[a]

The Western *Syrians have* forty marks, as metrical signs. Four radical, and they are, ܥܠܝܐ .: *above*, ܬܚܬܝܐ . *beneath*, ܫܘܝܐ : *equals*, ܦܣܘܩܐ *section*, and thirty six branches, which germinate from them. These are either simple or compound. There are twenty-eight simple *signs*, ܥܠܝܐ .: ܫܘܚܠܦ *variation of* ܥܠܝܐ, ܬܚܬܝܐ . ܫܘܚܠܦ *variation of* ܬܚܬܝܐ, ܫܘܝܐ : ܫܘܚܠܦ *variation of* ܫܘܝܐ, ܪܗܛܐ ܕܦܣܩ, *the* ܪܗܛܐ *which divides*, ܡܒܟܝܢܐ *weeping*, ܦܩܘܕܐ *commanding*, ܦܫܝܛܐ . *simple*, ܬܟܣܐ *reproof*, ܡܫܐܠܢܐ *interrogating*, ܪܗܛܐ ܕܠܐ ܦܣܩ ܘܕܦܣܩ, *the* ܪܗܛܐ *which does not divide and that which does divide*, ܬܠܬܐ ܪ̈ܗܛܐ *three* ܪ̈ܗܛܐ, ܡܫܒܚܢܐ *the praiser*, ܝܗܒ ܛܘܒܐ *giving happiness*, ܩܪܘܝܐ *calling*, ܡܚܘܝܢܐ *indicating*, ܡܨܠܝܢܐ *praying*, ܡܟܫܦܢܐ *supplicating*, ܡܢܚܬܐ *making to descend*, ܡܬܕܡܪܢܐ *admiring*, ܡܦܣܩܢܐ *discontinuing*, ܡܚܝܕܢܐ *uniting*, ܫܘܚܠܦ ܡܚܝܕܢܐ *variation of* ܡܚܝܕܢܐ, ܥܨܘܪܐ *tearing away* or *drawing out*, ܫܘܚܠܦ ܥܨܘܪܐ *variation of* ܥܨܘܪܐ, ܙܘܥܐ *motion*, ܣܡܟܐ *a prop*, ܫܘܚܠܦ ܣܡܟܐ *variation of* ܣܡܟܐ; ܙܘܥܐ ܘܣܡܟܐ, ܙܘܥܐ and ܣܡܟܐ; ܣܡܟܐ ܘܡܦܣܩܢܐ, ܣܡܟܐ and ܡܦܣܩܢܐ;

[a] The marks of many of the signs, through the ignorance or carelessness of the copyist, are not put with their names. They appear, however, in the description which follows.

ܕܦܣܘܩ ܘܪܗܛܐ ܘܙܘܓܐ ܡܫܐܠܢܐ, ܡܫܐܠܢܐ and ܘܗܒܐ and ܕܦܣܘܩ ܪܗܛܐ; ܕܠܐ ܘܪܗܛܐ ܘܗܒܐ ܘܦܣܘܩܐ ܦܣܘܩ, ܘܗܒܐ and ܦܣܘܩ ܕܠܐ ܪܗܛܐ and ܦܣܘܩܐ; ܦܘܡܐ *with the letters,* ܡܗܦܟܢܐ *turning back,* ܡܗܦܟܢܐ ܫܘܚܠܦ, *variation of* ܡܗܦܟܢܐ; ܬܫܒܘܚܬܐ ,ܙܪ ܥܡ ܬܫܡܫܐ, ܬܫܡܫܐ with ܬܫܒܘܚܬܐ ,ܙܪ.

A RAY.

The mark of the sign ܥܠܝܐ is two points, one under[b] the end of the clause, and the other before the end, above, thus ⁘

The mark of ܬܚܬܝܐ is two points, one under the end of the clause, and the other before the end, below, thus ∵.

The mark of ܙܘܓܐ, which is also named ܘܗܒܐ, is two points equal in position, thus :

The mark of ܦܣܘܩܐ is one point under the end of the sentence, thus .

The marks of these four acquire the denominations from the position of their points.

Observation. From the marks of these roots, the marks of their branches are composed. These may be distinctly known by examples of each one of them. Know, O reader, that Doctors perceive a vocal sign to be bound up in its mark, according to the logical purpose of every clause. But it is thought by me that they have not accurately com-

---

[b] It seems to have been the custom of at least some Syrians to write from the top of the page to the bottom, beginning at the left hand. Hence ܬܚܘܬ, *under*, would accurately express the position of this point of ܥܠܝܐ .

prehended, and, therefore, because knowledge such as this was difficult to be learned, they cut off opinion.[c] By the excision, they decreed and declared that it was not by human intelligence the measures were put in the Holy Scriptures, but as it appeared[d] they were inspired by the Holy Ghost, by whom was the placing of them. This thing is, therefore, confessed by those teaching it, that they are not to take the Holy Scriptures as immutable, as did the ancients. This is a very lofty *notion* and to which human power is unable to attain. But with respect to the signs, which *the marks* bind, let them be understood as they appear; and as they have heard from their masters, let *persons* learn to call these sounds.

Observation. In some places it is a possible matter to bring forth a logical reason for the signs. In the Old *Testament*, ܒܪܫܝܬ ܒܪܐ ܐܠܗܐ. ܝܬ[1] ܫܡܝܐ ܘܝܬ ܐܪܥܐ, *in the beginning God created the heaven and the earth.* Because that He, the lofty *one*, descended for the creation of heaven, the name ܐܠܗܐ is put with ܬܚܬܝܐ, the noun ܫܡܝܐ with ܦܣܘܩܐ, the ally of ܬܚܬܝܐ. In the New *Testament* we have ܟܬܒܐ[2] ܕܝܠܝܕܘܬܗ ܕܝܫܘܥ ܡܫܝܚܐ: ܒܪܗ ܕܕܘܝܕ[e] ܒܪܗ ܕܐܒܪܗܡ, *the book of the generation of Jesus Christ, the son of David, the son of Abraham.* Because that Christ the son enters into the family not *by* David emitting in the flesh, the noun

---

[1] Gen. i. 1. [2] Matth. i. 1.

[c] I.e. private judgment.

[d] Lit., according to that which has been seen.

[e] The ܪܬܒܐ of ܕܘܝܕ is omitted in the Text.

ܡܫܝܚܐ is bound with ܥܠܝܐ, and the name David with ܪܗܛܐ, the ally of ܥܠܝܐ. There are expressions suitable for two species of points, as in the Edessene copies of the prophet Isaiah, ܙܪܥܐ[f] ܡܒܐܫܐ[3] ܒܢܝܐ[g] ܡܚܒܠܐ, *a seed causing shame, children corrupting*, upon ܡܒܐܫܐ is put ܪܗܛܐ, and under ܒܢܝܐ, ܣܘܡܟܐ; but in the copies of Soba ܪܡܙܐ is on ܙܪܥܐ and ܒܢܝܐ.

I was acquainted at the same time with two old men at ܡܠܝܛܝܢܐ Melitene. There was a deliberation respecting the phrase ܫܒܘ ܥܠܡܐ ܗܢܐ. One, who was Michael, placed ܫܒܘ ܥܠܡܐ ܗܢܐ, with ܡܫܝܚܘܬܐ, as that he had received from his master and our master George. But the other, who was Basil, *placed* ܫܒܘ ܥܠܡܐ ܗܢܐ, with ܡܫܐܠܢܐ, as he had received from his master Constantine. And so every scribe measures according to what seems good to him.

THE THIRD SECTION.

On the suitableness of the positions of the four radical signs.

ܥܠܝܐ is put, when the first clause is finished by ܬܚܬܝܐ, and the second clause being long, it is therefore inserted between its members; as ܘܡܐ[4] ܕܡܨܠܐ ܐܢܬ. *and when thou prayest* (ܬܚܬܝܐ:), ܠܐ ܬܗܘܐ ܐܝܟ ܢܣܒܝ ܒܐܦܐ: *be not as the hypocrites* (ܥܠܝܐ:), ܕܪܚܡܝܢ ܠܡܩܡ ܒܟܢܘܫܬܐ ܘܒܙܘܝܬܐ ܕܫܘܩܐ ܠܡܨܠܝܘ: *who love to stand in the assem-*

---

[3] Isaiah i. 4.

[f] The ܪܡܙܐ of ܙܪܥܐ, the copyist has not put in the Text.

[g] The ܪܡܙܐ of ܒܢܝܐ, is also left out by the copyist. In the Bodleian MS. the mark upon ܙܪܥܐ and ܒܢܝܐ is ¨

[4] Matth. vi. 5.

blies, and in the corners of the streets to pray (:ܥܠܝܐ), ܕܢܬܚܙܘܢ ܠܒܢܝܢܫܐ.., *that they may be seen of men* (. ܦܣܘܩܐ). It is also put in a long question; as, ܡܢܘ ܡܢܟܘܢ ܓܒܪܐ ܕܐܝܬ ܠܗ ܥܪܒܐ ܚܕ :[6] *what man of you hath a sheep* (:ܥܠܝܐ), ܘܐܢ ܢܦܠ ܒܓܘܡܨܐ ܒܝܘܡܐ ܕܫܒܬܐ :, *and if it fall in the ditch on the Sabbath day* (:ܥܠܝܐ), ܐܠܐ ܐܚܕ ܘܡܩܝܡ ܠܗ . *but he taketh and raiseth it* (. ܦܣܘܩܐ). It is also put when many different thoughts come together. Theologus.[h] ܕܬܕܥܘܢ ܕܐܝܟܢܐ ܓܒܪ ܐܟܣܢܝܐ ܕܡܬܪܣܐ ܠܒܢܝ ܐܬܪܐ :, *that ye may know how a stranger may nourish the sons of the country* (:ܥܠܝܐ), ܘܠܩܘܪܝܝܐ ܡܕܝܢܝܐ :, *and a villager citizens,* (:ܥܠܝܐ), ܘܠܗܢܘܢ ܕܡܬܦܨܚܝܢ ܗܘ ܕܠܐ ܦܨܝܚ : *and he who is not mirthful those who are mirthful* (:ܥܠܝܐ) ܘܠܗܢܘܢ ܕܡܬܝܬܪܝܢ ܒܥܘܬܪܐ : ܡܣܟܢܐ ܘܒܪܒܝܬܐ . ܦܣܘܩܐ ., *and the poor man and the domestic* (:ܥܠܝܐ) *those who exceed in wealth.* (. ܦܣܘܩܐ).

A RAY.

ܬܚܬܝܐ is put at the end of the first clause, when the second ends with ܦܣܘܩܐ; as, ܘܐܬܘ ܒܬܪܗ[7] ܟܢ̈ܫܐ ܣܓܝܐܐ . ܘܐܣܝ ܐܢܘܢ ., *and many multitudes came after him* (. ܬܚܬܝܐ), *and he healed them* (. ܦܣܘܩܐ). But if the second be long, it will end with ܗܘܟܐ and ܫܡܟܐ and ܦܣܘܩܐ; as, ܘܩܪܒܘ ܠܘܬܗ ܦܪ̈ܝܫܐ . ܬܚܬܝܐ, *and the pharisees drew near to him* (ܬܚܬܝܐ), ܘܡܢܣܝܢ· ܗܘܟܐ, *and*

6 Matth. xii. 11.

7 Matth. xii. 15.

h Gregory Nazianzen.

tempted (ܙܘܓܐ), ܠܗ ܗܘܘ, *him* (ܦܩܘܕܐ), .ܘܐܡܪܝܢ, *and said* (.ܦܣܩ). There are *passages*, where two .ܬܚܬܝ̈ܬܐ may be put before ܦܣܘܩܐ; as, ܢܣܒ ܒܐܦ̈ܐ . ܬܚܬܝܬܐ . ܐܦܩ ܠܘܩܕܡ[8] ܩܪܝܬܐ ܡܢ ܥܝܢܟ . ܬܚܬܝܬܐ . ܘܗܝܕܝܢ ܬܬܚܙܐ ܠܟ ܠܡܦܩܘ ܓܠܐ ܡܢ ܥܝܢܗ ܕܐܚܘܟ . ܦܣܩ ., *thou hypocrite* (ܬܚܬܝܬܐ), *first cast out the beam from thine eye* (ܬܚܬܝܬܐ), *and then thou shalt see plainly to cast out the mote from the eye of thy brother.* (ܦܣܘܩܐ). There are *passages*, where there are three; as, ܘܬܡܢ[9] ܬܬܕܟܪ ܕܐܚܘܟ ܢܛܪ ܥܠܝܟ ܐܟܬܐ ܡܕܡ. ܬܚܬܝܬܐ . ܫܒܘܩ ܬܡܢ ܩܘܪܒܢܟ ܥܠ ܡܕܒܚܐ : ܬܚܬܝܬܐ . ܘܙܠ ܠܘܩܕܡ ܐܬܪܥܐ ܥܡ ܐܚܘܟ . ܬܚܬܝܬܐ . ܘܗܝܕܝܢ ܬܐ ܩܪܒ ܩܘܪܒܢܟ . ܦܣܩ . *and there thou rememberest that thy brother hath against thee any quarrel* (.ܬܚܬܝܬܐ), *leave there thy offering upon the altar* (.ܬܚܬܝܬܐ), *and go, first, be reconciled to thy brother* (.ܬܚܬܝܬܐ), *and then come, offer thy gift* (.ܦܣܩ). There are now found by Doctors more than three ܬܚܬܝ̈ܬܐ coming one after another.

A RAY.

ܙܠܝ̈ܩܐ are placed at the end of the first clause, when it is long, then comes ܬܚܬܝܬܐ, and then ܦܣܩ; as, ܘܐܠܘ[10] ܥܒ̈ܕܐ ܠܐ ܥܒܕܬ ܠܘܬܗܘܢ : ܙܠܝ̈ܩܐ . ܐܝܠܝܢ ܕܐܢܫ ܠܐ ܥܒܕ . ܬܚܬܝܬܐ . ܠܝܬ ܗܘܐ ܠܗܘܢ ܚܛܝܬܐ . ܦܣܩ, *and if I had not done in their eyes*

---

[7] Matth. xix. 3.
[8] Matth. vii. 5.
[9] Matth. v. 23, 24.
[10] John xv. 24.

(: ܙܘ̈ܓܐ), *those things which no other man hath done* (. ܬܚܬܝܐ), *they had not had sin* (ܦܣܩ̄). There are *passages*, where, after two ܙܘ̈ܓܐ, there follows ܬܚܬܝܐ, then ܦܣܩ̄; as, : ܡܐ ܕܐܬܐ ܕܝܢ ܦܪܩܠܝܛܐ[11]
ܙܘ̈ܓܐ . ܗܘ ܕܐܢܐ ܫܕܪ ܐܢܐ ܠܟܘܢ ܡܢ ܠܘܬ ܐܒܝ :
ܙܘ̈ܓܐ . ܪܘܚܐ ܕܫܪܪܐ ܗܘ ܕܡܢ ܠܘܬ ܐܒܝ ܢܦܩ .
ܗܘ ܢܣܗܕ ܥܠܝ . ܦܣܘܩܐ ., *but when there is come the Comforter* (: ܙܘ̈ܓܐ), *whom I send unto you from my Father* (: ܙܘ̈ܓܐ), *the Spirit of truth, who from my Father proceedeth* (. ܬܚܬܝܐ), *He shall testify of me* (ܦܣܘܩܐ). There are *passages*, where many ܙܘ̈ܓܐ follow one another, then ܬܚܬܝܐ, then ܦܣܩ̄; as, ܐܢ ܠܗܘܢ ܐܡܪ ܐܠܗ̈ܐ : ܙܘ̈ܓܐ[12]
ܘܠܐ ܡܫܟܚ ܟܬܒܐ ܕܢܫܬܪܐ : ܙܘ̈ܓܐ . ܠܡܢ
ܕܐܒܐ ܩܕܫܗ ܘܫܕܪܗ ܠܥܠܡܐ : ܙܘ̈ܓܐ . ܐܢܬܘܢ
ܐܡܪܝܢ ܐܢܬܘܢ ܕܡܓܕܦ ܐܢܬ : ܙܘ̈ܓܐ . ܥܠ ܕܐܡܪܬ
ܠܟܘܢ : ܕܒܪܗ ܐܢܐ ܕܐܠܗܐ . ܘܐܢ ܠܐ ܥܒܕ ܐܢܐ
ܥܒ̈ܕܐ ܕܐܒܝ ܠܐ ܬܗܝܡܢܘܢܢܝ . ܦܣܩ̄ ., *if he called them gods* (: ܙܘ̈ܓܐ), *and the Scripture cannot be broken* (: ܙܘ̈ܓܐ), *whom the Father hath sanctified and sent into the world* (: ܙܘ̈ܓܐ)*; ye say, Thou blasphemest* (ܙܘ̈ܓܐ), *because I said unto you that I am the Son of God* (. ܬܚܬܝܐ)*; and if I do not the works of my Father, believe me not* (ܦܣܩ̄).

Observation. ܙܘ̈ܓܐ are placed as the legs of sandals,[1] when there are many in the protasis,

---

[11] John xv. 26. [12] John x. 35, 36, 37.

[1] This expression is designed to represent the case when many members of a sentence come together, each bearing the mark of ܙܘ̈ܓܐ.

which being terminated by ܬܚܬܝܐ, the apodosis ending with ܦܣܘ̄. Theologus, ܟܕ ܫܒܩܝܢ ܐܢ ܫܦܝܪܐ ܠܟܠܗܘܢ ܗܢܘܢ ܐܚܪ̈ܢܐ : ܫܘܒܩܐ. ܠܡܘܫܐ : ܠܐܗܪܘܢ ܗܘ : ܫܘܒܩܐ . ܠܕ̈ܝܢܐ : ܫܘܒܩܐ . ܠܫܡܘܐܝܠ : ܫܘܒܩܐ . ܠܕܘܝܕ : ܫܘܒܩܐ . ܠܝܫܘܥ : ܫܘܒܩܐ . ܠܐܠܝܫܥ : ܫܘܒܩܐ . ܠܟܢܫܐ ܕܢܒ̈ܝܐ : ܫܘܒܩܐ . ܠܝܘܚܢܢ : ܫܘܒܩܐ . ܠܐܠܝܐ : ܫܘܒܩܐ . ܠܬܪܥܣܪ ܬܠܡܝ̈ܕܐ : ܫܘܒܩܐ . ܠܗܢܘܢ ܕܒܬܪ ܗܠܝܢ ܠܚܪܬܐ : ܗܢܘܢ ܕܒܣ̈ܓܝܐܬܐ ܥܡ̈ܠܐ ܘܥܡ̈ܠܐ ܢܦܩܘ ܠܟܘܡܪܘܬܐ ܒܙ̈ܒܢܐ ܕܠܗܘܢ ܟܠܚܕ ܡܢܗܘܢ : ܫܘܒܩܐ . ܟܕ ܠܗܠܝܢ ܟܠܗܘܢ ܥܒܪܝܢ . ܠܦܘܠܘܣ ܒܠܚܘܕ ܪܫܐ ܕܡܠܬܐ . ܦܣܘ̄ ., *we omit, if you please, all the others* (:ܫܘܒܩܐ), *Moses* (ܫܘܒܩܐ), *Aaron himself* (ܫܘܒܩܐ), *the Judges* (ܫܘܒܩܐ), *Samuel* (ܫܘܒܩܐ), *David* (ܫܘܒܩܐ), *Joshua* (ܫܘܒܩܐ), *Elisha* (ܫܘܒܩܐ), *the congregation of the prophets* (ܫܘܒܩܐ), *John* (ܫܘܒܩܐ), *Elias* (ܫܘܒܩܐ), *the twelve disciples* (ܫܘܒܩܐ); *lastly, those who were after them, who with much toil and labour went forth, each one of them in his time, to the (sacerdotal) office* (ܫܘܒܩܐ); *all these we pass by* (ܬܚܬܝܐ); *Paul only is at the head of the discourse.* (ܦܣܘ̄).

A RAY.

Every point which is placed at the end of the apodosis is ܦܣܘ̄ ܬܪܝܨܐ, *Posuqo proper* ܡܦܣܩܢܐ going before; as, ܐܠܗܐ܂ ܡܦܣܩܢܐ . ܠܐ . ܚܙܐ ܐܢܫ ܡܡ[13] ܡܬܘܡ . ܦܣܘ̄, *God* (ܡܦܣܩܢܐ) *no man hath seen at any time* (ܦܣܘ̄); or ܬܚܬܝܐ going before; as, ܗܘ ܕܠܐ ܡܝܩܪ ܠܒܪܐ . ܬܚܬܝܐ . ܠܐ ܡܝܩܪ ܠܐܒܐ[14]

---

[13] John i. 18.

[14] John v. 23.

. ܕܫܕܪܗ, *he who honoureth not the Son* (ܬܚܬܝܐ), *honoureth not the Father, who sent him* (ܦܣܘܩܐ). This sign also, where it is connected by a conjunction, occurs now and then after ܟܠܐ; as, (ܠܝܬ) ܠܝܬ ܓܝܪ ܐܢܫ ܕܥܒܕ ܚܝܠܐ ܒܫܡܝ : ܘܡܫܟܚ ܥܓܠ[15] . ܕܒܝܫ ܥܠܝ ܢܐܡܪ, *for there is not a man, who doeth miracles in my name* (ܟܠܐ), *and can lightly speak evil of me* (ܦܣܘܩܐ). Occasionally ܦܣܘܩܐ follows also ܫܘܝܐ, but ܡܫܐܠܢܐ is between; as, ܡܢ ܠܘܬ ܡܪܝܐ[16] ܗܘܬ ܗܕܐ : ܡܪܝܐ . ܘܐܝܬܝܗ ܕܬܕܡܘܪܬܐ ܒܥܝܢܝܢ . ܦܣܘܩܐ, *this is from the Lord* (ܫܘܝܐ), *and it is a marvel in our eyes* (ܦܣܘܩܐ). These are accurate ܦܣܘ̈ܩܐ.

. ܫܐܝܠܐ ܦܣܘܩܐ, *borrowed posuqo*, is that which falls in the beginning of a sentence, then follows ܬܚܬܝܐ, and after it is ܦܣܘܩܐ *proper;* as, ܦܘܠܘܣ[17] ܫܠܝܚܐ ܕܝܫܘܥ ܡܫܝܚܐ . ܦܣܘܩܐ . ܒܦܘܩܕܢܐ ܕܐܠܗܐ . ܡܚܝܢܢ . ܬܚܬܝܐ . ܘܕܡܫܝܚܐ ܣܒܪܢ ., *Paul, an Apostle of Jesus Christ* (ܦܣܘܩܐ), *by the commandment of God our Saviour* (ܬܚܬܝܐ), *and of Christ our hope* (ܦܣܘܩܐ *proper*). Several [k]ܫܐܝ̈ܠܐ ܦܣܘ̈ܩܐ follow each other, then ܬܚܬܝܐ, then ܢܝܚܬܬܐ ܦܣܘܩܐ; as, ܐܝܬܘ ܠܡܪܝܐ ܒܢܝ ܕܟܪܐ . ܦܣܘܩܐ . ܐܝܬܘ ܠܡܪܝܐ[18] ܝܩܪ ܘܐܝܩܪܐ . ܦܣܘܩܐ, *bring unto the Lord ye sons of the mighty* (*lit. of the males*) (ܦܣܘܩܐ), *bring unto the Lord glory and honour* (ܦܣܘܩܐ). This whole

---

[15] Mark ix. 39. [16] Ps. cxviii. 23. [17] 1 Tim. i. 1.

[j] Lit. one to how many.

[18] Ps. xxix. 1.

[k] Lit. *more than one.*

Psalm is divided by ܦܣܘ̈ܩܐ ܥܠ̈ܝܐ; lastly; ܡܪܝܐ ܢܬܠ ܚܝܠܐ ܠܥܡܗ . ܬܚܬܝܐ . ܘܡܪܝܐ ܢܒܪܟ ܠܥܡܗ . ܦܣܘ̄ ܡܪܢܝܐ., *the Lord will give power to his people* (ܬܚܬܝܐ), *and the Lord will bless his people* (ܦܣܘ̄ ܡܪܢܝܐ). There are passages, where instead of this ܬܚܬܝܐ, ܚܠܝܐ enters; as,[19] ܦܘ̄ ܥܒܕܐ ܕܝܫܘܥ ܡܫܝܚܐ . ܦܘ̄ . ܩܪܝܐ ܘܫܠܝܚܐ . ܦܘ̄ . ܕܐܬܦܪܫ ܠܐܘܢܓܠܝܘܢ ܕܐܠܗܐ . ܦܘ̄ . ܗܘ ܕܡܢ ܩܕܝܡ ܡܠܟ ܒܝܕ ܢܒܝܘܗܝ ܒܟܬ̈ܒܐ ܩܕ̄ : ܚܠܝܐ . ܥܠ ܒܪܗ ܗܘ ܕܐܬܝܠܕ ܒܒܣܪ ܡܢ ܙܪܥܐ ܕܒܝܬ ܕܘܝܕ . ܦܘ̄, *Paul, a servant of Jesus Christ* (ܦܘ̄), *called and sent* (ܦܘ̄), *who was separated to the Gospel of God* (ܦܘ̄), *which He had promised of old by His prophets in the Holy Scriptures* (ܚܠܝܐ), *concerning His Son, who was born in the flesh of the seed of the house of David* (ܦܘ̄).

Observation. When the protasis is long, it is divided by ܥܘ̈ܝܐ, finishing with ܬܚܬܝܐ; then follows the apodosis. But if the *apodosis* be long, ܚ̈ܠܝܐ are put in the middle between its members; then follows ܦܘ̄. The Acts;[20] ܘܗܘܐ ܕܟܕ ܣܠܩܝܢ ܫܡܥܘܢ ܟܐܦܐ ܘܝܘܚܢܢ ܐܟܚܕܐ ܠܗܝܟܠܐ : ܥܘ̈ܝܐ . ܒܥܕܢܐ ܕܨܠܘܬܐ ܕܬܫܥ ܫ̈ܥܝܢ . ܬܚܬܝܐ . ܘܗܘܐ ܓܒܪܐ ܚܕ ܚܓܝܪܐ ܕܡܢ ܟܪܣ ܐܡܗ : ܚܠܝܐ . ܡܫܩܠܝܢ ܗ̱ܘܘ ܐܢ̈ܫܐ ܐܝܠܝܢ ܕܡܥ̈ܕܝܢ ܗ̱ܘܘ ܡܝܬܝܢ ܘܣܝܡܝܢ ܠܗ : ܚܠܝܐ . ܠܬܪܥܐ ܕܗܝܟܠܐ ܕܡܬܩܪܐ ܫܦܝܪܐ . ܦܘ̄ ., *and it came to pass that when Simon Peter and John went up together to the temple* (ܥܘ̈ܝܐ), *at the time*

---

[19] Rom. i. 1.   [20] Acts iii. 1, 2.

of prayer, being the ninth hour (ܬܚܬܝܐ), *and behold a certain man lame from his mother's womb* (ܥܠܝܐ), *whom men took, who were accustomed to bring and place him* (ܥܠܝܐ) *at the gate of the Temple, which is called beautiful* (ܦܣܘܩ). But if the apodosis be not very long, one ܥܠܝܐ only is put in the middle of it. Theologus; ܐܠܐ ܗܘ ܡܟܐ ܕܠܢ ܙܒܢܐ ܕܒ ܡܡܪܕܝܬܐ
ܕܫܡܫܐ ܡܬܡܫܚ: ܫܢܝܐ. ܗܢܐ ܠܡܬܡܫܚܢܐ ܠܥܠܡ.
ܬܚܬܝܐ. ܗܘ ܕܝܢ ܗܘܝܢ ܕܐܝܬܝܗܘܢ ܡܬܡܫܚ:
ܥܠܝܐ. ܐܝܟ ܙܘܥܐ ܡܕܡ ܘܡܬܚܘܬܐ ܙܒܢܝܐ. ܦܣܘܩܐ.
But time which is measured to us by the course of the sun (ܫܢܝܐ), *this to eternals is for ever* (ܬܚܬܝܐ); *that which is extended to those who are existing* (ܥܠܝܐ), *is a certain motion, a temporary duration* (ܦܣܘܩܐ). These four radical signs are gathered together in these apostolical and instructive expressions.

THE FOURTH SECTION.

ON THE SIMPLE BRANCH SIGNS.

First. ܫܘܚܠܦ ܥܠܝܐ, *variation of* ܥܠܝܐ, is distinguished from ܥܠܝܐ by the length of its sound. It is placed after the protasis, ܦܣܘܩ following in the apodosis; then he who speaks returns to the thought. James the Apostle. ܟܠ ܚܕܘܐ ܬܗܘܐ ܠܟܘܢ ܐܚܝ: ܫܘܚܠܦ[21]
ܥܠܝܐ. ܟܕ ܬܦܠܘܢ ܠܢܣܝܘܢܐ ܡܫܚܠܦܐ ܘܡܣܓܝܐܐ.
ܦܣܘܩ. ܝܕܥܝܢܬܘܢ ܓܝܪ ܕܒܘܩܝܐ ܕܗܝܡܢ. ܬܚܬܝܐ
ܓܡܝܪܐ ܠܟܘܢ ܡܫܡܠܝܢܘܬܐ. ܦܣܘܩ. *all joy be to*

[21] James i. 1, 2.

you, brethren (ܥܨܘܠܐ ܚܠܐ), *when ye enter into many and divers temptations* (ܦܣܩܐ); *for ye know that the trial of faith* (ܬܚܘܝܬܐ) *worketh for you patience* (ܦܣܩܐ.).

ܥܨܘܠܐ ܬܚܘܝܬܐ, *variation of* ܬܚܘܝܬܐ, is distinguished from ܬܚܘܝܬܐ by its additional confirmation; and therefore the Eastern Syrians add a third point to it, and they call it ܬܚܘܝܬܐ ܬܠܝܬܝܬܐ. The Acts. ܗܝܕܝܢ ܐܙܠ ܚܢܢܝܐ ܠܘܬܗ. ܘܣܡ ܥܠܘܗܝ ܐܝܕܐ܂[22]
ܘܐܡܪ ܠܗ. ܫܐܘܠ ܐܚܝ܅ ܥܨܘܠܐ ܬܚܘܝܬܐ. ܡܪܢ
ܫܕܪܢܝ. ܘܫܪܟܐ., *then Ananias went to him, and put a hand upon him, and said to him, Brother Saul* (ܥܨܘܠܐ ܬܚܘܝܬܐ), *our Lord Jesus hath sent me*, &c. The Gospel. ܘܐܡܝܢ ܐܡܪ ܐܢܐ ܠܟ܅[23]
ܥܨܘܠܐ ܬܚܘܝܬܐ. ܕܠܐ ܬܦܘܩ ܡܢ ܬܡܢ ܥܕܡܐ ܕܬܬܠ
ܫܡܘܢܐ ܐܚܪܝܐ., *and verily I say unto thee* (ܥܨܘܠܐ ܬܚܘܝܬܐ), *that thou shalt not depart from thence, until thou shalt have paid the last farthing.*

ܥܨܘܠܐ ܫܘܝܐ, *variation of* ܫܘܝܐ, is distinguished from ܫܘܝܐ by the length of the sound, and is put at the end of the protasis, when the apodosis with ܦܣܩܐ follows, and there is not a return of the thought, and therefore it is called ܫܪܝܐ, *loosening*. Pentateuch. ܘܝܠܕ̈ ܠܗܘܢ ܓܢܒܪ̈ܐ ܕܡܢ ܥܠܡ: ܥܨܘܠܐ[24]
ܫܘܝܐ. ܓܢܒܪ̈ܐ ܕܫܡܗ̈ܐ. ܦܣܩܐ., *and they bore to them the Giants of old* (ܥܨܘܠܐ ܫܘܝܐ); *men of renown* (ܦܣܩܐ). Paul. ܘܕܚܠܘ ܘܫܡܫܘ:[25]
ܠܒܪܝܬܐ ܝܬܝܪ ܡܢ ܕܠܒܪܘܝܗܘܢ: ܥܨܘܠܐ ܫܘܝܐ.

---

[22] Acts ix. 17. [23] Matth. v. 26.
[24] Gen. vi. 4. [25] Rom. i. 25.

ܕܠܗ ܬܫܒ̈ܚܢ ܘܒܘܪ̈ܟܢ ܓܪ̈ܝܕܐ . ܠܥܠܡ ܥܠܡܝܢ ܐܡܝܢ .
. ܦܣܘܩ, *and they feared and served the creatures more than their creator* (ܥܘܕܐ ܥܣܘܩ), *to whom be praises and blessings* (ܓܪܝܕܐ) *for ever and ever, Amen* (. ܦܣܘܩ). This Pauline example is called ܥܘܕܐ of ܓܪܝܕܐ, because that in it ܓܪܝܕܐ follows ܥܘܕܐ.

ܪܗܛܐ ܕܦܣܘܩ establishes the flow of the protasis, and possesses the convenience of ܦܣܘܩ,[k] but it is distinguished from it by ܬܚܬܝܐ before it. Its mark is two points in a straight line below, and it is called ܪܗܛܐ ܕܦܣܘܩ, because with ܪܗܛܐ is joined ܦܣܘܩ; nevertheless another clause follows not tardily but quickly. Jeremiah. ܠܐ ܠܟܘܢ ܟܠ[26] ܥܒܪ̈ܝ ܐܘܪܚܐ: ܪܗܛܐ ܕܦܣܘܩ ܘܦܣܘܩ. ܐܣܬܟܠܘ ܘܚܙܘ, *not to you all ye passing the way* (ܪܗܛܐ ܕܦܣܘܩ ܘܦܣܘܩ), *understand and see.* ܦܣܘܩ indeed is not in some of the copies after ܐܘܪܚܐ; but that is not correct. Some put[1] ܪܗܛܐ ܕܒܪܬܗ before ܐܘܪܚܐ.

ܪܗܛܐ ܕܠܐ ܦܣܘܩ. Its sense and also its mark are as those which are before it; but it is distinguished in that the second *member* follows the first without ܦܣܘܩ; as, ܠܐ ܬܬܐܢܚܘܢ ܚܕ ܥܠ ܚܕ ܐܚ̈ܝ ܪܗܛܐ[27] ܕܠܐ ܦܣܘܩ. ܒܐܡܬܐ ܠܐ ܡܬܠܒܟ ܠܗ ܦܣܘܩ. ܕܠܐ ܬܬܕܝܢܘܢ., *do not grieve one another brethren* (ܪܗܛܐ ܕܠܐ ܦܣܘܩ, i.e. ܦܣܘܩ is not coupled with it)

---

k This sign has the force of ܦܣܘܩ, because the expression after which it is put may be said to be independent and complete in itself.

1 ܒܪܬܗ perhaps the same as the Greek ἀκρότης.

26 Lam. i. 12. 27 James v. 9.

that ye be not judged. ܐܘ ܚܣܝܪ̈ܝ، ܪܥܝܢܐ ܓܠܛܝܐ.[28] *O foolish Galatians.*

The Eastern Syrians recognise a third ܪܗܛܐ and its mark is three points as a triangle. They use it for ܫܘܪܪܐ, where they require additional assurance, and they call it ܪܗܛܐ ܕܪܝܫܬܗ from the form of its figure, and also ܪܗܛܐ ܕܬܠܬܬܐ; as, ܪܚܡ ܥܠܝ ܐܠܗܐ ∴ ܐܝܟ ܛܝܒܘܬܟ,[29] *have mercy on me, O God, according to thy goodness.* ܐܙܠܘ ܠܟܘܢ[30] ܡܢܝ ܠܝ̈ܛܐ ∴ ܠܢܘܪܐ ܕܠܥܠܡ., *depart from me ye cursed into everlasting fire.*

ܡܟܟܢܝܐ. It is also called ܡܣܟܢܝܐ, because that it is with a drooping and inclining figure, and affliction is poured forth. Its mark with us is ܬܚܘܬܝܐ, but with the Eastern Syrians ܬܚܘܬܝܐ ܕܬܠܬܐ; and it is distinguished from ܬܚܘܬܝܐ by a mournful sound, which is either by a kind of supplication, or by a kind of lamentation. Of the first, the Pentateuch. ܘܨܠܝ[31] ܝܥܩܘܒ ܘܐܡܪ. ܐܠܗܗ ܕܐܒܝ ܐܒܪܗܡ. ܐܠܗܗ ܕܐܒܝ ܐܝܣܚܩ., *and Jacob prayed and said, O God of my father Abraham, O God of my father Isaac.* Then after other mournful expressions he adds, ܦܨܢܝ ܡܢ ܐܝܕܘܗܝ، ܕܥܣܘ ܐܚܝ ܡܛܠ ܕܕܚܠ ܐܢܐ ܡܢܗ., *deliver me from the hand of Esau my brother, for I am afraid of him.* Of the second, Jeremiah. ܕܐ ܬܠܒܫܝܢ[32] ܙܚܘܪܝܬܐ. ܘܕܐ ܬܬܨܒܬܝܢ ܒܬܨܒܝܬܐ ܕܕܗܒܐ. ܕܐ ܬܟܚܠܝܢ ܒܟܘܚܠܐ ܥܝܢܝܟܝ. ܠܣܪܝܩܘܬܐ ܗܘ ܫܘܦܪܟܝ., *though thou clothest thyself with scarlet, though thou deckest thyself with ornaments*

[28] Gal. iii. 1. [29] Ps. li. 1. [30] Matth. xxv. 41.
[31] Gen. xxxii. 9. [32] Jer. iv. 30.

of gold, though thou colourest thy eyes with paint, in vain shalt thou make thyself fair.

ܦܩܘܕܐ. Its mark is one point at the head of the commanding word; as, ܙܠ ܐܝܟܢܐ ܕܗܝܡܢܬ ܢܗܘܐ[32] ܠܟ, *go, as thou hast believed, be it unto thee.* ܠܐ ܬܬܠܘܢ ܩܘܕܫܐ ܠܟܠܒܐ,[33] *give not that which is holy to dogs.* Know that a point such as this is put without a command, and is called by the name ܦܩܘܕܐ; but from the mark only, and not from the sense. Paul. .ܡܨܥܪܢܐ. ܫܒܗܪܢܐ[34] .ܡܫܟܚܝ ܒܝܫܬܐ. ܚܣܝܪܝ ܪܥܝܢܐ. ܕܠܐܒܗܝܗܘܢ ܠܐ ܡܬܛܦܝܣܝܢ, *despiteful, proud, boasters, inventors of evil things, foolish, who are disobedient to their parents.*

ܥܨܝܒܐ. This *sign* acquires a sound not its own, but it is found in that of the three radical signs, with ܪܬܡܐ cut off, at the end of a short protasis, even if the apodosis be long. In ܫܠܐ; as, ܘܒܪܢܫܐ[35] ܕܣܥܪܬܝܗܝ:, *and the son of man that thou didst visit him.* In ܬܢܝܬܐ; as, ܒܗܘ ܙܒܢܐ. ܡܗܠܟ ܗܘܐ[36] ܝܫܘܥ ܒܫܒܬܐ ܒܝܬ ܙܪܥܐ, *at that time Jesus walked on the sabbath day in the corn-fields.* In ܥܢܝܐ; as, ܠܐܚܪܢܐ ܐܚܝ: ܢܦܫܗ ܠܐ ܡܫܟܚ[37] .ܠܡܚܝܘ, *He saved others, himself he cannot save.* It is called ܥܨܝܒܐ because of the amputation of ܪܬܡܐ.

.ܬܚܡܐ is called by the Eastern Syrians ܡܒܕܠܢܐ ܪܒܐ, being compared with ܪܬܡܐ, which is ܡܒܕܠܢܐ ܕܫܘܪܐ; they also call it ܫܢܝܐ, and it is serviceable for perplexed matters. Its mark is two

---

[32] Matth. viii. 13. [33] Matth. vii. 7. [34] Rom. i. 30.
[35] Ps. viii. 5. [36] Matth. xii. 1. [37] Matth. xxvii. 42.

points, which are put obliquely under *the word* on the fore side, not on the end of the word, nor the beginning, nor the middle of it. This *sign* is found either in a kind of deliberating, chiding question; ܐܢ̇: ܫܪܝܪܐܝܬ ܙܕܝܩܘܬܐ ܡܡܠܠܝܢ ܐܢܬܘܢ,[37] *do ye, indeed, speak righteousness?* or in an interrogation, to which follows a chiding; ܗܐ ܟܠܟܘܢ ܥܘ̇ܠܐ ܡܡܠܠܝܢ ܐܢܬܘܢ ܒܐܪܥܐ. ܘܫܪ., *behold all of you speak iniquity in the earth,* &c.; or in a kind of caustic question; as, ܨܒܝܬܐ ܕܐܝܣܪܝܠ: ܥܠ ܪ̈ܡܬܟ[38] ܩܛܝܠܐ, *the honour of Israel is slain upon thy high places;* or in a kind of wailing; Jeremiah, ܐܢ̇:[39] ܢܐܟܠܢ ܢܫ̈ܐ ܦܐܪ̈ܝܗܝܢ. ܬܠܘ̈ܕܐ ܕܡܬܒܥܬܝܢ. ܐܢ̇: ܢܬܩܛܠܘܢ ܒܡܩܕܫܗ ܕܡܪܝܐ. ܟܗܢܐ ܘܢܒܝܐ., *shall the women eat their fruit? and children be beaten? the priest and the prophet be slain in the sanctuary of the Lord?* ܬܟܫܦܬܐ is joined with ܫܪ, ܬܫܥܝܬܐ; as, ܥܕ, ܐܬܐ: ܬܟܫܦܬܐ. ܘܐܡܚܝܘܗܝ ܠܐܪܥܐ ܠܓܡܪ.,[40] *until I come* (ܬܟܫܦܬܐ) *and smite the earth with destruction.*

ܡܦ̣ܩܠܣܝܢܐ.; as, ܓܘܪܝܐ ܕܐܪܝܐ ܝܗܘܕܐ,[41] *Judah is a lion's whelp.* In Greek it is called παροξύτονος, that is, before the last syllable, for that it (ܝܗܘܕܐ) has three points ܡܫܒܚܐ, ܪܗܛܐ, and the third is ܡܦܩܠܣܝܢܐ.* The , of ܝܗܘܕܐ is pronounced mutteringly. The Greeks put in the place of this point ܡܦܩܠܣܝܢܐ, a little line. Some of us put it on this word only, i.e. on ܝܗܘܕܐ .

---

[37] Ps. lviii. i. [38] 2 Sam. i. 19. [39] Lam. ii. 20.
[40] Mal. iv. 6. [41] Gen. xlix. 9.

* If these three points were named in the order of collocation, they would be, first ܪܗܛܐ, second ܡܦܩܠܣܝܢܐ, and third ܡܫܒܚܐ.

---

[38], [39] These examples should change places with each other.

ܡܒܥ ܛܘܒܐ; as, ܛܘܒܘܗܝ ܠܡܢ ܕܐܫܬܒܩ ܠܗ ܥܘܠܗ,[42] *blessed is he whose iniquity is forgiven;* ܛܘܒܘ̄ ܠܡܢ ܕܚܐܪ ܒܡܣܟܢܐ, *blessed is he who looketh on the poor.* Its mark is one point at the head of the first syllable, and its accent is ܡܢܓܪ.[m] According to the opinion of Thomas of Ḥarḳel, ܡܫܠܡܢܐ and ܡܒܥ ܛܘܒܐ are one; and this is correct, for they are equal in the sign, although in ܡܫܠܡܢܐ, the point is mentioned afterwards upon that which is the praising noun, but in ܡܒܥ ܛܘܒܐ upon the protasis in the beginning of the sentence.

ܩܪܘܝܐ; as, ܬܘ ܠܘܬܝ, ܟܠܟܘܢ ܠܐܝ̈ܐ ܘܫܩܝ̈ܠܝ ܡܘܒܠܐ ܘܐܢܐ ܐܢܝܚܟܘܢ[43] *come to me, ye that are wearied and laden, and I will give you rest.* Of this again the mark is one point at the head of the calling word, which is protracted by its accent.

ܡܚܘܝܢܐ; as, ܗܐ ܐܡܪܗ ܕܐܠܗܐ. ܗܢܘ ܗܘ[44] ܕܐܡܪܬ ܥܠܘܗܝ, ܕܒܬܪܝ, ܐܬܐ, *behold the lamb of God! This is He of whom I said, that he cometh after me.* Of this *sign* also the mark is one point, distinguished by its sound, from that which is without it.

ܡܓܠܝܢܐ. Its mark is one point, before the head, and two behind[n] in a straight line at the end of the protasis; but upon the clauses, which follow, the one *point* only is put; as, ܐܒܘܢ ܕܒܫܡܝܐ.[45]

---

[42] Ps. xxxii. 1, 2.

[m] This word and ܦܢܓܪܐ occurring just before are forms derived from the root ܢܓܪ, for the sense of which see Castell.

[43] Matth. xi. 28. [44] John i. 29, 30.

[n] When the writing is from the top to the bottom, a point to the left of a letter may be said to be *before*, ܡܩܕܡ, and when it is to the right to be *behind*, ܡܣܬܪ.

[45] Matth. vi. 9, 10.

ܢܬܩܕܫ ܫܡܟ . ܬܐܬܐ ܡܠܟܘܬܟ . ܢܗܘܐ ܨܒܝܢܟ.
Our Father, who art in heaven, hallowed be Thy name, Thy kingdom come, Thy will be done.

ܡܦܝܣܢܐ. Its mark is similar to that of ܡܟܠܝܢܐ; as, ܡܪܝܐ ܬܬܠ ܠܢ ܫܠܡܐ, *Thou, O Lord, wilt keep us in peace.* When the protasis is long, ܬܚܬܝܐ follows, and at the conjunction of the apodosis, is ܬܚܘܬܐ; as, ܡܪܝܐ ܐܝܟ ܟܠܗ ܙܕܝܩܘܬܟ · ܬܚܬܝܐ . ܕܥܒܕܬ ܥܡܢ .[46]
ܬܚܘܬܐ . ܢܗܦܘܟ ܪܘܓܙܟ ܘܚܡܬܟ ܡܢ ܡܕܝܢܬܟ
ܐܘܪܫܠܡ ܘܡܢ ܛܘܪܐ ܩܘܕܫܟ . ܗ̄ܢ, O *Lord, according to all Thy righteousness, which Thou hast done to us, let Thine anger and Thy wrath be turned away from Thy city Jerusalem, and from Thy holy mountain.*

ܡܥܠܝܢܐ. Of this also the mark is one point, at the head before; and it is joined, among many, to ܡܢܘ, ܡܢܐ, ܐܝܟܢܐ and ܐܝܟܐ; as, ܘܐܬܪܟܢܬ[47] ܪܦܩܐ ܡܢ ܥܠ ܓܡܠܐ ܘܐܡܪܬ ܠܥܒܕܐ . ܡܢܘ ܓܒܪܐ ܗܢܐ ܕܐܬܐ ܒܚܩܠܐ ܠܐܘܪܥܢ., *and Rebecca lighted off the camel, and she said to the servant, who is this man, who cometh in the field to meet us?* ܘܣܓܕ ܘܐܡܪ ܡܢܐ ܐܡܪ ܡܪܝ ܠܥܒܕܗ :,[48] *and he made obeisance and said, what saith my lord unto his servant?* ܡܢ ܐܝܟܐ ܐܢܬ.,[49] *from whence art thou?* ܐܝܟܢܐ ܠܐ ܕܚܠܬ ܠܡܘܫܛܘ ܐܝܕܟ ܠܡܚܒܠܘ[50] ܠܡܫܝܚܗ ܕܡܪܝܐ, *how wast thou not afraid to stretch forth thy hand to destroy the Lord's anointed.* ܐܝܟܐ ܗܘ ܗܒܝܠ ܐܚܘܟ,[51] *where is Abel thy*

---

[46] Dan. ix. 16. [47] Gen. xxiv. 64, 65. [48] Josh. v. 14.
[49] 2 Sam. i. 13. [50] 2 Sam. i. 14. [51] Gen. iv. 9.

brother? ܐܢ̇ܬܬܟ ܣܪܐ ܗ̱ܝ، ܐܝܟܐ,[52] *where is Sarah thy wife?*

ܡܟܝܟܘܬܐ. It is derived from humility, gentleness and contrition of heart. The holy Jacob has said: "it is proper to read the word, upon which is ܡܟܝܟܘܬܐ, not suddenly and with much emotion, but protractedly." Its mark is one point, at the head of the word behind, and as with many, it is placed before ܬܚܘܬܝܐ. Isaiah. ܕ̣ܠܡܐ ܝܘܡܐ ܟܠܗ̇· ܪܕܐ·[53] ܐܟܪܐ ܠܡܙܪܥ. ܘܦܬܚ ܘܡܦܩ ܐܪܥܗ., *doth the ploughman plough all day to sow? doth he open and break the clods of his ground?* ܘ̣ܠܐ ܐܬ̣ܐܡܪ ܠܟܘܢ[54] ܡܢ ܪܫܝܬܐ., *and was it not said to you from the beginning?* But ܡܟܝܟܘܬܐ and ܬܚܘܬܝܐ follow one another in a solitary noun; as, ܡܪܢ. ܐܡܬܝ،[55] ܚܙܝܢܟ ܕܟܦܢ ܐܢܬ ܘܙܪܢܢܟ., *Lord, when saw I Thee hungry, &c.* There are *passages* where ܥܠܝܐ follows next to ܡܟܝܟܘܬܐ. The Pentateuch. ܢܚܙܐ ܡܪܝܐ[56] ܥܠܝܟܘܢ ܘܢܕܘܢ: ܕܐܒܐܫܬܘܢ ܠܪܝܚܢ ܒܥܝܢܝ ܦܪܥܘܢ ܘܒܥܝܢܝ ܥܒܕܘܗܝ،: ܠܡܬܠ ܠܗ ܣܝܦܐ ܒܐܝܕܝܗܘܢ ܠܡܚܪܒܢ., *the Lord shall look upon you and judge, for ye have made our savour to be abhorred in the eyes of Pharaoh and in the eyes of his servants, to put a sword in their hands to destroy us.* There are *passages* where ܦܣܘܩܐ follows next. Jer. ܐܣܬܟܠܘ[57] ܘܚܙܘ. ܐܢ ܐܝܬ ܟܐܒܐ ܐܝܟ ܟܐܒܝ ܕܐܟܐܒ ܠܝ ܡܪܝܐ., *understand and see, if there is sorrow as my sorrow, which the Lord hath done to me.*

ܡܬܟܪܟܢܐ. Its mark is similar to that of ܬܚܘܡܐ,

---

[52] Gen. xviii. 9. [53] Is. xxviii. 24. [54] Is. xl. 21.
[55] Matth. xxv. 37. [56] Ex. v. 21. [57] Lam. i. 12.

but it is distinguished from it, in that it has position at the head of the word; as, ܐܝܟܢܐ ܢܦܠܘ ܓܢܒܪܐ.[58] *how have the mighty fallen!* ܐܝܟܢܐ ܐܚܫܟ ܡܪܝܐ[59] ܒܪܘܓܙܗ ܠܒܪܬ ܨܗܝܘܢ., *how hath the Lord obscured in His anger the daughter of Zion!* There are *passages* where ܟܠܐ follows next; as, ܐܝܟܢܐ[60] ܡܬܒܣܪܬܐ ܕܗܒܐ ܠܛܒܐ : ܘܫܢܐ ܨܒܥܐ ܫܦܝܪܐ., *how is the fine gold despised, and the beautiful colour changed!* But some of us make its mark one point, as that of ܡܫܐܠܢܐ. Then it acquires a distinction by the accent, not by the mark.

ܡܦܣܩܢܐ from ܦܣܩ *a cessation* of motion,[o] where it is thought that there is motion, although not obtained; as, ܠܐ ܬܬܕܡܪ ܕܐܡܪܬ ܠܟ ܕܘܠܐ ܠܟܘܢ[61] ܠܡܬܝܠܕܘ ܡܢ ܕܪܫ., *marvel not that I say unto you, it is needful for you to be born again.* Here the necessity of motion is apparent, of ܟܠܐ or ܬܚܬܝܐ or some other, for the apodosis is not yet completed; but motion ceases, because that it (the apodosis) is presented to the mind, very lofty, elevated, and too far removed by the protasis, to be plainly understood; as, ܪܘܚܐ·[62] ܐܬܪ ܕܨܒܝܐ ܢܫܒܐ ܘܢܫܒܐ., *the wind bloweth where it willeth,* &c.

ܡܫܝܢܐ is put when there is one word only in Greek, but two in Syriac. Its mark is one point after the first member,[p] and by it, *the member* is woven

---

[58] 2 Sam. i. 19. [59] Lam. ii. 1. [60] Lam. iv. 1.

[o] *Motion* seems here to mean, continuance of the subject. It ceases at the end of John iii. 7, for the reason above stated, and ܦܘܣܩܐ is therefore put instead of ܟܠܐ or some other minor point.

[61] John iii. 7. [62] John iii. 8.

[p] I.e. the first member of the expression.

with the other, and therefore Thomas calls it ܦܘܣܩܐ ; as, . ܫܘܐ . ܒܐܘܣܝܐ *equal in substance,* . ܫܠܝܛ ܒܟܠ *omnipotent,* ܠܐ . ܡܝܘܬܐ *immortal,* ܠܐ . ܝܠܝܕܐ *unbegotten,* ܠܐ . ܡܫܬܚܠܦܢܐ *unchangeable.*

ܫܘܚܠܦ ܡܫܝܚܢܐ , *the variation of* ܡܫܝܚܢܐ . Its mark is the same as that of ܡܫܝܚܢܐ , but it is distinguished from it in the mind, namely, that in Greek, as in Syriac, its expression has two members; as, . ܡܙܕܪܥ . ܒܚܒܠܐ ܘܩܐܡ . ܒܠܐ ܚܒܠܐ,[63] *sown in corruption, raised in incorruption.*

ܬܠܘܪܐ joins single disjointed members, attracted to one another, and its mark is one point, similar to that of ܦܩܘܕܐ , before the moveable letter, which is at the head of every member. Paul. ܐܠܐ[64] ܒܟܠ ܡܕܡ ܢܚܘܐ ܢܦܫܢ . ܕܡܫܡܫܢܐ ܚܢܢ ܕܐܠܗܐ . ܒܡܣܝܒܪܢܘܬܐ ܣܓܝܐܬܐ . ܒܐܘܠܨܢܐ . ܒܐܢܢܩܣ . ܒܡܚܘܬܐ . ܒܐܣܘܪܐ . ܒܫܓܘܫܝܐ . ܒܥܡܠܐ . ܒܫܗܪܐ . ܒܨܘܡܐ . ܒܕܟܝܘܬܐ . ܒܝܕܥܬܐ . ܒܢܓܝܪܘܬ ܪܘܚܐ . ܒܒܣܝܡܘܬܐ . *But in every thing we approve ourselves as the ministers of God, in much patience, in afflictions, in necessities, in prison, in stripes, in bonds, in tumults, in labour, in watching, in fasting, by pureness, by knowledge, by longsuffering, by kindness.* So far we have ܬܠܘܪܐ ; from here and beyond, although the members are joined together, ܬܠܘܪܐ ceases, and ܙܘܓܐ , whose mark is a line above, is introduced, especially by the Eastern Syrians; as, ܒܪܘܚܐ ܕܩܘܕܫܐ . ܒܚܘܒܐ

---

[63] 1 Cor. xv. 42. [64] 2 Cor. vi. 4—6.

ܕܠܐ ܢܟܠܐ. ܒܡܠܬܐ ܕܩܘܫܬܐ, *by the Holy Ghost, by love unfeigned, by the word of truth.*

ܫܘܚܠܦ ܙܘܘܓܐ, *variation of* ܙܘܘܓܐ, is similar in that it joins single disjointed members, which are bound to one another by the letter Vau; but it is read with ܬܚܬܝܐ and ܡܫܡܫܢܐ; as, ܝܘܡܐ܆ ܘܝܪܚܐ܆[65] ܘܙܒܢܐ܆ ܘܫܢܝܐ ܢܛܪܝܢ ܐܢܬܘܢ. *days and months and times and years ye observe.*

ܓܢܝܚܐ. Its mark is similar to that of ܦܩܘܕܐ, but it is put in close proximity to ܫܐܠܐ. Isaiah. ܘܐܠܘ ܠܐ ܡܪܝܐ ܕܚܝܠܬܢܐ ܐܘܬܪ ܠܢ ܫܪܟܢܐ܆ ܐܝܟ[66] ܣܕܘܡ ܗܘܝܢ ܗܘܝܢ ܓܢܝܚܐ ܗܘܝܢ: ܫܐܠܐ. ܘܠܥܡܘܪܐ ܡܬܕܡܝܢ ܗܘܝܢ. *except the Lord of Hosts had left us a remnant, we should have been as Sodom, and we should have been like unto Gomorrah.* The Gospel. ܡܛܠ ܕܟܠ ܐܡܬܝ܆ ܕܒܥܒܘܕܐ ܘܒܫܫܠܬܐ[67] ܡܬܐܣܪ ܗܘܐ. ܫܫܠܬܐ ܡܦܣܩ ܗܘܐ܆ ܓܢܝܚܐ ܗܘܐ: ܫܐܠܐ. ܘܥܒܘܕܐ ܡܬܦܣܩܝܢ܆ ܓܢܝܚܐ ܗܘܐ: ܫܐܠܐ. ܘܠܐ ܡܫܟܚ ܗܘܐ ܠܡܐܣܪܗ. *because that every time, when he was bound with fetters and chains, he broke the chains, and the fetters he cut off, and no (man) was able to bind him.*

ܫܘܚܠܦ ܓܢܝܚܐ, *variation of* ܓܢܝܚܐ.[q] Its mark is one point, like ܬܚܬܝܐ; and it is distinguished from ܓܢܝܚܐ by the feebleness of the sound. As with many, it falls in close proximity to ܫܐܠܬܐ; as, ܚܠ ܕܡܗܠܟܬܝ܆ ܒܐܘܪܚܗ ܕܚܬܟܝ. ܐܬܠ ܟܣܗ[68]

[65] Gal. iv. 10. [66] Is. i. 9. [67] Mark v. 4.

[68] Ezek. xxiii. 31.

[q] This sign is called ܓܢܝܚܐ by Jacob and in Appendix i.

ܒܐܝܕܝ̈ܟܝ. , *because that thou hast walked in the way of thy sister, I will deliver her cup into thy hands.*
69 ܘܗܐ ܩܠܐ ܡܢ ܫܡܝܐ܀ ܕܐܡܪ. ܗܢܘ ܒܪܝ ܚܒܝܒܐ
ܕܒܗ ܐܨܛܒܝܬ܀, *and behold a voice from heaven, which said, This is my beloved son in whom I am well pleased.* But it falls also before ܥܠܝܐ in close proximity; as,
70 ܒܗܘ ܝܘܡܐ ܬܕܥܘܢ ܕܐܢܐ ܒܐܒܝ܁
ܘܐܢܬܘܢ ܒܝ ܘܐܢܐ ܒܟܘܢ, *in that day, ye shall know that I am in my Father, and, ye are in me, and I in you.*

ܥܠܝܐ, by the Eastern Syrians is named ܪܗܛܐ, and in the intonation it possesses the power (use) of half of ܥܠܝܐ, and its mark is one point on the fore side; as,
71 ܘܐܙܠܘ ܒܬܪܗ ܟܢܫ̈ܐ ܣܓܝ̈ܐܐ. ܡܢ ܓܠܝܠܐ܁
ܥܠܝܐ. ܘܡܢ ܥܣܪ ܡܕ̈ܝܢܬܐ ܘܡܢ ܐܘܪܫܠܡ܁ ܥܠܝܐ
ܘܡܢ ܝܗܘܕ, *and many multitudes went after Him, from Galilee* (ܥܠܝܐ), *and from Decapolis, and from Jerusalem* (ܥܠܝܐ), *and from Judah.*

ܡܫܡܫܢܐ. It possesses the power (use) of half of ܬܚܬܝܐ in softness *of sound.* Its mark is one point behind; as,
72 ܠܐ ܒܫܡܝܐ ܡܫܡܫܢܐ. ܕܟܘܪܣܝܐ ܗܘ
ܕܐܠܗܐ. ܘܠܐ ܒܐܪܥܐ ܡܫܡܫܢܐ. ܕܟܘܒܫܐ ܗܘ
ܕܬܚܝܬ ܪ̈ܓܠܘܗܝ. ܘܠܐ ܒܐܘܪܫܠܡ ܡܫܡܫܢܐ. ܕܡܕܝܢܬܗ
ܗܝ ܕܡܠܟܐ ܪܒܐ., *not by heaven* (ܡܫܡܫܢܐ), *for it is God's throne, neither by earth* (ܡܫܡܫܢܐ), *for it is His footstool, neither by Jerusalem* (ܡܫܡܫܢܐ), *for it is the city of the great king.* And so,
73 ܘܐܡܪ ܠܗ
ܠܝܘܚܢܢ ܡܕܡ ܕܫܡܥܬܘܢ ܘܚܙܝܬܘܢ. ܣܡܝ̈ܐ.
ܕܚܙܝܢ. ܘܚܓܝ̈ܣܐ ܡܗܠܟܝܢ. ܘܓܪ̈ܒܐ ܡܬܕܟܝܢ.

---

69 Matth. iii. 17. 70 John xiv. 20. 71 Matth. iv. 25.
72 Matth. v. 34, 35. 73 Matth. xi. 4, 5, 6.

ܘܚܪ̈ܫܐ ܫܡܥܝܢ. ܘܡܝ̈ܬܐ ܩܝܡܝܢ. ܘܡܣ̈ܟܢܐ ܡܣܬܒܪܝܢ. ܬܚܬܝܐ ܦܫܝܛܐ. ܘܛܘܒܘܗܝ ܠܐܝܢܐ ܕܠܐ ܢܬܟܫܠ ܒܝ., *go, say to John every thing which you have seen and heard* (ܦܣܘ̄); *that the blind see, the lame walk, the lepers are cleansed, the deaf hear, the dead are raised, and the poor are preached to* (simple ܬܚܬܝܐ), *and blessed is he, whosoever shall not be offended in me.* But if a verb with ܕ follows a noun in such as these, not ܡܫܡܥܢܐ but ܚܠܝܐ follows; as, ܕܢܬܕܡܪܘܢ[74] ܟܢܫ̈ܐ ܚܙܘ: ܚܠܝܐ. ܕܫܪܝܢ, ܚܪ̈ܫܐ ܕܡܡܠܠܝܢ: ܘܩܛܝ̈ܥܐ ܕܡܬܚܠܡܝܢ: ܚܠܝܐ. ܘܚܓܝ̈ܣܐ ܕܡܗܠܟܝܢ: ܚܠܝܐ. ܘܣܡ̈ܝܐ ܕܫܪܝܢ. ܦܣܘ̄. ܘܫܒܚܘ ܠܐܠܗܐ ܕܐܝܣܪܝܠ., *That the multitude* (ܚܠܝܐ) *wondered, when they saw the dumb speaking, the maimed made whole* (ܚܠܝܐ), *the lame walking* (ܚܠܝܐ), *the blind seeing* (ܦܣܘ̄); *and they glorified the God of Israel.*

ܫܘܚܠܦ ܡܫܡܥܢܐ, *variation of* ܡܫܡܥܢܐ, is distinguished from ܡܫܡܥܢܐ by the extension of the single and simple sound (ܙܘܥܐ);† but is not as ܬܚܬܝܐ double of the sound. Its mark is as the mark of ܡܫܡܥܢܐ; as, ܠܐ[75] ܡܘܬܐ. ܘܠܐ ܚܝ̈ܐ. ܘܠܐ ܡܠܐܟ̈ܐ. ܘܠܐ ܐܪ̈ܟܘܣܐ. ܘܠܐ ܚܝܠܘ̈ܬܐ. ܘܠܐ ܕܩܝܡܢ. ܘܠܐ ܕܥܬܝ̈ܕܢ. ܘܠܐ ܪܘܡܐ. ܘܠܐ ܥܘܡܩܐ. ܘܐܦܠܐ ܒܪܝܬܐ ܐܚܪܬܐ ܬܫܟܚ ܬܦܪܫܢ ܡܢ ܚܘܒܗ ܕܐܠܗܐ ܕܒܡܪܢ ܝܫܘܥ ܡܫܝܚܐ; *neither death, nor life, nor angels, nor principalities,*

---

[74] Matth. xv. 31.

† ܙܘܥܐ is *motion;* here it seems to mean the motion of the sound. Bar Hebræus is speaking of an extension of the motion of the sound, i.e. an extension of the sound.

[75] Rom. viii. 38, 39.

nor powers, nor things present, nor things to come, nor height, nor depth, nor any other creature shall be able to separate me from the love of God, which is in Christ Jesus our Lord.

ܦܣܩܐ is distinguished from ܥܐܠܐ . ܦܣ̄ܩ in that the clause which follows it, is united to it by the letter Vau; as, ܘܚܙܐ· ܘܗܐ ܢܓܒܘ ܐܦ̈ܝ ܐܪܥܐ .[76] ܦܣܩܐ . ܘܒܝܪܚܐ ܕܬܪܝܢ . ܒܥܣܪܝܢ ܘܫܒܥܐ ܒܗ ܒܝܪܚܐ ܝܒܫܬ ܐܪܥܐ, *and he saw, and behold the face of the earth was dry* (ܦܣܩܐ), *and in the second month, in the twenty-seventh day of the month, the earth was dried.* ܘܒܢ̈ܝ ܕܒܠܗܐ ܐܡܬܗ ܕܪܚܝܠ .[77] ܕܢ ܘܢܦܬܠܝ . ܦܣܩܐ . ܘܒܢ̈ܝ ܙܠܦܐ ܐܡܬܗ ܕܠܝܐ . ܓܕ ܘܐܫܝܪ, *and the sons of Bilhah, the handmaid of Rachel, Dan and Naphtali* (ܦܣܩܐ); *and the sons of Zilpah, the handmaid of Leah, Gad and Asher.*

ܡܗܦܟܢܐ . I wished to hear the reading of this sign from a distinguished old man in Melitene. He confessed, "I do not know it, nor have I heard it in my time. But formerly a pious man learned it from a Greek, and he called it ܡܒܪܘܣܝܐ. But now, as concerns the various sounds of its expressions, *the sign* is not known in our regions even by the Greeks." An example of it is, "ܨܘܬܘ ܫܡܝܐ[78]
ܘܐܡܠܠ . ܘܬܫܡܥ ܐܪܥܐ ܡܐܡܪ̈ܐ ܕܦܘܡܝ . ܢܪܣܦ .
ܐܝܟ ܡܛܪܐ ܝܘܠܦܢܝ . ܘܢܚܘܬ ܐܝܟ ܛܠܐ ܡܐܡܪܝ .
Give ear, O ye heavens, and I will speak, and hear, O earth, the word of my mouth. My doctrine shall drop as the rain, and my speech shall descend as the dew.

---

[76] Gen. viii. 13, 14. [77] Gen. xxxv. 25, 26.
[78] Deut. xxxii. 1, 2.

The pious man taught that the measure of the first expression was ܡܗܦܟܢܐ, of the second ܥܘܫܠܐ ܡܗܦܟܢܐ by letters, and the third ܥܘܫܠܐ ܡܗܦܟܢܐ by lines. But we, not knowing these, call the first expression by ܪܗܛܐ ܕܠܐ ܦܘܣܩ, the second by ܦܘܣ̄. ܫܐܝܠܐ, and the third by ܡܬܚܬܐ.

Observation. With the Eastern Syrians there is another sign, which they call ܢܘܚܐ; because *one* proclaiming its sign, thrusts forth as much in the reading as he can of strength of voice and shouting. And this is either ܫܪܝܪܐ *proper*, when it is not fitting that the sign should be disregarded; or ܫܐܝܠܐ *borrowed*, when the reader stays for those, who are wishing for his strength. But ܢܘܚܐ *proper* is constantly joined to ܐܡܪ, and ܢܘܚܐ *borrowed* to what is without ܐܡܪ; as, ܐܡܼܪ ܗܘ ܥܘܡܝܫܘ ܐܢܫ ܣܟܘܠܣܛܝܩܐ ܕܥܠܝܗܘܢ, *Romishu a scholastic said of them*, where there is with ܢܘܚܐ either ܐܡܼܪ, or ܐܡ̇ܪ; or, as, ܥܢܐ ܝܫܘܥ ܘܐܡܼܪ. *Jesus answered and said*, ܘܡܟܪܙ ܗܘܐ ܒܡܕܒܪܐ ܕܝܗܘܕ ܘܐܡ̇ܪ, *and preached in the wilderness of Judea, saying*, ܘܗܢܘܢ ܕܝܢ ܥܢܘ ܘܐܡ̇ܪܝܢ, *and they answered, saying*, ܘܥܢܝ̈ ܗܢܝܢ ܚܟܝ̈ܡܬܐ ܘܐܡ̇ܪ̈ܢ, *and the wise women answered, saying*. Where ܦܘܩܕܐ and ܢܘܚܐ come together, read first ܦܘܩܕܐ, and then if you wish, read ܢܘܚܐ; as ܘܠܥܒܕܝ ܕܥܒܕ[79] ܗܕܐ ܘܥܒܕ. *and to my servant, do this, and he doeth* (*it*). So far these our signs. It is not right *for people* to estimate *them*, as they hear *them*.

---

79 Matth. viii. 9.

SECTION V.

ON THE COMPOUND BRANCH SIGNS.

ܪܗܛܐ ܕܠܐ ܦܣܩ ܘܕܦܣܩ. Isaiah. ܨܘܬܝ، ܠܝܫ̈ ܘܥܢܝ[60] ܥܢܬܘܬ̈ ܐܬܬܙܝܥܬ ܡܕܡܢܐ, *attend, O Laish, and answer, O Anathoth, Madmena is removed.* ܠܝܫ is read with ܪܗܛܐ ܕܠܐ ܦܣܩ, and ܥܢܬܘܬ with ܪܗܛܐ ܕܦܣܩ; then follows the expression "Madmenah is removed."

ܬܠܬܐ ܪܗܛ̈ܐ. Proverbs. ܡܢ ܒܪܝ̈ ܘܡܢ ܒܪ ܟܪܣܝ̈ ܘܡܢ[81] ܒܪ ܢܕܪ̈ܝ ܠܐ ܬܬܠ ܚܝܠܟ ܠܢܫ̈ܐ: ܘܐܘܪ̈ܚܬܟ ܠܡܐܟܘܠܬܐ ܕܡ̈ܠܟܐ. *O my son! O son of my womb! O son of my vows! Give not thy strength to women, nor thy ways for the food of kings.* Here the first and second, their ܪܗ̈ܛܐ do not divide; but the third, its ܪܗܛܐ does divide. But the Eastern Syrians do not read these with ܪܗ̈ܛܐ; but the first and second with ܬܪܥܐ and the third with ܦܣܩ. Theologus. ܫܡܥܘ ܗܕܐ ܟܠܟܘܢ ̈ܥܡܡܐ: ܫܡܥܘ ܥܡ̈ܡܐ ܠܫ̈ܢܐ ܫܪ̈ܒܬܐ: ܠܟܠܗ ܓܢܣܐ ܕܒܢܝ̈ܢܫܐ ܘܟܠ ܦܘܡܐ, *hear this all ye people; hear ye nations, tongues, families, the whole race of men, and every thing existing.* Here the first does not divide, but the second and third do divide.

ܘܒܥܡܐ ܕܐܝܟ ܗܢܐ ̈ܠܐ — ܬܬܦܪܥ ܢܦܫܝ. ܬܫܘܝܬܐ ܐܝܟܢܝܐ.[82] *and shall not my soul be avenged upon such a people as this?* (ܬܫܘܝܬܐ ܐܝܟܢܝܐ).

---

[80] Is. x. 30. [81] Prov. xxxi. 23. [82] Jer. v. 9.

ܐܢ ܚܢܢ ܪܘܚܢܝܬܐ — ܫܐܠܬܐ ܘܬܟܫܦܬܐ ܘܡܩܒܠܢܝܬܐ[83]
ܙܪܥܢ ܒܟܘܢ : ܫܐܠܬܐ . ܪܒܐ ܗ̈ܝ . ܬܟܫܦܬܐ . ܐܢ ܚܢܢ
ܡܢܟܘܢ ܕܦܓܪܢܝܬܐ ܢܚܨܘܕ . ܡܩܒܠܢܝܬܐ ., *if we sow in you spiritual things* (ܫܐܠܬܐ), *is it a great matter* (ܬܟܫܦܬܐ), *if we reap of you carnal things?* (ܡܩܒܠܢܝܬܐ).

There are *passages*, where ܬܗܝܬܐ not interrogative is put for ܬܗܝܬܐ interrogative; as, ܐܟܡܢ[84]
ܠܥܡܒܪܐ ܕܚܩܠܐ ܕܝܘܡܢܐ ܐܝܬܘܗܝ ܘܡܚܪ ܢܦܠ
ܠܬܢܘܪܐ : ܫܐܠܬܐ . ܐܠܗܐ ܗܟܢܐ ܡܠܒܫ . ܬܗܝܬܐ .
ܠܐ ܣܓܝ ܝܬܝܪ ܠܟܘܢ ܙܥܘܪܝ ܗܝܡ̄ ., *but if God so clothe the grass of the field, which to-day is, and to-morrow is cast into the oven; shall He not much more* (*clothe*) *you, O ye of little faith?* But the Eastern Syrians read the verb ܢܠܒܫ with ܫܐܠܬܐ.
ܘܐܢ ܢܗܘܐ̈ ܬܗܝܬܐ . — ܬܗܝܬܐ ܘܦܢܝܐ ܘܬܟܫܦܬܐ
ܦܘܢܝܐ̈ ܗܘܐ . ܦܢܝܐ . ܠܒ̈ܢܝ ܐܝܣܪܝܠ : ܬܟܫܦܬܐ ., *and will there be* (ܬܗܝܬܐ) *an answer* (ܦܢܝܐ) *to the children of Israel?* (ܬܟܫܦܬܐ). This compound the Eastern Syrians name ܡܣܐܢܢܝܬܐ; because the sole of the expression is adorned with ܦܢܝܐ as with a sandal.
ܕܠܡܐ̈ . ܬܗܝܬܐ . ܛܝܒܘܬܗ — ܬܗܝܬܐ ܘܬܟܫܦܬܐ ܘܡܩܒܠܢܝܬܐ[85]
ܡܩܒܠ ܗܘ ܥܒܕܐ ̈. ܬܗܝܬܐ . ܕܥܒܕ ܡܕܡ
ܕܐܬܦܩܕ ܠܗ . ܡܩܒܠܢܝܬܐ, *whether* (ܬܗܝܬܐ) *does that servant receive his thanks* (ܬܟܫܦܬܐ), *because that he hath done whatsoever has been commanded of him?* (ܡܩܒܠܢܝܬܐ).
ܘܐܡܪܝܢ ܗܘܘ . ܡܢ . ܕܠܡܐ . — ܡܫܐܢܝܬܐ ܘܡܩܒܠܢܝܬܐ[86]
ܒܥܐܕܐ. ܗܘܘ ܐܡܪܝܢ ܐܢܫ̈ . ܕܠܐ ܡܫܐܢܝܬܐ . ܐܬܐ

---

[83] 1 Cor. ix. 11. [84] Matth. vi. 30.
[85] Luke xvii. 9. [86] John xi. 56.

ܠܚ̈ܕܕܐ. ܒܗܝܟܠܐ. , *and they said one to the other in the temple; what think ye, that he doth not* (ܕܐܬܝܐ) *come to the feast?* (ܒܗܝܟܠܐ).

ܐܒܪܗܡ܇ ܝܠܕ. ܐܘܠܕ ܐܝܣܚܩ. ܝܠܕ ܘܐܝܣܚܩ[87]
ܠܐܝܣܚܩ. , *Abraham* (ܝܠܕ) *begat* (ܐܝܣܚܩ) *Isaac.*
ܘܬܩܪܐ܇ ܫܡܗ ܝܫܘܥ ,[88] *and thou shalt call his name Jesus.* ܫܡܥ ܗܪܘܕܣ ܡܠܟܐ ܘܐܬܬܙܝܥ. ,[89] *Herod the king heard and was troubled.* This compound more than any other is placed in Syriac books.
ܒܪܫܝܬ ܡܠܬܐ. ܐܝܬܘܗܝ ܗܘܐ — ܡܠܬܐ ܘܡܠܬܐ[90]
ܡܠܬܐ. ܡܠܬܐ ܘܗܘ ܡܠܬܐ ܐܝܬܘܗܝ ܗܘܐ ܠܘܬ
ܐܠܗܐ. , *in the beginning* (ܡܠܬܐ) *was the word* (ܡܠܬܐ); *and the word was with God.* ܐܠܗܐ܇[91]
ܡܠܬܐ. ܠܐ ܚܙܝܗܝ ܐܢܫ ܡܡܬܘܡ. ܡܬܘܡ. ܝܚܝܕܝܐ
ܐܠܗܐ ܗܘ ܕܐܝܬܘܗܝ ܒܥܘܒܐ ܕܐܒܘܗܝ, ܗܘ ܐܫܬܥܝ
God (ܡܠܬܐ) *no man hath seen at any time* (ܡܡܬܘܡ); *the only begotten Son of God, He who is in the bosom of His father, He hath declared.*
ܐܝܟܐ ܗܘ. — ܐܝܟܐ ܙܟܘܬܐ ܘܙܟܘܬܟ ܕܡܘܬܐ[92]
ܐܝܟܐ. ܙܟܘܬܟ܇ ܙܟܘܬܐ. ܡܘܬܐ̈ ܙܟܘܬܟ ܕܡܘܬܐ.
where (ܐܝܟܐ) *is thy victory* (ܙܟܘܬܐ) *O death?*
ܪܚܡܘ. ܟܐܢܘܬܐ— ܟܐܢܘܬܐ ܘܙܟܘܬܐ ܕܐܪܥܐ ܕܝܢܝ.
ܘܕܝܢܝ܇ ܙܟܘܬܐ ܕܝ̈ܢܝܐ ܕܐܪܥܐ̈ ܐܪܥܐ ܕܐܪܥܐ
ܕܝܢܝ. , *love* (ܟܐܢܘܬܐ) *righteousness* (ܙܟܘܬܐ), *ye judges of the earth* (ܕܝܢܝ ܕܐܪܥܐ ܐܪܥܐ).

Observation. Of the compound signs, which the Eastern Syrians only use, there is that which they call ܡܫܠܡܢܘܬܐ *tradition;* because it was delivered by the readers of the Persian school at Nisibis. Where

---

[87] Matth. i. 2. [88] Luke i. 31. [89] Matth. ii. 3.
[90] John i. 1. [91] John i. 18. [92] 1 Cor. xv. 55.

they found an adherence to one another, of ܪܬܡܐ before ܬܚܬܝܐ, followed by ܦܣܘ, they read and taught to read in a restrained way, for ornament and excellence. This *sign* however was not in every place; but in some rare passages; as, ܢܬܟܢܫܘܢ[94] ܡ̈ܝܐ ܠܬܚܬ ܡܢ ܫܡܝܐ ܠܐܬܪܐ ܚܕ. ܘܬܬܚܙܐ ܝܒܝܫܬܐ., *let the water be gathered together under heaven to one place, and let the dry land be seen.* Zechariah; ܐܝ̈ܕܘܗܝ[95] ܕܙܘܪܒܒܠ. ܣܡ ܫܬܐܣ̈ܘܗܝ ܕܒܝܬܐ ܗܢܐ, *the hands of Zerubbabel laid the foundations of this house.* ܘܐܬܬ[96] ܡܢ ܥܒܪ̈ܘܗܝ ܕܐܪܥܐ ܕܬܫܡܥ ܚܟܡܬܗ ܕܫܠܝܡܘܢ. ܘܗܐ ܕܝܬܝܪ ܡܢ ܫܠܝܡܘܢ ܗܪܟܐ., *and she came from the uttermost parts of the earth to hear the wisdom of Solomon, and behold a greater than Solomon is here.*

---

[94] Gen. i. 9. [95] Zech. iv. 9. [96] Matth. xii. 42.

APPENDIX I.

Immediately following the Tract of Jacob in the MS. is a fragment of a Letter on the subject of the accents, the author of which is not mentioned. I say a fragment, for the beginning of the Letter as Dr. Land has observed, is evidently wanting.* It may be and probably is the case; that the fragment comprises most of the Letter; but in the beginning, there is no mention, according to custom, of the person by whom the Letter was written, nor of the person to whom it was addressed. Again, the second word ܕܐܦ of the fragment, intimates that there was something previously treated of. Those who are addressed are called spiritual brethren, and, therefore, it is probable that it was written for the use of a Monastery.

Although we cannot say by whom the letter was written, most likely, because it has not been given entire, yet there is decisive evidence, that it is one of the earliest writings on the subject of the accents. I am disposed to think that it belongs to the sixth century, and that it was written about the time of Thomas the Deacon. There are correspondences in the list of accents given in this Letter with the list of Thomas, which do not exist with the list of Jacob, or with that of Bar Hebræus, and which are of such a kind, as to suggest that they were con-

---

* See *Anecdota Syriaca.* Tom. i. p. 16.

temporaneous. For instance, both in this Letter, and in the list of Thomas, ܩܘܒܠܐ ܚܒܫ and ܡܬܘܠܝܐ are two names of the same sign; but by Jacob and Bar Hebræus they are made, each the name of an independent sign. In the two former lists, ܡܒܗܪܢܐ is mentioned as another name of the sign ܡܛܠܠܢܐ; but in the two latter, it is not given. In the two former, ܢܩܘܪܐ is said to be a second name of the sign ܡܫܚܚܢܐ; but in the two latter it is not mentioned. In the two former we have ܦܪܐܐܘܦܬܘܢܘܣ as another name for the sign ܬܚܘܪܐ; whilst in the two latter it is the second name of ܡܬܘܠܝܐ. These correspondences in the two former lists afford some evidence that they were written about the same time, and as it is said that Thomas the Deacon flourished in the sixth century, I think that early in that century, this Letter first saw the light. Further; in this Letter there is nothing said about compound signs, and the reason for not treating of them is stated. The reason was because the subject was new, and that there existed ܠܐ ܡܫܘܕܥܘܬܐ ܘܠܐ ܡܥܩܒܘܬܐ ܕܐܢܫܝܢ ܕܥܠܝܗܝܢ *no publication, nor disquisition of men on these* (accents). This statement is a proof that the Letter must have been written before the compound signs had obtained much consideration, and consequently before the Tract of Mār Jacob, who lived in the succeeding century, and who has therein entered into this subject, perhaps as fully, or nearly so, as any subsequent writer on the accents. On account of the antiquity of this Letter, it is of great importance, and I, therefore, insert it here. It is, like the Discourse of Bar Hebræus, a very useful commentary to the Tract of Jacob, which precedes it in the MS. We have nothing said in the Tract about the position of the mark. The metrical points are given, and a passage of Scripture for each accent. If these passages were correctly pointed, they would not be sufficient for a student to learn the accents; but from the carelessness and ignorance of the copyist, several of them are without the points, and there are several in which the points are wrongly placed. Towards the end of the Tract, some of the signs are put in groups, each sign of the same group having the same mark in the same place; but no intimation is given, as to where that place is. Hence the information contained here is valuable.

ܬܘܒ ܡܛܠܠܬܗܘܢ ܕܠܗܘܢ ܕܢܘܩܙܐ ܗܠܝܢ ܕܐܡܕܢܚܐ
ܬܫܡܫܬܐ ܕܩܪܝܬܐ ܕܟܠ ܚܕ ܚܕ ܡܢܗܘܢ ܗܢܘܢ ܕܡܢ
ܐܝܠܝܢ ܢܩܝܦܐ ܐܬܬܚܝܒܘ.

ܐܝܬܐ ܕܐܦ ܗܠܝܢ ܐܚܪܢܐ ܕܐܬܪܫܡܬ ܡܢ ܦܝܠܘܣܘܦܐ
ܝܘܢܝܐ. ܗܠܝܢ ܕܠܡܣܒܐ ܠܐܪܓܘܡܢܛܝܩܐ ܚܒܪܘ:
ܕܟܕ ܡܠܡܠܬܐ ܕܠܐ ܗܘܕܐ ܒܝܕܥܬܐ ܐܬܥܒܕܬ ܠܐܣܛܟܣܝܣ
ܐܠܗܐ ܕܐܠܝܢ: ܐܝܠܝܢ ܗܟܝܠ ܡܢ ܦܝܠܘܣܘܦܐ:
ܡܬܚܫܒܢܬ ܕܝܢ ܐܪܝܣܛܘܛܠܝܣ: ܕܡܚܫܒܢܐ ܝܘܢܝܐ
ܕܡܠܬܐ ܐܝܬܝܗܘܢ ܐܪܒܥ. ܗܢܘ ܕܝܢ. ܡܚܘܝܢܝܬܐ.
ܦܘܩܕܢܐ. ܡܫܐܠܢܐ. ܩܪܝܢܐ. ܒܥܘܬܐ. ܡܛܠ ܗܢܐ
ܕܝܢ ܐܝܠܝܢ ܕܫܡܫܝ ܥܡ ܥܒܕ ܡܠܬܐ: ܐܝܟ ܡܢ
ܗܢܘܢ ܐܝܠܝܢ. ܐܝܠܝܢ ܕܝܢ ܠܐܪܝܣܛܘܛܠܝܣ ܬܚܘܡܝܗ،
ܒܡܠܬܐ: ܕܗܠܝܢ ܕܐܝܟ ܗܢܐ. ܒܥܠܡܐ ܡܫܝܚܐ

ܐܫܠܡܘ ܟܕ ܒܬܘܠܬܐ ܕܠܗܘܢ: ܠܗܠܝܢ ܕܒܕܐܝܢ ܗܠܝܢ
ܢܨܒܢ ܕܢܬܒܥܘܢ. ܕܐܦ ܗܘܕܐ ܐܦܝܣܩܘܦܘܣ ܘܟܗܢܐ
ܕܥܕ̈ܬܐ: ܘܡܫܡ̈ܫܢܐ ܕܡܫܝܚܘܬܐ ܫܪ̈ܝܪܬܐ
ܘܬܪܝܨܘܬ ܫܘܒܚܐ: ܘܕܠܝ̈ܠܐ ܡܣ̈ܩܝܢܐ ܘܠܐ
ܡܫܬܘܕܝܢܐ: ܠܫܪ̈ܝܐ ܕܟܪ̈ܝܐ ܘܕܐܟ̈ܠܐ ܡܬ̈ܘܪܐ
ܘܡܫ̈ܡܫܢܐ: ܘܕܗܠܝܢ ܕܠܗܘܢ ܫܒܝܚܝܢ ܢܨܒܢ ܕܐܦ
ܒܐܣ̈ܝܐ ܢܒܥܘܢ: ܪܓܐ ܘܐܒܝܢ، ܠܟܠܗ ܪܘܚܢܘܬܐ
ܘܡܫܝܚܘܬܐ ܕܡܫܝܚܐ. ܟܕ ܒܬܘܠܬܐ ܪܥܝܢܬܐ ܟܕ
ܡܬܬܘܣܒܢ ܕܪܘܚܐ ܩܘܫܐ ܥܠܡ ܠܐܢܫܝܢ ܕܡܥܬܡܪܝܢ.
ܡܛܠ ܕܝܢ ܕܒܗܠܝܢ ܐܢܫܝܢ ܫܘܪܝܐ ܕܐܝܟܢܘܬ ܠܐ
ܟܢܫܝܢ. ܡܬܪ̈ܬܐ ܡܬܚܝܐ ܠܝ: ܕܗܫܐ ܡܛܠ
ܦܘܠܚܢܐ ܕܗܠܝܢ ܕܠܐ ܙܕܩܐ ܐܘ ܗ̇ܝ ܕܟܠܗ ܡܢܗܘܢ
ܚܕܐ ܡܢ ܗܠܝܢ ܫܒܥ ܘܐܝܠܝܢ. ܐܘ ܗ̇ܝ ܕܗ̇ܢܘܢ ܗܠܝܢ
ܕܡܬܚܙܝܢ ܚܕܐ ܫܒܠܐ ܦܢܝܐ ܟܠܗ ܡܢܗܘܢ ܐܘ ܕܟܠ
ܐܝܠܝܢ ܦܘܠܓ̈ܢܐ ܗܢܘ ܕܢܬܦܫܟܘܢ ܐܘܟܝܬ ܚܕܐ
ܕܘܟ̈ܝܬܐ ܦܢܝܐ ܟܠܗ ܡܢܗܘܢ ܢܓܡܪ. ܡܛܠ ܕܝܢ ܗ̇ܝ
ܕܒܕܐܝܢ ܗܠܝܢ ܢܬܒܥܐ: ܐܬܚܙܝܬ ܒܐܝܢܐ ܕܠܘ
ܕܗܟܢܐ ܗ̇ܝ ܗܫܐ: ܡܛܠ ܠܐ ܒܦܘܩܕܢܘܬܐ ܘܠܐ
ܡܕܪܫܘܬܐ ܕܐܢܫܝܢ ܕܒܗܠܝܢ: ܡܛܠ ܗܠܝܢ ܕܟܢܫܝܢ
ܒܗܘܢ ܚܝ ܫܘܪܝܐ: ܐܬܚܙܝ ܕܙܕܩܐ ܕܐܦܫܪ ܓܝܪ
ܚܘܒܗܘܢ ܐܠܗܐ. ܫܡܥܐ ܐܘܟܝܬ ܠܘܩܒܠ ܕܒܗܘܢ
ܡܬܚܫܚܝܢ ܚܝ ܫܘܪܝܐ: ܒܕܡܐ ܠܟܠܗܝܢ ܘܬܠܬܐ
ܐܬܟܫܠ. ܡܚܝܝܢܐ ܕܠܗܘܢ. ܡܢ ܐܢܫܝܢ ܡܩܒܠܢܐ.
ܫܘܝܐ ܟܪ ܡܢܗܘܢ ܬܚܝܬ ܚܙ̈ܕܐ ܢܦܠܝܢ. ܡܢ ܚܙ̈ܕܐ
ܒܝܬ ܡܬܚܡܝܢ ܘܡܬܬܚܙܝܢ ÷ ܐܝܬܘܗܝ، ܕܝܢ ܫܘܡܠܝܐ
ܕܠܗܘܢ ܗܟܢܐ ÷ ܟܠܗ. ÷ ܒܝܬܐ ÷ ܘܐܚܐ ÷

ܬܫܝܬܐ ܀ ܫܡܟܝܐ ܀ ܡܪܠܝܢܐ ܀ ܬ̈ܘܪܐ : ܬܘܟܣܐ ܀
ܥܪܝܐ ܀ ܪܗܛܐ ܕܦܣܩ ܀ ܘܕܠܐ ܦܣܩ ܀ ܡܟܐܠܝܢܐ ܀
ܡܣܘܝܢܐ ܀ ܦܪܘܫܐ ܀ ܦܣܘܕܐ ܀ ܡܦܝܣܢܐ ܀ ܗܘܢ
ܦܠܓܘܬܐ ܐܘܟܝܬ ܡܦܠܓܢܐ ܀ ܡܬܕܪܟܢܐ ܀ ܡܢܝܢܬܐ ܀
ܡܫܠܠܢܐ ܐܘܟܝܬ ܡܢܗܪܢܐ ܀ ܘܦܘܪܫܐ ܐܘܟܝܬ
ܡܣܝܒܪܢܐ ܀ ܕܝܘܪܐ ܐܘܟܝܬ ܦܐܪܐܒܘܠܘܣ ܀
ܦܣܘܩܐ ܀ ܗܠܝܢ ܐܬܡܢܝܘ ܫܘ̈ܡܗܐ ܕܡܠܘܐܐ.
ܕܐܫܬܡܥܬ ܕܐܫܬܕܪܒ ܘܐܬܟܢܫ ܠܟܘܢ ܕܫܟܝܢܬܐ. ܐܘ̈
ܐܝܟܢܐ ܕ̈ܘܝܫܐ. ܡܛܠ ܕܝܢ ܕܬܠܬ ܓܠܝܬܐ ܗܘܝܐ ܠܟܘܢ
ܡܢܛܠܬܐ ܫܬܝܬܬܐ ܕܡܛܠ ܗܠܝܢ: ܘܕܕܐܝܟ ܐܝܟ ܐܡܝܢ
ܡܬܬܩܢܢ ܫܒܥܐ ܘܒܐܝܢܐ. ܢܩܘܕܢ ܚܠܝܨ ܡܬܬܩܢܢ
ܗܐ ܒܬܪ ܫܒܥܐ ܠܟܘܢ: ܚܠܝܨ ܢܩܘܕܢ ܡܢ ܦܬܓܡܐ
ܕܡܢ ܟܬܒܐ ܐܠܗܝܐ: ܘܕܡܢ ܙ̈ܘܓܐ ܡܕܥܐ ܐܬܬܟܠܠ
ܘܒܐܝܕ̈ܝ ܩ̈ܕܡܝܐ ܘܕܥܡܗܘܢ ܠܗܠܝܢ ܬ̈ܟܠܝܬܐ ܐܫܬܠܡ
ܠܟܠܗ̇ ܟܬܒܬܐ ܀ ܐ̄ ܀ ܫܡܟܐ ܟܝܬ ܐܘ ܢܩܘܕܐ ܕܠܟܠ
ܡܢ ܟܬܒܬܐ ܐܝܬܝܬܐ ܕܗܕܟܐ ܐܝܟܢܐ: ܕܡܬܬܣܝܡ
ܥܠ ܦܣܘܩܐ. ܠܗܢܐ ܥܠܝܐ ܦܪܝܢ. ܐܝܟ ܕܐܡܝܪܐ
ܠܡܕܥܐ ܡܬ݂، ܟܕܘܪ، ܟܬܒܐ ܕܐܘܢܓܠܝܘܢ ܕܠܘܩܐ ܀
ܒ̄ ܀ ܟܕ ܕܝܢ ܗ̣ܘ ܢܩܘܕܐ ܒܬܚܘܬ ܕܫܡܟ ܐܟܘܬ ܕܐܡܪ:
ܫܠܝܡ ܡܢ ܗ̇ܘ ܕܦܣܩ ܠܦܬܓܡܐ: ܟܕ ܠܝܬ ܫܘܘܟܠܗ
ܕܗܢܐ ܟܝܢܐ ܡܢ ܗܕܟܐ ܗ̇ܘܢ ܕܒܬܪܗ. ܠܗܢܐ
ܚܝܠܐ ܡܫܡܫܝܢ ܣܝܢ. ܐܝܟ ܗ̇ܝ ܕܐܡܝܪܐ: ܒܗ̇ܘ
ܬܕܒܚܘܢ ܕܐܝܢܐ ܒܐܢܐ: ܘܐܢܬܘܢ ܒܗ ܐܢܬܘܢ ܀
ܓ̄ ܀ ܐܡܬܝ، ܬܘܒ ܕܗ̇ܘ ܫܡܟܐ: ܐܝܟ ܕܐܬܡܘܗܝ،
ܢܦܬܪ: ܘܫܘܘܟܠܗ ܕܗܢܐ ܒܬܚܘܬ ܟܕ ܡܢ ܗܕܟܐ
ܕܟܬܪܘ. ܠܗܢܐ ܘܡܟܐ ܦܪܝܢ. ܐܝܟ ܕܐܡܝܪܐ. ܕܠܐ

ܐܬܝܬ ܕܐܒܪܐ ܢܒܗܘܬܐ܆ ܐܠܐ ܕܐܬܓܠܐ. ܗܕܐ
ܐܬܬܣܝܡ ܬܫܠܡܘܬ ܫܦܝܪܐ ܗ̇ܝ܆ ܡܩܒܠܬܐ ܀ ܕ̄ ܀ ܕܐܬܬܣܝܡ
ܕܝܢ ܗܕܐ ܐܬܝܗ̇ܒ. ܟܕ ܚܙܝܢ ܢܘܗܪܐ ܥܡ ܦܨܚܐ
ܡܬܬܣܝܡ: ܠܬܫܥ ܡܢ ܐܬܘܬܐ ܐܚܪܝܬܐ ܕܗܕܡܐ
ܐܚܪܝܐ ܕܦܬܓܡܐ: ܐܝܟ ܕܡܨܪܝܐ ܟܬܒܐ ܩܕܝܫܐ
ܕܐܦܪܣܘܢ. ܗܢܝ ܬܫܥܬܐ ܕܚܫܘܢ ܡܫܬܒܚܗ ܀ ܗ̄ ܀
ܐܡܪܬ܆ ܕܝܢ ܕܣܦܪ ܡܢ ܦܨܚܐ: ܢܗܘܐ ܗ̇ܘ ܢܘܚܐ ܐܝܟ
ܕܐܬܘܗܝ܆ ܡܫܒܚܐ. ܐܝܟ ܗ̇ܝ܆ ܕܡܬܒܥܐ ܠܢܒܝܐ
ܐܠܗܐ ܕܐܡܪ. ܠܡܫܒܚ ܦܨܚܢ ܠܗ ܕܒܢܝܐ ܀ ܘ̄ ܀
ܐܡܪܬ܆ ܬܘܒ ܕܗ̇ܝ܆ ܕܠܬܐ ܠܬܐܠܗܐ ܫܢܝܐ ܐܘܩܕܬ
ܬܫܒܘܚܬܐ: ܘܗ̣ܘ ܢܘܚܐ ܐܝܟ ܬܘܕܝܬܐ ܕܫܒܚܢ
ܕܡܫܡ: ܐܝܟ ܐܢܫ ܕܐܡܪ ܒܐܕܢܐ ܥܡܐ ܡܢܢ ܡܪܐ.
ܗܢܐ ܡܢ ܠܢܝܐ ܐܘܩܝܬ ܡܬܦܩܕܢܐ ܕܡܫܬܒܚܐ ܀ ܙ̄ ܀
ܬܫܠܡܘܬ ܫܦܝܪܐ ܡܢ ܕܠܬܬ ܗܕܐ ܐܬܝܗ̇ܒ. ܐܝܟܢܐ
ܕܬܫܥ ܢܘܗܪܐ ܢܚܬܘܢ ܕܡܫܒܚܝܢ ܡܘܐܡܬ:
ܒܡܘܠܟܢܐ ܕܦܬܓܡܐ ܒܗܝܢܐ ܙܢܐ: ܟܕ ܠܦܘܪܟܢܐ
ܕܡܠܬܐ ܪܘܡܢ ܕܢܘܪܒܐ. ܠܗܢܐ ܥܘܢܐ ܡܫܒܚܝܢ
ܠܗ. ܐܝܟ ܗ̇ܝ܆ ܕܐܡܪܬܐ: ܕܟܘܢ ܡܢ ܕܘܐ ܟܡܐ ܕܐܦܩܬ
ܥܢܝܬܐ ܕܐܪܒܥܐ ܒܐܪܒܥܐ: ܕܠܫܥܐ ܕܒܗ ܡܫܬܒܪܢܐ
ܠܥܦܢܐ ܫܢܬܐ ܕܫܠܝܚܘܬ ܕܐܒܕܘܢ ܀ ܚ̄ ܀ ܐܡܪܐ ܕܝܢ
ܕܠܟܠ ܡܢ ܐܬܘܬܐ ܐܚܪܝܬܐ ܕܗܕܡܐ: ܡܢ ܗܠܝܢ
ܕܟܡܝܢܬܐ ܡܫܬܒܚܝܢ ܠܗ ܕܡܫܒܚܝܢ. ܘܙܒܢܐ ܕܫܪܬܐ
ܠܐܠܝܢ ܕܡܠܐܟܘܬ ܡܫܡܫܝܢ: ܐܢܫܝܢ ܢܫܝܐ ܕܐܘܢܝ. ܗ̇ܘ
ܕܫܢܐ ܫܢܝܐ ܕܠܒܫܐ܆ ܠܐ ܫܢܐ. ܠܗܢܐ ܬܫܡܫܬܐ ܦܪܝܢ.
܀ ܛ̄ ܀ ܀ ܐܡܪܐ ܕܝܢ ܕܡܫܠܡ ܬܫܡܫܬܐ ܙܢܝܐ ܕܦܬܓܡܐ:
ܘܐܝܟ ܗ̇ܘ ܡܦܩܢܐ ܢܫܬܒܚ ܕܫܪܝ. ܐܝܟ ܗ̇ܝ܆ ܕܫܦܝܪܐ

ܠܥܠܝܢܐ ܐܠܗܝܐ ܒܐܓܪܬܐ ܕܠܘܬ ܥܒܪ̈ܝܐ : ܕܠܗ
ܬܫ̈ܒܚܢ ܘܝܩ̈ܪܢ : ܠܥܠܡ ܥܠܡܝܢ ܐܡܝܢ . ܠܗܢܐ ܫܪܒܐ
ܐܚܪ̈ܝܢ ܠܗ ܀ ܝ̄ ܀ ܬܫܥܝܬܐ ܢܩܪܐ ܕܝܢ : ܗܿܝ ܕܐܬܪ̈ܟܒ
ܗܿܝ ܕܪ̈ܗܛܠܐ ܕܠܐ ܣܘܦ ܘܕܗܿܘ ܕܣܘܦ ܗܕܐ ܗܝ . ܗܿܘ
ܡܢ ܡܕܢܚܐ ܚܘܪ ܡܙ̈ܢܐ ܘܫܝ ܡܢܟܐ ܦܘܩܐ ܠܝ .
܀ ܟ̄ܐ ܀ ܗܿܘ ܕܝܢ ܕܐܬ̈ܪܝܢ ܠܐ ܬܦܠܓܐ ܠܝ ܡܢܝܢܐ.. ܀ ܟ̄ܒ ܀
ܥܬܘܬܘܬ ܢܩܪܐ ܕܝܢ ܗܿܝ ܕܫܡܥ : ܗܿܝ ܕܐܫܘܝܢܐ .
ܘܡܫܐܠܢܐ . ܘܦܪܘܥܐ . ܘܦܩܘܕܐ . ܘܡܦܫܩܢܐ . ܘܗܘܒ
ܦܠܚܐ ܐܘܪܚܬ ܡܫܠܡܢܐ . ܗܕܐ ܐܝܬܝܗܿ . ܗܠܝܢ
ܒܠܗܘܢ ܫܕܐ ܕܗܘܟܬܐ ܐܚܝܕܝܢ : ܗܿܝ ܕܠܟܠ ܡܢ
ܒܬܚܒܬܐ ܡܕܚܠܬܐ ܕܗܕܡܐ ܡܕܚܢܐ ܒܬܫܘܒܚܢ
ܘܬܬܡܪܐ ܣܟܐ ܕܠܗܘܢ ܫܒܠܐ ܠܗܘܬ ܕܗܘ̈ܟܠܐ
ܕܟܬ̈ܒܐ ܐܝܠܝܢ ܕܠܬ̈ܚܝܢ ܀ ܘܦܪܘܫܐ ܦܝ ܗܿܝ ܕܟܕ
ܦܪܘܩ ܡܬܚܘܝܬܐ ܗܘܐ ܡܢ ܢܘܚ ܡܡܕܡܢܐ ܠܒܢܝܢܐ
ܗܿܘ ܕܠܐ ܡܛܘܦ ܗܘܐ ܒܗ ܐܝܟ ܕܒܡܒܘܠܐ ܘܐܬܪ̈ܐ .
ܗܐ ܐܡܪܗ ܕܐܠܗܐ ܗܿܘ ܕܩܛܠ ܫܠܝܛܗ ܕܡܠܟܐ ܀
ܟ̄ܗ . ܀ ܕܐܬܪ̈ܝܢ ܕܝܢ ܐܝܟ ܗܿܝ ܕܡܫܐܠ ܗܘܐ ܦܘ ܦܪܘܩ
ܡܠܠ ܠܒܪ ܐܘܒܐ ܫܡܬܘܢܝܗܝ ܀ ܟ̄ܘ ܀ ܀ ܕܬܠܬܐ ܕܝܢ
ܐܝܟ ܗܿܝ ܕܐܡܣܪܐ ܠܦܪܘܩ ܡܠܬܐ ܐܠܗܝܐ
ܒܐܘ̈ܐܢܓܠܝܐ ܕܠܗ : ܕܪܘ ܠܟܘ ܠܐܚܪ̈ܐ ܘܥܩܝܠ
ܡܩ̈ܒܠܐ ܘܡܫܪܐ ܡܐܬܝܢ ܀ ܟ̄ܙ ܀ ܕܐܪ̈ܒܥܐ ܐܝܟ
ܗܿܝ ܐܬܬܐ ܕܐܡܦܪܐ ܡܢ ܡܘܬܗ ܠܗܘܬ ܛܠܝܬܐ : ܕܪܒ
ܠܟܢܫܐ ܐܪ̈ܒܥܐ ܕܫܢ̈ܝܐ ܐܝܬܐ . ܀ ܟ̄ܚ ܀ ܕܚܡܫܐ ܕܝܢ ܕܐܝܟ
ܗܘܢܐ ܐܝܬܘܗܝ . ܐܡܪܬ ܕܡܢ ܗܿܘ ܕܒܪܝܢ ܠܗܿ ܘܗܘ ܕܪܒ
ܒܬܘܪܒܐ ܡܠܬܐ : ܐܝܟ ܗܿܢܝܢ ܕܗܿܘ ܒܪܐ ܐܘܫܦܐ
ܠܘܬ ܐܒܘܗܝ ܒܬܫܥܝܬ ܗܘܐ ܕܒܐܡܪ . ܕܦܠܠ ܐܝܟ

ܚܕ ܡܢ ܐܚ̈ܘܗܝ. ܘܗܘ ܕܡܢ ܐܬܥܝܪ ܒܒܥܘܬܐ ܠܘܬ
ܐܠܗܐ ܡܬܘܕܝܢܐ ܕܐܡܪܝܢ ܫ̈ܠܝܚܐ. ܠܒܪ ܥܘܕ̈ܪܢܘܬܐ.
ܠܐ ܬܐܡܪ ܠܠܐ ܢܚܫ̈ܘܫܘܬܐ ܗܢܐ ܡܫܝܚܐ ܡܬܘܕܝܢܐ.
ܡܕܝܢ ܗܘ ܒܪ ܗܘ ܦܫܝܛܐ ܘܡܫܝܚܐ. ܒܪ ܡܢ ܗܘ ܕܪܒ
ܠܘܬ ܗܘ ܕܐܒܘܗܝ ܡܬܐܡܪ ܦܫܝܛܐ ܗܘ. ܡܛܠ
ܕܦܫܝܛܘܬܗ ܡܬܐܡܪ. ܐܝܕܝܢ ܐܝܟ ܕܡܣܦܩܐ
ܡܫܝܚܐ ܀ ܝܐ ܀ ܡܫܠܡܢܐ ܕܝܢ ܐܘܪܚܗ ܢܗܘܐ ܬܘܒ ܠܡܐܡܪ.
ܐܝܟ ܗܠܝܢ ܬܘ̈ܒܐ ܕܒܐܘܢܓܠܝܘܢ ܡܢ ܡܪܢܐ ܕܒܠ
ܠܡܦܪ̈ܝܘ ܬܘ̈ܒܐ ܐܬܦܩܕܘ ܒܗ ܡܫܠܡܢܐ ܀ ܝܒ ܀
ܬܠܬܝܘܬ ܢܩܘܡܐ ܕܝܢ ܗܘ ܕܐܒܐ ܗܘ ܕܡܬܝܕܥܢܐ.
ܘܡܫܝܚܐ. ܘܡܫܬܠܡܢܐ. ܗܕܐ ܐܝܬܝܗ̇. ܒܠܗܘܢ ܗܢܘܢ
ܩܢܘ̈ܡܝܢ ܕܗܠܝܢ ܕܡܬܝܕܥܝܢ ܡܬܬܩܢܢ. ܗ̄ ܠܬܠܬ
ܡܢ ܒܬܪܗܢ ܡܫܝܚܬܐ ܕܗܕܡܐ ܡܫܝܚܐ ܕܒܬܪ ܪܘܚܐ ܀
܀ ܝܓ ܀ ܘܡܫܝܚܐ ܕܝܢ ܐܝܟ ܗܘ ܕܒܗ ܡܬܕܡܪ ܢܒܝܐ
ܐܡܪ. ܒܝܕ ܢܚܬܐ ܢܦܠܘ ܒܪܚܡܐ: ܘܐܝܟ ܪܘܚܐ ܕܡܪܝܐ.
܀ ܝܕ ܀ ܕܬܪ̈ܝܢ ܗܘܝ ܬܘܒ ܐܝܟ ܕܐܝܬ ܒܬܪ ܪܘܚܐ ܦܢܝܐ:
ܘܐܫܪܝܐ ܕܢܐܠ ܒܬܪܗ. ܘܡܢ ܗܝܟܠ ܦܘܪܫܢܐ
ܕܡܠܬܐ. ܐܝܟܢܐ ܕܗ̇ܝ ܕܢܒܝܐ ܐܡܪ ܡܫܝܚܐ ܠܒܪܢܫܐ
ܗܘ ܕܝܗܒ ܕܝܠܗܘܢ ܕܡܬܩܢܝܢ ܡܬܩܕܫܝܢ
܀ ܝܗ ܀ ܀ ܕܬܠܬܐ ܬܘܒ ܐܝܟ ܗܘ ܕܠܘܩܣܝܢ
ܐܘܐܘܢܓܠܝܣܛܐ ܐܡܪ ܒܟܬܒܐ ܕܐܘܢܓܠܝܘܢ ܕܝܠܗ:
ܒܪܫܝܬ ܐܝܬܘܗܝ ܗܘܐ ܡܠܬܐ. ܀ ܝܘ ܀ ܗܕܝܢ ܡܦܪܐ
ܐܘܪܚܬ ܚܘܫܒܢܐ ܗܘ ܕܡܠܘܐ ܘܡܦܩܢܐ. ܬܠܝܬܝܘܬ
ܢܩܘܡܐ ܗܘ ܕܐܒܐ. ܗܠܝܢ ܡܫܠܡܢܘܬ ܡܬܬܩܢܝܢ
ܘܕܠܝܬܘܬ ܐܝܟ ܒܠܚܘܕ ܕܠܗ. ܘܕܘܒܪܐ ܕܝܢ
ܕܗܘ ܡܫܝܚܐ ܗܕܐ ܐܝܬܝܗ̇. ܡܛܠ ܕܐܝܬ ܬܠܬܐ ܒܠܚܘܕ

ܗܟܢܐ: ܕܚܕ ܠܠܫܢܐ ܕܝܠܢ ܣܘܪܝܝܐ ܢܦܩ. ܠܐ ܡܨܝܐ
ܕܣܦܪ ܡܢ ܬܘ̈ܡ ܩܕܡܝܢ ܒܬܦ̈ܩܣ. ܐܝܟܢܐ ܕܗܠܝܢ
ܐܦܘ̈ܦܣܝܣ: ܗ̄ ܡܬܡܟܢܢܘܬܐ. ܐܝܟ ܗ̇ܝ ܕܠܟ ܒܠܫܢܐ
ܘܠܟ ܡܫܬܠܡܢܐ. ܘܠܟ ܡܬܪܓܡܢܐ ܘܕܐܪܟܐ. ܐܬܚܣܝܬ
ܠܐܟܘ̈ܬܐ ܡܩܪ̈ܝܢܐ: ܘܡܦܩ̈ܢܐ ܕܟܬ̈ܒܐ ܐܠܗ̈ܝܐ
ܕܢܘܩܙܐ ܚܕ ܢܬܬܣܝܡ ܠܬܚܬ ܡܢ ܐܬܘܬܐ ܐܚܪ̈ܢܝܬܐ
ܕܗܪܟܐ ܡܪܟܒܢ̇. ܘܢܘܩܙܐ ܐܚܪܢܐ ܠܬܚܬ ܡܢ
ܐܬܘܬܐ ܡܪܟܒܬܐ ܕܗܪܟܐ ܕܬܘ̈ܡ. ܕܬܚܘܡ ܕܐܦ
ܟܠܥܢܐ ܣܘܪܝܝܐ ܬܘ̈ܡ ܐܝܟ ܗܪ̈ܟܐ. ܐܠܐ ܒܗܘܢܐ ܚ̣ܕ
ܗܪܟܐ ܐܬܩܒܠܘ ܐܝܟ ܕܗܡܘܠܐ ∴ ܩ̄ܠ ∴ ܗ̇ܘ ܬܘܒ
ܚܢ ܕܟܘܪܐ ܡܢ ܣܘܪ̈ܝܝܐ ܡܬܩܪܝܐ: ܘܟܠ ܡܘܕܐ
ܟܠܗܘܢ ܡܢ ܐܝܟܢ ܡܬܬܩܢܝܢ: ܗܢܐ ܒܗ̇ ܕܡܢ ܠܟܠ
ܣܒܟܐ ܘܡܬܩܪܝܐ ܐܘܟܡܢܐ ܚܕ. ܘܬܠܬ ܕܟܬ̈ܒܬܐ
ܐܝܬ ܠܗ ∴ ܗ̄ ܣܘܟܠܐ ܐܚܪܢܝܬܐ ܒܬܬܣܝܡ. ܘܟܠ
ܕܦܕܡ ܗ̇ܝ ܐܚܪܢܝܬܐ. ܘܟܠ ܗ̇ܝ ܕܦܕܡ ܗܢܐ ܕܟܠ
ܣܘܕܐ ܡܬܬܩܢ̈ܝܢ ܡܬܩܪܝܐ.

Again: concerning these points; how the place of each one of them is known, as they have been fixed by studious men.[a]

There are also those, as I have ascertained from foreign philosophers, who have worked out grammatically the position *of these points*, which I will, therefore, in this my short writing, make known, for the love of God, to you men, from the philosophers.

---

[a] This Title to the Letter was most likely put by the copyist, and was intended to apply only to the fragment which he copied.

Aristotle[b] very wisely said, that there are five signs of discourse, viz. ܡܫܐܠܢܝܐ *interrogating*, ܩܪܘܝܐ *calling*, ܡܬܟܫܦܢܐ *supplicating*, ܦܩܘܕܝܐ *commanding*, ܦܣܘܩܝܐ *a section*. With respect to this last *sign*, it perfects the discourse much more exactly than the others. But there are other grammarians, distinguished for knowledge of such matters as these, who have in their writings delivered ten points (or accents) for those who wish to become conversant with these things.

Epiphanius,[c] also, holy and a worker of wonders, who in the pastures of the true and orthodox faith, and in the folds strong and inaccessible to the wild (field) swine and ravenous and tearing wolves, and with those, who are found willing to work for the sake of others, fed and did good to the dear and beloved flock of Christ—in the writings engraven by the inspiration of the Holy Spirit, he has delivered (signs or accents) to boasting men. But because Syrian men, such as we, are not familiar

---

[b] In the commentary of Probus on Aristotle περὶ ἑρμηνείας, just published by Dr. Hoffmann, p. 66, he says: *the object of Aristotle in this book is to teach us concerning speech; but not concerning all speech; for there are five kinds of speech,* ܩܪܘܝܐ, ܡܫܐܠܢܝܐ, ܦܣܘܩܝܐ, ܦܩܘܕܝܐ, ܡܬܟܫܦܢܐ.

[c] Epiphanius was bishop of Salamis in the 4th century. Jerome speaks of him in high terms, and says that he was called πεντάγλωττος, *a man of five languages*, viz. Greek, Syriac, Hebrew, Egyptian and Latin. It seems probable from the context and from the time in which Epiphanius flourished, although he knew Syriac, that what he wrote on accents, was on Greek accents. In the *Bibliotheca Orientalis, Tom.* ii. p. 499, by Assemani, there is mention of a MS. in the Vatican by Epiphanius, *de punctis: de ponderibus et mensuris, et de significatione literarum alphabeti*, a Syriac version.

with these matters, it has appeared to me, that to speak now of the distribution of these *points*, or of how many of these and what each one of them comprises, or of those which are embraced *in the same sentence*, how much power each one of them possesses, or upon what syllables it is right that they should be put, viz. how many places each one of them acquires, would be unseasonable. It seems to me that to occupy ourselves now with such things as these would be ill timed; because there is no publication,[d] and no disquisition of men in these matters.

Concerning those *signs*, with which we Syrians are familiar, it is right that I should speak in holy love to you. The ܡܢܩ̈ܕܢܐ, namely ܢܘ̈ܩܙܐ *points*, which we Syrians use, the number of those imposed by men, has attained to twenty three; many of them falling under[e] one another, being bound and held by one another.

The naming of them is thus, ܥܠܝܐ *above*, ܚܪܝܢܐ *contention*, ܙܘܥܐ *motion*, ܬܚܬܝܐ *beneath*, ܣܡܟܐ *a fulcrum*, ܡܨܠܝܢܐ *praying*, ܫ̈ܘܝܐ *equals*, ܬܡܗܐ

---

[d] What is here said, is to be understood of compound signs. The writer excuses himself for not treating of these signs, because the subject was new, or at least, there had been no work published on it. He, therefore, invites the attention of those, who are addressed, only to simple or single signs. The treatment of signs, two, three, four, &c., combined in a sentence, and the consideration of all the circumstances of their combination would, he says, be *unseasonable*. We infer from what has been here mentioned, that this must have been one of the first writings on the subject.

[e] It is said to have been a custom with many Syrians to write from the top of the page to the bottom. This practice will explain what is here said of signs falling under one another.

reproof, ܫܪܝܐ *loosening,* ܪܗܛܐ ܕܦܣܩ, i.e. ܪܗܛܐ *which divides,* ܘܕܠܐ ܦܣܩ *and* (ܪܗܛܐ) *which does not divide,* ܡܫܐܠܢܐ *interrogating,* ܡܚܘܝܢܐ *indicating,* ܩܪܘܝܐ *calling,* ܦܩܘܕܐ *commanding,* ܡܟܫܦܢܐ *supplicating,* ܝܗܒ ܛܘܒܐ *giving happiness,* or ܡܫܒܚܢܐ *praising,* ܡܬܕܡܪܢܐ *admiring,* ܡܚܬܬܐ *making to descend,* ܡܒܛܠܢܐ *discontinuing,* or ܡܢܗܪܢܐ *shining,* ܙܩܘܪܐ *a weaver, or* ܡܚܝܕܢܐ *uniting,* ܓܪܘܪܐ *drawing out,* or ܦܪܐܟܣܘܛܘܢܘܣ,* *παροξύτονος,* ܦܣܘܩܐ *a section.**

These are the names of the points, O spiritual brethren, which I have been able to make known and collect for you on the instant. But that an accurate knowledge may be more manifested to you concerning these, and of how each one of them (ܦܢ̈ܝܡܐ) is placed, and by what accent it is read; behold I write for you each one of them with a passage from Holy Scripture, which was spoken by the Holy Spirit and delivered to all the earth by hands holy and fit for these exalted matters.

1. The point which is above the last writing† of the last member, being placed by ܦܣܘܩܐ; this they call ܫܠܐ, according to that which is said by St. Matthew in the beginning of the book of his gospel.[a]

2. But when the point is found placed, where it is said (in 1), without that (*the point* ܦܣܘܩܐ) which divides the expression, there being not any

---

* In MS. ܦܪܐܟܣܘܛܘܢܘܣ is omitted, and ܦܩܘܕܐ is by mistake for ܦܣܘܩܐ.

† ܟܬܒܬܐ here, as in many other places in this Tract, means a *letter*, or *consonant*.

[a] ܟܬܒܐ ܕܝܠܝܕܘܬܗ ܕܝܫܘܥ ܡܫܝܚܐ: *the book of the generation of Jesus Christ.*

thing contrary to *this member* in one of those members, which are after it; this we name ܚܘܝܐ; as, that which is said, ܒܗܘ ܬܕܥܘܢ ܕܐܢܐ ܒܐܒܝ·[b] ܘܐܢܬܘܢ ܒܝ ܐܢܬܘܢ, *in that (day) ye shall know that I am in my father, and ye are in me.*[c]

3. Again: when the point remains as it was, but there is found something contrary to *this member* in one of the members, which are after it; this they call ܢܘܚܐ, as that which is said, ܠܐ[1] ܐܬܝܬ ܕܐܫܪܐ ܢܡܘܣܐ· ܐܠܐ ܕܐܡܠܐ, *I came not to destroy the law, but to fulfil.* This is the first triad of points.

4. The second *triad* is thus. When the point is put with ܦܘܣܩܐ, below the last letter of the last member of the expression, as that which begins the Holy Book of the Acts; this is named by them (the accentuators) ܬܚܬܐ.

5. But when it is without ܦܘܣܩܐ, the point will be ܡܫܡܥܐ;[d] as that which is written by the holy prophet David, ܠܚܡܐ ܡܣܥܕ ܠܒܗ ܕܒܪܢܫܐ,[2] *bread sustaineth the heart of man.*

6. When again the speech looketh unto God, that is, is supplicating, then the point is found placed as ܬܚܬܐ; as one would say, ܒܥܐ ܐܢܐ ܡܢܟ ܡܪܝܐ. *I beseech Thee, O Lord.* This is named ܡܨܠܝܢܐ *praying*, or ܡܬܟܫܦܢܐ *supplicating.*

7. The third triad of points is this: where two points are found placed equally, at the end of an expression, in this way (:), being incited to

---

[b] In the margin is ܥܒܕܐ. [c] John xiv. 20.

[d] Literally: "as that which is ܡܫܡܥܐ."

[1] Matth. v. 17. [2] Ps. civ. 15.

tread on the apodosis of the discourse, this they name ܫܘܝܐ *equals;* according to that which is said, ܘܚܙܐ ܡܪܝܐ ܕܣܓܝܐܬ ܒܝܫܘܬܐ ܕܐܢ̈ܫܐ[3] ܒܐܪܥܐ, *the Lord saw that the wickedness of men was great in the earth,* which has respect to sinners, and by placing it in the beginning, seems to tread lightly on the flood.[e]

8. But where that they are above the last letter of the member of those which are found by me placed in the middle, and one purposes to rebuke those, who conduct themselves amiss, *as* the prophet David said, ܗܘ ܕܒܪܐ ܥܝ̈ܢܐ ܕܠܡܐ܀ ܠܐ ܚܙܐ,[4] *he who created the eyes, doth he not see?* this they call ܬܡܗܐ.

9. Where one wishes to make an end of the discourse, and it is found placed as the preceding one; as that which is placed by the holy Apostle in the Epistle to the Romans, : ܕܠܗ ܬܫ̈ܒܚܢ ܘܒܘܪ̈ܟܢ[5] ܠܥܠܡ ܥܠܡܝܢ ܐܡܝܢ, *to whom be glory and blessing for ever and ever, Amen;* this they call ܦܪܝܐ.

10. The fourth *group* is a duality of points. It consists of ܪܗܛܐ ܕܠܐ ܦܣܩ, *the* ܪܗܛܐ *which does not divide,* and of ܗܘ ܕܦܣܩ, *that which does divide.* The first is as, ܚܘܪ ܡܪܝܐ̈ ܘܚܙܝ ܡܢܐ ܗܘܐ ܠܢ,[6] *look, O Lord, and see what has happened to us.*

---

[3] Gen. vi. 5.

[e] The example of ܫܘܝܐ here given is from Gen. vi. 5. This passage serves as an introduction to the subject of the flood, and a reason for bringing the flood on the earth. The subject itself may be considered to have its commencement at the 6th verse. There is, then, an interval between ܫܘܝܐ and the apodosis, and this interval explains what is meant by *treading lightly on the flood.*

[4] Ps. xciv. 9. [5] Rom. xi. 36. [6] Lam. v. 1.

11. The second is as, .. ܠܐ ܬܛܥܐ ܠܢ ܡܪܝܐ, *O Lord, suffer us not to go astray.*

12. The fifth *group* consists of a sextuple of points. They are ܡܚܘܝܢܐ, ܡܫܐܠܢܐ, ܩܪܘܝܐ, ܦܩܘܕܐ, ܡܦܝܣܢܐ, and ܝܗܒ ܛܘܒܐ or ܡܛܘܒܢܐ. All these take one place; they are put above the first consonant of the first member, and their accent is called according to the particular sense, *which is* in the words which are written. The first is, as when our Saviour was pointed at by John the Baptist, as with the finger, to the multitude, who were not persuaded concerning him, and he said, ܗܐ ܐܡܪܗ[7] ܕܐܠܗܐ ܗܘ ܕܫܩܠ ܚܛܝܬܗ ܕܥܠܡܐ, *behold the Lamb of God, that taketh away the sin of the world.*

13. The second *sign* is as that which our Saviour asked concerning Lazarus, ܐܝܟܐ ܣܡܬܘܢܝܗܝ,[8] *where have ye placed him?*

14. The third is according to that which is said by our Saviour, the Word God, in His Gospels, ܬܘ ܟܠܟܘܢ ܠܐܢܝܐ ܘܫܩܝܠܝ ܡܘܒܠܐ ܘܐܢܐ ܐܢܝܚܟܘܢ, *come ye that are wearied and heavy laden, and I will give you rest.*[9]

15. The fourth is as the sign, which was mentioned by Jonathan to the boy, ܪܗܛ ܠܩܘܛ ܠܓܐܪܐ ܕܫܕܐ ܐܢܐ, *go, gather the arrows, which I cast.*[10]

16. The fifth signifies, when the matter is brought forward by one who is inferior to one who is superior; as, those *words* which the prodigal son devised to say to his father, ܥܒܕܝܢܝ ܐܝܟ ܚܕ ܡܢ ܐܓܝܪܝܟ, *receive me as one of thy hired servants.*[11]

---

[7] John i. 29. [8] John xi. 34. [9] Matth. xi. 28.
[10] 1 Sam. xx. 36. [11] Luke xv. 19.

Also the petition which is brought forward by man to God; ܐܥܒܪ ܚܛܗ̈ܝܢ, *cause our sins to pass away;* ܥܛܝ ܣܘܪ̈ܚܢܝܢ, *blot out our offences;* ܠܐ ܬܥܗܕ ܣܟܠ̈ܘܬܢ, *remember not our iniquities.* This is called ܡܦܝܣܢܐ. Therefore as to ܦܩܘܕܐ and ܡܦܝܣܢܐ, when *the expression* is said by one who is superior to another who is inferior, it is ܦܩܘܕܐ, because that it is said imperatively; but if the contrary, then it is ܡܦܝܣܢܐ.

17. ܡܫܒܚܢܐ or ܥܒܕ ܛܘܒܐ. Such are those beatitudes, which are given with praise in the Gospel by the Lord of all to those doing good works.[f]

18. The sixth group consists of a triad of points (accents). These are ܡܬܕܡܪܢܐ and ܡܫܝܚܬܐ and ܡܦܠܠܐ. All these are placed the contrary of those which are before them, i.e. *below* the first letter of the first member of the expression.

19. The first is according to that which the prophet wondering said; ܐܝܟܢܐ ܢܦܠܘ ܓܢܒܪ̈ܐ. ܘܐܒܕܘ[12] ܡܐܢ̈ܐ ܕܩܪܒܐ, *how have the mighty fallen and the vessels of war perished!*[g]

20. The second is, where there is a simple expression, and another following it, thus completing the apodosis of the discourse; as that *passage,* where

---

[f] ܡܫܒܚܢܐ is made here another name for the sign which is called ܥܒܕ ܛܘܒܐ; but in Jacob's Tract, and by Bar Hebraeus, ܡܫܒܚܢܐ is treated as an independent sign. See note to ܡܫܒܚܢܐ in the Tract.

[12] 2 Sam. i. 27.

[g] The mark of this sign is put *above* the first letter by Bar Hebraeus, where see, under ܡܬܕܡܪܢܐ.

Christ saw those Apostles, whom he wished to choose, mending their nets.[h]

21. Again, the third is as the point by John the Evangelist in the beginning of his Gospel; ܒܪܫܝܬ ܐܝܬܘܗܝ ܗܘܐ ܡܠܬܐ[13] *in the beginning was the word.*[i]

22. Then ܙܘܥܪܐ or ܡܙܥܪܢܐ, ܛܪܘܪܐ and ܦܣܘܩܐ make the triad of points of the seventh group. These are differently put, and each one takes its appropriate place. The place of the first is this. Because there are words in the Greek language, which, when translated into our Syriac language, it is not possible to render, except by two members,—as those prominent negations ܠܐ[j] ܝܠܝܕܐ *unbegotten*, ܠܐ[k] ܡܫܬܚܠܦܢܐ *immutable*, ܠܐ[l] ܡܬܕܪܟܢܐ *incomprehensible*, &c.,—it has appeared to the holy fathers and translators of the holy Scriptures, that one point should be placed below the

---

[h] This passage is an example of meekness and humility on the part of the disciples in immediately leaving all, and following Christ, and its sign is ܡܟܝܟܬܐ.

[13] John i. 1.

[i] See this sign explained and illustrated by Bar Hebræus.

The Syriac Text of ܛܪ, i.e. of ܛܪܘܪܐ is evidently mutilated. I have not, therefore, attempted a translation. I believe that the text in its integrity is found a folio or two further on in the MS. which contains the Tract of Thomas the Deacon. I have inserted it and given a translation in Appendix II., where see.

[j] Greek, ἀγέννητος. [k] Greek, ἀμετάτροπος.

[l] Greek, ἀσύλληπτος.

The sign ܦܣܘܩܐ is mentioned in the list, but there is not subsequently given any description of it. I have therefore put in Appendix II. the account of it found in the Tract of Thomas the Deacon, as probably similar to what we should have here, if mentioned at all.

last letter of the first member, and the other point below the first letter of the second member, which show that in the Syriac language there are two members, but in the Greek they are one member, *as is the case* with many.

APPENDIX II.

ܫܡ̈ܗܐ ܕܢܘ̈ܩܙܐ ܕܒܝܢܝܢ ܠܬܐܘܡܐ ܡܫܡܫܢܐ.
ܚܪܝܢܐ .. ܙܘܥܐ .. ܬܚܝܬܐ .. ܬܚܘܬܝܐ̇ . ܫܘ̈ܝܐ :
ܪܗܛܐ ܕܠܐ ܦܣܩ .. ܡܫܐܠܢܐ . ܡܣܟܢܢܐ .
ܦܘܩܕܐ .. ܦܩܘܕܐ . ܡܦܝܣܢܐ . ܢܗܒ ܠܦܘܡܐ ܐܘܟܝܬ
ܡܠܝܠܐ . ܡܬܕܡܪܢܐ . ܡܢܝܚܢܐ . ܡܡܠܠܢܐ ܐܘܟܝܬ
ܡܗܪܢܐ .. ܘܦܩܘܕܐ ܐܘܟܝܬ ܡܣܝܒܪܢܐ . ܙܩܦܐ
ܐܘܟܝܬ ܡܐܪܟܣܛܘܦܘܣ ܘܡܦܣܩܢܐ .
ܙܩܦܐ ܬܘܒ ܡܢ ܗܘ̈ܝܐ ܡܬܬܪܝܡ̇. ܘܥܠ ܡܘܕܝܐ
ܒܠܚܘܕ ܡܢ ܐ̈ܢܫܝܢ ܡܬܬܣܝܡ̣. ܗܢܐ ܒܗ̇ ܕܡܬܩܪܝܐ
ܐܘܟܣܝܣ ܢܩܝܦ ܕܐܝܬ ܠܗ̇. ܗ̄. ܥܠ
ܡܠܐܟܐ ܐܪܚܝܬܐ ܡܬܬܣܝܡ̣. ܘܥܠ ܗ̇ ܕܦܩܕ ܐܪܚܝܬܐ̣.
ܘܥܠ ܗ̇ ܕܦܩܕ ܗ̇ ܕܦܩܕ ܗ̇ ܐܪܚܝܬܐ. ܘܗܢܐ ܕܥܠ
ܡܘܕܝܐ ܡܬܬܣܝܡ ܦܪܐܣܛܘܡܘܣ . ܗܢܐ ܟܘܢܝܐ
ܥܠ ܫܡ̈ܗܐ ܐܝܟ̈ܢܐ ܡܫܬܟܚܝܢ ܕܦܩܕ . ܘܐܟܘܬ̄
ܡܪܦܝܢܐ .

There is the sign, which is called ܙܩܦܐ by us Syrians, and is put by some on ܡܘܕܝܐ only. This is bound in that which is called ὀξύς, which has three places, i.e., it is put upon the last syllable, upon that which is before the last, and upon that which is before that, which is before the last. This which is placed on ܦܘܕܐ is ܦܪܘܣܘܕܝܐ. It is found put in Greek over many nouns.

ܗܘ ܬܘܒ ܕܡܬܩܪܐ ܦܣܘܩܐ܆ ܗܘ ܕܥܠܗ ܦܝܠܣܘܦܐ ܚܦܛܘ ܠܘܬܗ܂ ܦܝܠܣܘܦ̈ܐ܆ ܘܡܝܬܪܐܝܬ ܐܪܣܛܘܛܠܝܣ ܗܘ ܕܐܡܪ ܕܡܣܒܪܐ ܫܪܪܐ ܐܘ ܕܓܠܬܐ܂ ܗܢܐ ܐܝܬܘܗܝ ܗܘ ܕܦܣܩ ܡܠܬܐ ܘܐܡܪ܆ ܘܕܬܬܗܦܟ ܠܐ ܡܫܟܚܐ ܡܢ ܐܢܫ܂ ܕܐܟܢ ܐܡܪ܂ ܛܒܐ ܐܝܬܘܗܝ ܐܠܗܐ܂ ܢܦܫܐ ܠܐ ܡܝܘܬܬܐ ܐܝܬܝܗ܂

Again, that which is called ܦܣܘܩܐ is that upon which philosophers have been solicitous, especially Aristotle, who said that it announces a truth or falsehood. This is that which divides the discourse, and he said that it cannot be overturned by man; such as, *God is good; the soul is immortal.*

ERRATUM.

In page 13, *for* names of accents; for the Syrians give names to points, *read* metrical points; for the Syrians call points ܢܘ̈ܩܙܐ.

APPENDIX III.

In the British Museum is a volume of MSS. marked Additional 25,876, consisting of a series of Tracts on Syriac Grammar. The compiler of them (see Assemani, Bibl. Orient. tom. iii. p. 307) was John Bar Zugbi. The fifth Tract of this compilation is one on the great metrical points. Its title, according to Assemani, is ܫܡܗ̈ܐ ܕܦܘ̈ܣܩܐ ܕܢܘ̈ܩܙܐ ܪ̈ܘܪܒܐ ܕܦܫܩ ܐܝܟ ܩܕܝܫܐ ܡܪܝ ܐܠܝܐ ܩܬܘܠܝܩܐ ܦܛܪܝܪܟܝܣ, *the names of the great metrical points, which the holy Mār Elias, the catholic patriarch, explained.* On p. 265 of the same volume of Assemani, he gives a list of the works written by Elias the first patriarch of the name. Of the works which are found mentioned in this list, the last is ܡܐܡܪ̈ܐ ܓܪܡܛܝܩܝ̈ܐ, *Grammatical Discourses.* On the same page is Note 7, as follows: "Exstat unus *de punctis* sub Eliæ Catholici nomine, quem Joannes Bar Zugbi suæ Grammaticæ inseruit." The evidence then is complete that Elias the catholic patriarch was the same as Elias the first.

The chief object of this Tract appears to be to explain etymologically the names of many of the Accents, of which some are exclusively Nestorian. These Syrians, it is known, carried out in comparatively later times the accentuation system in great detail, exclusively for the purpose of regulating the voice and adapting it to all the varieties and niceties of reading. As this Tract is, however, taken up with merely giving the derivation of the names of the Accents, without saying any thing about the mark and the position belonging to each Accent, it is of itself too imperfect for publication. I shall, therefore, content myself with making extracts. Some of these may be of use for illustrating what has been already treated of, whilst others will introduce three or four additional Nestorian Accents to the reader.

ܐ. ܙܘܓܐ ܗܘ: ܡܢ ܡܢܝܢܐ ܕܢܘܩܙܐ ܐܬܩܪܝ ܗܟܢܐ. ܗܢܘ ܕܝܢ. ܬܪܝܢ ܢܘܩܙܐ. *Zaugo is so named from the number of the points,* i. e. *two points.* The word ܙܘܓܐ signifies a pair, here of course a pair of points. It seems to be employed in this Tract to express a pair of points, varying very considerably in their position. It may be regarded as a general designation; a name for a number of Accents, each of which has for its mark two points, each of which too has an especial name, derived from the position of the mark, or a name suggesting either the sense of the passage, or the regulation of the voice. For the sake of example I make the following extracts. ܙܘܓܐ ܥܠܝܐ ܐܬܩܪܝ. ܡܛܠ ܕܟܘܫܚܬܐ ܗܘ̄ ܕܢܘܩܙܘܗܝ. ܪܡܝܐ. ܗ̄. ܫܫܠܬܐ ܕܠܥܠ ܀ ܙܘܓܐ *is named* ܥܠܝܐ *because the metre of its points is elevated,* i.e. *the chain is above.*

ܒ. ܙܘܓܐ ܓܢܝܒܐ. ܐܘ ܟܡܝܪܐ. ܡܛܠ ܕܒܟܝܬܐ ܗ̄ܝ ܩܪܝܢܗ. ܐܘ ܕܝܢ ܕܓܢܒ ܠܒܪܬ ܡܠܬܐ ܩܠܝܠ ܀ ܙܘܓܐ ܓܢܝܒܐ *or* ܟܡܝܪܐ is so called, *because that the reading is mournful, or because it steals a little from the word.* From this explanation of the accent, I infer that it is only another name for either of two accents treated of in previous pages, i.e. either for ܬܚܘܬܝܐ or ܡܟܝܟܐ. In both cases the etymology of the name is suggested by the situation of the mark, the mark being a little withdrawn from the

word, and lying rather furtively or secretly under it.
ܕ. ܗܘܦܟܐ ܒܝܢܝܐ. ܡܛܠ ܕܟܠܝܐ ܠܩܪܘܝܐ ܡܢ ܡܫܘܦܦܐ ܕܩܪܝܢܗ ܀ ܗܘܦܟܐ ܒܝܢܝܐ is so named, *because it obstructs the reader in the progress of his reading.* This is another instance, which shows that ܗܘܦܟܐ is employed by Elias as a general name for a class of Accents. Bar Hebræus speaks of ܗܘܦܟܐ as only another name for ܥܨܝܐ. See p. 37.

ܡܙܝܥܢܐ ܀ ܗ. ܡܙܝܥܢܐ. ܡܢ ܙܘܥܗ ܕܠܫܢܐ ܀ is so named *from the motion of the tongue.* There are two Accents bearing this name, one of which is called ܡܙܝܥܢܐ ܪܒܐ, and the other ܡܙܝܥܢܐ ܕܩܘܪܒܐ. According to Bar Hebræus, the former is the name given by the Eastern Syrians to the Accent ܬܟܣܐ, and the latter to that which is more generally called by the name ܪܗܛܐ. See p. 50.

ܙ. ܢܝܫܐ. ܡܙܝܥܢܐ ܐܚܪܢܝܐ. ܘܦܪܫ ܠ
ܡܙܝܥܢܐ *is* ܢܝܫܐ ܀ ܥܘܗܕܢܐ ܡܢܗ. ܐܝܟ ܕܠܦܘܪܫܢܐ ܀ *and receives this denomination for distinction.*

ܟܒܫܐ ܀ ܝܐ. ܟܒܫܐ. ܡܛܠ ܕܟܒܫ ܠܩܠܐ ܓܪ ܡܬܡܪܐ ܀ *is so called because it depresses the voice.* The mark of this Accent is not given; but it can be ascertained from another quarter. When Ewald was at Rome in the year 1836, he observed in a Syriac MS. in the Vatican, an account given of the names of the Accents. The MS., it seems, contained the Nestorian edition of the Epistles of St. Paul. In the first leaf of this MS. there appeared the names of eighteen Accents with the mark of each of them placed together in a row. There was also seen by him a second copy of these Accents in a different handwriting from that of the first. Hence he observes: "dass man nicht zweifeln kann hier die echten Namen und Zeichen zu sehen." In pp.

206, 207 of the "Zeitschrift für die Kunde des Morgenlandes," erster Band, Ewald has given these two lists. The first consists of the names and marks of eighteen Accents, the other of the names and vowel points of the same Accents. He states that he has given these two lists to prevent any mistake being made as to what are vowel points and what are Accents. Of the Accents mentioned in these lists ܟܡܝܫܐ is one, and the mark attached to it is ܁ thus ܟܡܝ̈ܫܐ.

ܗ. ܢܩܝܫܐ. ܡܛܠ ܕܢܩܫ ܠܠܫܢܐ ܒܡܩܪܝܢܘܬܐ ܀

ܢܩܝܫܐ is so called *because that it strikes on the tongue in the reading*. This Accent is one of those constituting Ewald's list, and the mark attached to it is ܂ thus ܢܩܝ̣ܫܐ. See p. 61 for the account given of this Accent by Bar Hebræus.

ܚ. ܨܒܥܐ ܕܚܒܩܬܗ. ܡܛܠ ܕܨܒܥܐ ܗܢܘܢ ܢܩܘܙܘܗܝ. ܨܒܥܐ ܕܚܒܩܬܗ ܀ ܠܚܒܩܬܐ ܕܚܒܝܩܐ is so called *because the position of its points is similar to the thumb restrained*, or *bridled*. According to Bar Hebræus its mark is three points ∴ making a triangle. See p. 49. As ܚܒܩܬܗ is derived by Elias from ܚܒܩܬܐ, we infer that ܗ is the pronominal affix of the third person singular. See Note A, p. 96. When the thumb is *restrained* or *bridled*, the position will correspond to the form of the mark of this Accent. The first joint will be the vertex of a triangle, the three points of which will be the first joint, the second joint and the end of the thumb. ܚܒܝܩܐ is the pass. part. of ܚܒܩ. The root is not found in the Lexicons; but it is perhaps cognate in sense with ܚܢܩܐ and ܚܢܩ. In like manner ܟܡܝܫܐ is from ܟܡܫ, which is also not found in the Lexicons; although it is no doubt cognate in sense with ܟܢܫܐ. But if we cannot state precisely the sense of ܚܢܝ by analogy with ܚܢܩܐ and ܚܢܩ; we are assisted by finding ܚܢܝܩܘܬܐ in Castell with the meaning *constrictio*, which he gives. If the sense of the participle be corresponding to this, we may translate it *restrained* or *bridled* as above.

ܚܠ ∴ ܦܣܘܩܐ ܕܬܠܬܐ. ܡܢ ܡܢܝܢ ܢܘܩܙܘܗܝ ܐܬܩܪܝ. ܦܣܘܩܐ ܕܬܠܬܐ ∴ ܗ. ܬܠܬܐ ܢܘܩܙܐ ∴ *is named from the number of its points*, i.e. *three points*. According to the Vatican MS. as copied by Ewald, its mark is ⁘ the same as that of ܬܚܘܬܐ ܕܬܠܬܐ. See p. 47.

ܕܐ ∴ ܡܩܝܡܢܐ. ܗܢܐ ܕܡܩܘܐ ܠܫܡܐ. ܘܐܝܟ ܗܘ ܕܦܣܩ ܡܢ ܗܘ ܕܒܬܪܗ. ܡܩܝܡܢܐ ∴ is so named, *because that it abides on the noun, and as that which cuts off* the expression *from what is after it.* Its mark consists, on the authority before mentioned, of two points; thus, : ܡܩܝܡܢܐ. This Accent and those marked ܠ, ܫ, ܐ, ܪܫ, ܩ, ܫܫ, and ܚܠ are exclusively Nestorian.

ܚܬ ∴ ܡܚܬܢܝܬܐ. ܡܢ ܢܚܬܘܬܐ ܐܫܬܘܫܛ ܫܡܗ. *its name is derived* (lit. *germinates*) *from* ܢܚܬܘܬܐ *descent.*

The Tract concludes with the following observation. ܗܫܐ ܗܟܝܠ ܕܢܫܠܡ ܠܡܠܬܐ ܕܥܠ ܦܠܓܘܬܐ ܩܕܡܝܬܐ ܕܡܫܘܚܬܢܝܘܬܐ ܕܢܘܩܙܐ ܪܘܪ̈ܒܐ ∴, *now, therefore, we end the discourse on the first part of the accentuation of the great metrical points.* We infer from this remark that Elias compiled a second Tract on this subject. It is probable that the two Tracts together made a complete work on the accents. Concerning the time in which Elias lived, Assemani in his Bibl. Orient., tom. iii. p. 262, says, "Elias hujus appellationis primus Nestorianorum Patriarcha anno Christi 1028, ordinatus, sedit unum supra viginti annos." He then makes a quotation from the Syriac Chronicle of Bar Hebræus, of which the following is an extract. ܘܩܡ ܒܬܪܗ ܐܘܟܝܬ ܒܬܪ ܝܫܘܥܝܗܒ ܐܠܝܐ ܩܕܡܝܐ ܕܐܝܬܘܗܝ ܗܘܐ ܐܦܝܣܩܘܦܐ ܕܛܝܪܗܐܢ: ܓܒܪܐ ܣܒܐ ܘܡܠܦܢܐ ܡܗܝܪܐ, *and there arose after him,* viz. *after Jeshuayab, Elias the first, who was bishop of Tirhan, an old man and an excellent scholar.*

THOMAS THE DEACON.

In Appendix I, I have used as an argument for the antiquity of the Letter there published, the points of resemblance between it and the Tract on Accents by Thomas the Deacon. The antiquity of the Letter, indeed, may be established quite independently of this argument; for the internal evidence for it brought forward on p. 67, is, I think, sufficient to show that it must have been written at a time anterior to that of Jacob of Edessa. I have in that Appendix spoken of Thomas the Deacon as living in the vi[th] century. I have, however, offered no proof in confirmation of this statement, and it may be thought by some persons that I should have done so. It seems to me that it is, therefore, desirable that I should produce such evidence as I have to give, especially as it has been recently asserted in a French Periodical, that Thomas the Deacon is known only by name. In seeking for information of this kind, it is usual to have recourse to the Biblioth. Orient. of Assemani, as the storehouse for supplying such intelligence. On consulting that work, I observe that he has mentioned in several places Thomas the Deacon of Edessa; yet I do not find there that anything whatever is said of a Thomas the Deacon as the author of a Tract on Accents. The heading of the Tract of Thomas is simply, ܫܡܗܐ ܕܦܘܩܕܐ ܕܥܒܝܕܝܢ ܠܬܐܘܡܐ ܡܫܡܫܢܐ. His name and office are only mentioned. Hence establishing the time in which he lived can, I apprehend, be done only by inference. In conducting an inquiry into the circumstances of the life of Thomas, it is fair to suppose that he might at some period or other have changed his designation. By this supposition, we get a Thomas, who has written on Accents, and written, so far as we know, according to the Tract of Thomas the Deacon. The inference which I shall endeavour to draw, and which I shall be able to support by evidence, is that Thomas the Deacon was the same as Thomas of Ḥarḳel. This Thomas, it is true, is no where spoken of as Thomas the Deacon, but as Bishop of Germanicia. In the life of this Thomas by an anonymous author, given in Assem. Biblioth. Orient. tom. ii. p. 90, it is not said that he wrote a Tract on Accents; but then the account is a very brief one, and, as Assemani has pointed out, although short, yet contains three serious errors. In such a biography we can only expect to meet with a bare statement of the leading points of the life. Again, the Tract itself is very short, and therefore the circumstance that no record of it is found in the biography ought to excite no surprise. It contains only three or four pages, and assuming that it was written by Thomas, it would not be likely to appear as a separate publication; but would be most probably appended to some larger work, such as his Syriac Version of the New Testament. Instances of small works being placed in a volume comprising a large treatise are not unfrequent. One instance we have in the Letter of Jacob edited in this Volume. It was originally appended to his translation of the λόγοι ἐπιθρόνιοι of Severus. The scribes copying the Letter were to place it before the middle book of the Epithronian discourses. See Letter on Syriac Orthography, p. 10. The version of the New Testament was made A.D. 616, when Thomas was Bishop and probably advanced in life. The Tract on Accents was no doubt written at a much earlier period, when the Author was only a Deacon of the Church, and very probably in the latter half of the sixth century.

Although the particular Tract on Accents with the Title as given in Appendix II. is nowhere spoken of as written by Thomas of Ḥarḳel; yet we learn from Bar Hebræus, that he certainly wrote on Accents. On p. 53 Bar Hebræus says, "according to the opinion of Thomas of Ḥarḳel ܡܫܠܡܢܐ and ܩܘܡ ܠܥܠܐ are one." This is exactly what is stated in the list of Accents by Thomas the Deacon, p. 83. Again on p. 56, Bar Hebræus remarks that the Accent ܡܫܝܕܢܐ is also called by Thomas by the name ܢܗܘܪܐ. This too is the second name of the Accent ܡܫܝܕܢܐ in the list of Thomas the Deacon. This coincidence must appear still stronger, when I observe that ܡܫܠܡܢܐ and ܩܘܡ ܠܥܠܐ are treated of as independent Accents by Jacob and all other writers with whom we are acquainted, with the exception of the author of the Letter given in Appendix I.

The inference I draw from all the circumstances which I have here enumerated is that Thomas the Deacon, the Author of the Tract on Accents, was the same as Thomas of Ḥarḳel.

ADDITIONAL EXPLANATORY NOTES AND CORRECTIONS.

Page viii. l. 3, *for* 720 l, *read* 7201.

p. ܒ, l. 5. ܕܐܟܘܬ ܐܡܪ. ܐܡܪ ܐܢܐ. ܡܢ ܗܠܝܢ ܕܥܬܝܕ ܐܢܐ ܕܐܡܪ ܐܫܬܥܝܘ. ܟܠܟܘܢ ܗܠܝܢ ܕܠܗܠܝܢ ܩܪܝܢ ܐܢܬܘܢ. The punctuation of this passage causes much perplexity. The Vat. MS. too has ܘ prefixed to ܟܠܟܘܢ, which must be an error. After a very full consideration of the passage, it seems to me that the translation in p. 1 may be improved as follows. I would finish the third paragraph of the page with the word *it*, in line 23. I would then for the rendering there given, viz. "more, I say, than such as those I am about to speak of. Understand all ye, who read these things that," substitute the following: *Understand all ye who read those things of which I am about to speak, I speak for the sake of example.* That the words ܕܐܟܘܬ ܐܡܪ may be rendered *for the sake of example*, see Payne Smith's *Thesaurus Syriacus* p. 149. The next sentence begins with the word *With* in l. 26.

p. ܐ, l. 14. Here for the negative particle ܠܐ, the Vatican copy has the preposition ܠܘܬ, which is no doubt correct, and which makes the sense obvious. But in accepting this reading, my explanatory note[k] of this passage in p. 10 becomes evidently incorrect. The defence I have to offer, I think a fair one, is, that I was led astray by the particle ܠܐ, and that I could only deal with the Syriac which was before me, not having seen the Vat. copy at the time the note was written. With the Syriac of my copy, I do not see that I could do otherwise than I did. Adopting the reading ܠܘܬ, as of course I do, I would in page 10, l. 4, have instead of: "For the sake of argument, I attempt to suppose something, which is not significant of that which I wish to teach," the following: *For the sake of example, I attempt to put words different in signification* (in juxta-position), *which is what I wish to teach.* Then follows the next sentence, which is correctly translated, but which in connection with the preceding one must be thus explained. In this sentence the word ܟܒܪܐ occurs four times, and each time in a different sense. This difference is indicated by the points, and by them only. Hence this sentence affords a happy illustration of the justice of Jacob's previous remark to the copyists, that the points should be put in the right places, and not where there is a vacant place, whether it be suitable or unsuitable.

P. 22, note za. For *admonitory* read *chiding.*

P. 25, l. 1. In the Vatican copy there is no point under ܐ of ܐܝܬܘܗܝ, and I think that it is correct.

P. 26, l. 19. For *or* read *and of.*

P. 32, l. 11. Jacob means that ܗܘܒܐ is constantly found in the way mentioned by him in this paragraph as accompanying ܪܗܛܐ ܕܦܣܘܩ, and also ܪܗܛܐ ܕܠܐ ܦܣܘܩ. In the first example we have ܗܘܒܐ with the latter named accent, and in the second we have ܗܘܒܐ with the former named accent.

P. 38, l. 3. For *By* read *With.*

P. 39, l. 11. ܡܢܘ ܫܠܡܐ ܗܢܐ, *what is this peace?* The difference between Michael and Basil could not have been with respect to the sense of this expression, because it is obvious that it must be interrogative. It is impossible to strip it of that character.

The difference, therefore, which existed must have been rather with respect to the reading or chaunting. An explanation of this difference may be found, if we turn to p. 54, and observe what is there said. Of ܡܢܝܚܬܐ it is stated, that "its mark is one point, at the head of the word, behind, and as with many it is placed before ܫܐܠܬܐ," i.e. before ܫܐܠܬܐ interrogative. Several examples are there given of ܡܢܝܚܬܐ before ܫܐܠܬܐ interrogative. I have, therefore, no doubt that Michael put ܫܐܠܬܐ after ܗܢܐ and that he accentuated the expression thus: . ܡܢܘ ܥܠܬܐ ܗܢܐ.

P. 39. Dele note *g*. Bar Hebræus means us to understand that the nouns ܙ̈ܒܢܐ and ܒܢܝܐ are in the nominative case according to the Edessene copies, and in the vocative according to the copies of Soba.

P. 43, l. 1. For *being* read *are*.

P. 51, l. 6. Dele *or in*.

„ l. 10. For *caustic* read *mournful*.

„ l. 23. Dele ܦܩܘܕܐ. Some explanation of the paragraph on ܡܦܩܢܐ is necessary to make it intelligible. What is required for this purpose may be found in p. 83 on ܙܩܦܐ. We learn there that what has three places is not the Syriac accent ܙܩܦܐ, or as it is here called, ܡܦܩܢܐ, but the Greek accent ʼοξεῖα, which is found, sometimes on the last syllable, sometimes on the penultimate, and sometimes on the antepenultimate. Bar Hebræus gives to these different positions the respective names of ܣܡܟܐ, ܡܦܩܢܐ and ܪܗܛܐ.

P. 52, ll. 9, 10. Instead of "mentioned afterwards upon that which is the praising noun," it would be more correct to translate, *upon the praising noun, which is last mentioned.* In p. 81, in the paragraph on this accent, reference is made to the beatitudes in Matth. v. They afford a happy illustration of the difference of position of the accents ܫܗܒ ܛܘܒܐ and ܡܫܠܝܢܐ as stated by Bar Hebræus. The word ܛܘܒܝܗܘܢ occurs several times. According to him, the mark of ܫܗܒ ܛܘܒܐ is on the first ܛܘܒܝܗܘܢ mentioned in this passage, and that of ܡܫܠܝܢܐ on the last.

P. 53, l. 23. For *my lord* read *the lord.*

P. 79, l. 4. For ܒܐܪܬܐ read : ܒܐܪ̈ܬܐ.

„ l. 9. For *me* read *us.*

„ l. 16. For *preceding* read *first.*

„ l. 19. For *glory and blessing* read *praises and blessings.*

NOTE A.

The pronominal affix ܗ in ܒܪܬܗ seems to be pleonastic. A similar construction is met with in Assem. Bibl. Orient. tom. i. p. 252, Note 1, where Simeon the Stylite is called ܫܡܥܘܢ ܕܐܣܛܘܢܗ. Dr. Bickell, in the glossary to his edition of the Nisibene Hymns, page 41, under ܐܢܬܬܐ ܕܕܡܫܗ has the following note: "Eadem constructio apparet in ܢܡܪܐ ܕܚ̈ܟܠܬܗ panthera maculosa, versicolor, ܩܛܘܠ ܪܘܓܙܗ occisor furiosus, immo cum nominibus propriis, ܐܦܪܝܡ ܕܚܟ̈ܝܡܘܬܗ, Ephraem sapientissimus."

In concluding this work, I beg to say that I believe it contains the substance of all which native writers have left us on the subject of the Accents. I doubt if any thing really new could be added to what is here to be found. As there is no other printed book which treats fully and didactically on the Syriac Accents, I hope that it may be long useful to those who desire to engage in the study of them.

ܕܦܫܛ. ܐܡܪܐ ܗܘ ܡܬܒܐܠܢܐ. ܕܡܬܦܢܐ· ܘܦܢܐ.
ܥܒܕܬܐ̈ ܕܗܠܝܢ ܕܦܫܛ. ܦܫܝܛܐ ܘܙܘܥܐ ܘܕܗܠܝܢ
ܕܠܐ ܦܫܛ. ܕܫܡܘ ܦܫܝܛܐ. ܘܕܡܣܩܬܐ· ܘܦܢܐ.
ܕܢܬܘܗ ܕܐܘܪܚܐ̈ ܕܗܠܝܢ ܕܠܐ ܦܫܛ. ܡܬܒܪܢܘܬܐ.
ܘܡܢ ܢܦܫܐ ܡܬܚܡܐ ܕܡܬܢܫܝܐ ܥܠܝܗ̇. ܡܬܢܟܣܝܢ
ܒܗ ܐܢܬܘ. ܗܘ ܕܥܠܡܝܢܘܬܐ ܦܪܫ ܠܗ. ܒܕܡ
ܥܡܘܪܝܢܐ ܕܐܣܟܘܠܐ ܦܪܫܘܬܐ ܠܝܚܡ ܐܬܬܥܠܡܬ:
ܒܕ ܐܡܪܐ ܕܢܣܝܒܘܬ ܕܬܒܥܐ ܠܣܒܪܐ ܡܢܡ ܬܫܘܬܐ
ܕܢܦܩ ܠܗ ܦܫܛ ܐܥܒܕܗ ܬܟܣܐܝܬ ܐܝܟ ܕܠܝܒܬܐ
ܘܦܕܪܐ ܦܢܘ ܘܐܡܢܝܗ. ܠܐ ܫܘܐ ܒܢܡ ܒܠܒܘܟ.
ܐܠܐ ܒܬܟܬܒܐ ܡܢܡ ܕܠܒܠܐ. ܐܝܟ ܢܬܟܢܫܘܢ ܡ̈ܫܝܐ:
ܠܬܒܝܬ ܡܢ ܥܡܝܢܐ ܠܐܬܪܐ ܚܕ. ܘܬܬܚܬܢܐ ܢܒܥܬܐ.
ܘܪܢܐ. ܐܢ̈ܫܘܗܝ ܕܘܪܒܝܢ. ܗܢܘܢ ܥܒܐ̈ܦܝܗܘܢ ܕܒܝܬܐ
ܗܢܐ. ܘܐܬܬ· ܡܢ ܒܢ̈ܝܢ ܕܐܘܪܚܐ̈ ܕܬܒܥܒܪ
ܢܒܥܬܗ ܕܥܠܝܡܐ. ܘܗܘܐ ܕܬܬܪ ܡܢ ܥܠܝܡܐ
ܦܘܪܫܐ ܀ ܘ ܀

ܬܫܬܐ ܡܫܬܐܠܢܐ. ܥܢܝܐ ܘܬܟܫܦܬܐ ܘܡܫܬܐܠܢܐ.
ܐܘܢ ܣܡ ܕܦܘܫܐ ܘܐܦ ܟܠܗܘܢ: ܥܢܝܐ. ܙܟܝܐ̈ ܬܟܫܦܬܐ.
ܐܘܢ ܣܡ ܡܢܟܘܢ ܕܦܠܓܐ ܢܦܫܘܬ. ܡܥܐܠܢܐ. ܘܐܝܬ
ܐܢܟܐ ܕܣܠܩ ܬܫܬܐ ܡܫܬܐܠܢܐ. ܬܫܬܐ ܠܐ
ܡܫܬܐܠܢܐ ܡܬܒܝܢ. ܐܝܟ ܐܢܫ ܠܟܡܒܪܐ ܕܢܦܠܐ
ܕܡܟܢܐ ܐܝܬܘ ܘܡܢܫ ܢܦܠ ܒܬܘܪܐ: ܥܢܝܐ.
ܐܠܗܐ̈ ܗܟܢܐ ܡܠܟܐ. ܬܫܬܐ. ܠܐ ܦܠܛ ܢܬܒ
ܠܟܘܢ ܘܟܘܪ̈ܗ ܗܢܐ. ܘܡܕܢܚܐ ܠܟܠܬ ܡܠܟܐ
ܬܦܢ ܟܥܢܝܐ ܦܪܡ. ܬܟܫܦܬܐ ܘܘܟܐ ܘܥܢܝܢܐ. ܘܐܘܢ
ܢܦܘܐ̈ ܬܟܫܦܬܐ. ܦܘܢܝܐ ܘܟܠܐ. ܠܟܠ ܡܫܐܠ:
ܥܢܝܐ. ܘܠܗܢܐ ܙܘܟܐ ܡܕܢܚܐ ܡܫܟܠܢܐ ܡܟܝܢ.
ܟܕ ܘܠܐ ܐܚܪܢܐ ܐܝܟ ܕܡܦܢܝܢܐ ܡܬܠܟܬܐ ܦܫܛ
ܦܬܓܡܐ. ܬܪܝܢ ܬܟܫܦܬܐ ܘܡܫܬܐܠܢܐ. ܕܠܟܐ̈
ܬܟܫܦܬܐ. ܠܡܦܘܬܗ ܡܦܠܠ ܕܗܘ ܟܕܒܐ̈ ܬܟܫܦܬܐ.
ܕܟܕܒ ܡܕܡ ܕܐܬܦܣܩ ܠܗ. ܡܫܬܐܠܢܐ. ܡܢܣܬܐ
ܘܡܫܬܐܠܢܐ. ܘܐܡܪܝܢ ܗܘܘ ܣܝ ܠܣܝ ܒܦܘܠܐ. ܡܟܐ
ܦܪܝܢ ܐܢܬܘܢ. ܕܠܐ ܡܢܣܬܐ. ܐܬܬܐ ܠܟܕܒ.
ܡܫܬܐܠܢܐ. ܙܘܟܐ ܘܦܫܟܐ. ܐܟܪܗܢ. ܘܘܟܐ.
ܐܘܠܝ ܫܡܟܐ. ܠܐܒܫܣܐ. ܘܬܦܪܐ ܥܡܟܝ ܢܥܒܕ.
ܥܒܕ ܐܢܘܫܐ ܡܠܟܐ ܘܐܬܬܘܒ. ܘܗܢܐ ܙܘܟܐ
ܬܢܝ ܟܡ ܟܠ ܙܘܟܐ ܡܬܦܢ ܟܦܘܪܐ ܫܘܪܢܐ. ܫܡܟܐ
ܘܡܬܠܠܢܐ. ܟܪܥܝܢ ܫܡܟܐ. ܐܝܬܘܗܝ ܗܘܐ ܡܠܬܐ.
ܡܬܠܠܢܐ. ܘܗܘ ܡܠܬܐ ܐܝܬܘ ܗܘܐ ܠܟܠܗ ܐܠܗܐ.
ܐܠܗܐ ܫܡܟܐ. ܠܐ ܝܕܥ ܐܢܫ ܟܡ ܡܬܬܦ.
ܡܬܠܠܢܐ. ܝܫܘܥܐ ܐܠܗܐ̈ ܗܘ ܕܐܝܬܘ ܟܟܦܟܐ
ܕܐܟܦܗܝ ܗܘ ܐܝܬܘܟ. ܡܫܬܐܠܢܐ ܘܙܘܟܐ ܘܦܪܫܬܐ

ܗܘ . ܘܠܐ ܦܠܐ ܗ̱ܘܐ ܕܢܬܦܫܩܘܢ ܗܟܢ . ܐܘ ܡܫܐܠܢܐ
ܦܠܓܝܢ ܦܪܘܫܐ ܥܒܪܝܢ ܠܒܪܗ . ܘܢܦܩܐ ܗܘ ܡܪܘܢܐ
ܒܡܫܝܚܐ ܠܡܐܡܪ ܢܦܫܗ . ܘܡܫܐܠܢܐ ܠܕܗܠܝܢ ܗܟܢ ܐܡܪ .
ܐܝܟ ܕܐܡܪܝ ܐܪܫܥܘܬ ܐܢܫ ܡܫܡܠܝܘܬܐ ܡܢܗܘܢ .
ܕܐܡܬܐ ܠܟ ܕܐܡܪܬ ܕܢܦܩܐ ܐܡܪ ܐܘ ܐܡܪܐ . ܐܘ ܐܝܟ
ܕܢܐ ܢܦܩ ܘܐܡܪ . ܘܕܚܪ ܗ̱ܘܐ ܒܡܫܪܝܐ :
ܕܡܘܗܝ . ܘܐܡܪ . ܘܦܢܗ ܕܝܢ ܒܗ ܘܐܡܪܝܢ . ܘܕܢܐ
ܦܠܓ ܢܣܒܝܢܘܬܐ ܘܐܡܪܝܢ . ܘܐܡܬܐ ܕܐܡܪܬ ܦܘܕܐ
ܘܢܦܩܐ ܡܪܝ ܠܡܘܕܥ ܦܘܕܐ . ܟܝ ܐܢ ܥܠܝܒܐ ܡܪܝ
ܢܦܩܐ . ܐܝܟ ܘܠܒܢܘܗܝ ܕܒܢܘܗܝ ܗܘܐ ܘܚܒܪܘܗܝ . ܘܠܗܘܢ
ܢܒܝܐ ܦܠܓ ܕܠܝ ܠܐ ܦܐܫܐ ܢܫܒܘܩ ܒܗ ܥܒܕܝܢ . ܦܫܘ
ܗ ܡܠܠ ܢܒܝܐ ܒܝܘܡܢܐ ܒܝܬܡܢܐ . ܘܡܢ ܪܘܚܐ ܕܠܐ
ܦܫܘ ܘܕܦܫܘ . ܐܫܟܚܐ . ܫܘܬܐ ܠܢܫ̈ ܘܡܢܝ ܒܢܘܬܐ̈
ܐܬܪܘܬܐ ܡܕܒܪܢܐ ܠܢ̈ ܒܪ ܪܘܚܐ ܕܠܐ ܦܫܘ .
ܡܬܢܒܝܢ . ܘܒܢܘܬܐ̈ ܪܘܚܐ ܕܦܫܘ . ܐܝܟܐ ܢܦܩ
ܦܬܟܡ ܐܬܪܘܬܐ ܡܕܒܪܢܐ . ܬܠܬܐ ܪ̈ܘܚܐ .
ܡܬܠܐ . ܢ ܒܪ̈ ܘܢ ܒܪ ܒܪܫܐ̈ ܘܢ ܒܪ ܢܒܪ̈ ܠܐ
ܬܬܠ ܢܒܝܘܬ ܠܢܒܝܐ : ܘܐܘܪܫܬܟ ܠܡܐܩܠܬܐ ܕܡܠܟܐ .
ܘܡܪܟܐ ܡܕܒܪܢܐ ܘܬܪܢܐ ܠܐ ܦܫܩܝܢ ܪ̈ܘܚܝܗܘܢ .
ܘܬܠܝܬܝܐ ܦܫܘ ܪܘܚܗ . ܘܡܕܒܪܢܐ ܠܐ ܗ̱ܘܐ
ܒܪܘܚܐ ܦܪܝ ܗܠܝܢ . ܐܠܐ ܠܡܕܒܪܢܐ ܘܬܪܢܐ
ܒܪܬܡܐ . ܘܬܠܝܬܝܐ ܒܦܫܘ . ܬܐܘܠܐ . ܥܡܟܘ ܗܕܐ
ܦܠܓܘ̈ ܒܡܟܡܐ . ܥܡܟܘ ܒܡܟܡܐ .· ܠܢܒܝܐ .· ܥܡܟܬܐ :
ܟܠܗ ܓܒܫܐ ܕܒܢܝܢܫܐ . ܘܟܠ ܦܘܡܐ . ܘܡܪܟܐ ܡܕܒܪܢܐ
ܠܐ ܦܫܘ . ܘܬܪܢܐ ܘܬܠܝܬܝܐ ܦܫܩܝܢ . ܬܦܫܘܬܐ
ܘܡܫܐܠܢܐ . ܘܟܡܟܡܐ ܕܗܡܢܐ ܠܐ ܬܬܪܗܡ ܢܦܫܟ .

ܕܦܬܟܡ . ܘܠܐ ܙܘܥܐ . ܘܠܐ ܕܚܠܬܐ̈ . ܘܠܐ
ܟܘܪܗܢܐ . ܘܐܦܠܐ ܟܪܝܘܬܐ ܐܝܟ ܬܒܥܝܢ ܠܦܓܪܐ
ܡܢ ܚܘܒܗ ܕܐܠܗܐ ܕܡܫܪܐ ܫܘܚܪ ܡܚܝܠܐ .
ܦܘܡܐ . ܦܪܝܫ ܡܢ ܦܓܪܐ ܥܐܠܐ . ܗܘ̇ ܕܡܬܚܫܒܐ
ܕܢܦܫ ܠܗ ܒܗ ܘܐܦ ܐܬܬܘܬܐ ܡܢ ܚܫܒܬܐ ܒܗ . ܐܝܟ
ܘܡܢܐ ܗܘܐ ܡܢܫܐ ܐܟܐ ܐܪܥܐ . ܦܘܡܐ . ܘܒܢܝܢܐ
ܕܬܪܝܢ . ܒܦܓܪܐ ܘܒܫܪܢ ܒܗ ܒܢܝܢܐ ܡܢܫܬ ܐܪܥܐ .
ܘܒܢܝܗ ܕܐܠܗܐ ܐܡܬܘܗܝ ܕܫܝܢܐ . ܕ ܘܢܦܬܠܢ .
ܦܘܡܐ . ܘܒܢܝ ܐܠܗܐ ܐܡܬܘܗܝ ܕܠܒܐ . ܒܗ ܘܐܥܒܪ .
ܦܘܡܒܐ . ܠܗܢܐ ܢܦܫܐ ܒܗ ܡܢ ܦܘܪܢܣܐ ܐܝܟ ܦܓܪܐ
ܠܒܢܝܐ ܒܡܠܠܢܝܬܐ ܕܒܢܬ ܕܐܣܬܟܠ . ܐܘܕܝ ܕܠܐ
ܢܦܫ ܐܝܟ ܠܗ ܐܦܠܐ ܫܒܚܬܗ ܡܢ ܐܚܪ . ܘܒܬܪ ܡܢ
ܢܦܫܐ ܢܦܫ ܢܦܫܐ . ܘܡܦܪܢܣܢܐ ܬܘܒ ܦܪܐ ܠܗ .
ܘܒܬܪ ܡܛܠ ܩܠܐ ܕܬܒܥܐ ܕܡܬܚܫܒܐ . ܘܒܐܬܪܘܬ
ܐܦ ܡܢ ܡܘܢܐ ܠܐ ܢܒܥ . ܘܬܘܣܦܬܗ ܒܡܘܬ ܫܡܝܢܐ
ܘܐܬܟܠܠ . ܬܫܡܫܬ ܐܪܥܐ ܡܐܡܪܗ ܕܦܘܩܕ .
ܢܦܫ ܐܝܟ ܕܡܠܐܐ ܡܘܠܕܝ . ܘܢܦܫܬ ܐܝܟ ܡܠܠܐ
ܡܐܡܪܝ . ܘܢܦܫܐ ܡܠܟ ܕܦܘܩܕ ܡܬܚܫܒܐ ܡܥܡܪܢܐ
ܢܦܫܢܝܐ ܗܘ̄ . ܘܕܬܪܬܝܢܐ ܫܘܠܛ ܡܢܦܫܢܝܐ ܒܝܕ
ܐܬܘ̈ܬܐ . ܘܬܠܝܬܝܐ ܫܘܠܛ ܢܦܫܢܝܐ ܒܝܕ
ܡܘܬܠܐ . ܣܡ ܕܝܢ ܒܗ ܡܠܟ ܠܐ ܢܕܥܝܢ ܠܡܬܚܫܒܐ
ܡܥܡܪܢܐ ܒܪܘ̇ܡܐ ܕܠܐ ܦܫܛ ܦܪܝܢ . ܘܠܬܪܝܢܐ
ܒܦܓܪ ܥܐܠܐ . ܘܠܬܠܝܬܝܐ ܒܡܘܬܐ . ܡܫܪܝܢܘܬܐ .
ܠܡܥܡܪܢܐ ܗܘ ܢܦܫܐ ܐܝܬ ܐܝܟ ܐܝܢܐ ܕܦܓܪ̈ܐ
ܦܪܝܢ ܠܗ . ܒܥܠܡܐ ܠܡܬܚܫܒ ܒܦܪܢܝܐ . ܐܡܟܢ ܕܡܬܘܕܥܐ
ܘܠܐ ܘܡܬܘܬܐ ܡܫܪܐ ܢܦܫܗ . ܘܗܘ ܗܢܐ ܐܘ ܡܫܪܢܐ

ܟܕ ܘܐܢܫܘܗܝ. ܒܐܬܪ ܕܐܢܫܐ: ܒܘܚܕܢܗܘܢ ܫܘܡܥܐ
ܐܢܫܘܗܝ: ܘܐܢܫܐ ܓܒܘܗܝ. ܙܘܥܐ. ܓܡ ܡܬܢܫܝܐ
ܬܪܓܡܐ ܡܬܓܒܝܐ. ܘܫܥܝܬܐ ܕܦܠܓܘܬ ܟܠܝܐ ܒܪܘܚܡܐ
ܦܝܠܝ. ܘܡܢ ܗܘ ܢܘܡܘܣܐ ܡܘܕܒܪܢܐ ܢܕܒܪܗ. ܐܝܟ
ܘܐܙܠܗ ܒܬܪܗ ܒܢܫܐ ܦܓܪܢܝܐ. ܡܢ ܟܠܠܐ· ܙܘܥܐ.
ܘܡܢ ܒܬܪܗ· ܡܬܒܢܝܢܘܬܐ ܘܡܢ ܐܘܪܥܠܡ· ܘܙܘܥܐ. ܘܡܢ
ܡܛܠ. ܡܫܡܫܐ ܫܥܝܬܐ ܕܦܠܓܘܬ ܬܫܡܫܬܐ
ܒܪܘܚܡܘܬܐ ܦܝܠܝ. ܘܡܢ ܗܘ ܢܘܡܘܣܐ ܒܡܫܬܪܝܐ ܢܕܒܪܗ.
ܐܝܟ ܠܐ ܡܫܡܫܢܐ ܫܡܫܐ. ܕܡܘܪܫܢܐ ܗܘ ܕܐܠܗܐ.
ܘܠܐ ܒܐܘܪܚܐ ܫܡܫܐ. ܕܡܘܫܒܐ ܗ̄ܘܝ ܕܬܒܝܬܐ
ܬܟܠܬܗ. ܘܠܐ ܒܐܘܪܥܠܡ ܫܡܫܐ. ܕܡܢ ܒܝܬܗ ܗ̄ܘܝ
ܕܬܠܡܐ ܪܒܐ. ܘܗܡܢܐ ܗܠܝ ܐܡܪܘ ܠܢܦܫܗ ܟܠܡܕܡ
ܕܒܝܫܬܗ ܦܪܢܣܝܬܗ. ܦܫܛܐ. ܕܫܡܫܢܝ ܫܘܡ.
ܘܫܡܫܝ ܡܬܠܒܟܝܢ. ܘܠܡܬܒ ܡܬܕܒܪܝܢ. ܘܢܒܕܝܢ
ܥܡܠܝܢ. ܘܡܫܬܒܥܝܢ ܦܠܓܝܢ. ܘܡܦܫܩܢܝ ܡܦܬܟܪܝܢ.
ܬܫܡܫܬܐ ܥܣܩܬܐ. ܘܠܡܥܡܘܗܝ ܠܐܢܫܐ ܕܠܐ ܢܬܥܒܠ
ܟܕ. ܘܐܢܫܘ ܕܒܢܝ ܕ̄ ܢܦܫܐ ܠܥܡܪܐ ܡܟܬܒܐ ܒܕܐܝܟ
ܡܠܝܢ. ܠܐ ܢܦܫ ܫܡܫܐ. ܐܠܐ ܟܠܝܐ. ܗܟܢܐ ܐܝܟ
ܕܡܬܕܒܪܘܢ ܒܢܫܐ ܫܡܫܘܢ: ܟܠܝܐ. ܕܫܘܡ ܢܬܓܫܐ
ܕܡܬܠܠܝܢ. ܘܦܫܛܐ ܕܡܬܢܠܡܝܢ: ܟܠܝܐ. ܘܫܡܫܬܐ
ܕܡܫܠܓܝܢ: ܟܠܝܐ. ܘܡܫܬܢܝܐ ܕܫܘܡ. ܦܫܛܐ. ܘܢܦܫܗ
ܠܐܠܗܐ ܕܢܦܪܐܠ. ܫܘܠܛ ܫܡܫܐ. ܒܡܬܢܫܘܬ
ܙܘܥܐ ܫܒܝܠܐ ܘܦܫܛܠܐ ܦܪܝ ܡܢ ܫܡܫܐ. ܘܠܘ ܐܝܟ
ܬܫܡܫܐ ܬܪܝܢ ܘܫܡܐ ܗܘ. ܘܢܬܒܥ ܗܘܦܟ ܒܗ ܗܘ
ܢܕܒܪ ܕܫܡܫܡܫܐ. ܐܝܟ ܠܝ ܡܢܘܬܐ. ܘܠܝ ܢܦܫܐ.
ܘܠܝ ܡܠܬܝܗܐ. ܘܠܝ ܥܘܠܬܢܐ. ܘܠܝ ܚܝܠܐ. ܘܠܝ

ܒܡܦܩܢܘܬܐ ܫܟܝܪܬܐ. ܒܐܘܠܨܢܐ. ܒܐܢܢܩܐ.
ܒܫܘܥܒܕܐ. ܒܢܓܕܐ. ܒܐܣܘܪܐ. ܒܥܠܘܒܝܐ.
ܒܠܐܘܬܐ. ܒܥܡܪܐ. ܒܨܘܡܐ. ܒܕܚܝܠܘܬܐ.
ܒܕܚܠܬܐ. ܒܢܟܪܝܘܬ ܐܪܥܐ. ܒܡܣܟܢܘܬܐ. ܒܕܡܥܐ
ܠܡܪܝܐ ܬܘܕܝܐ. ܘܡܟܐ ܘܠܗܠ ܟܕ ܡܬܬܠܘܬܝܢ
ܡܕܒܪܐ ܬܘܕܝܐ ܟܠܠ. ܘܢܓܘܕܐ ܕܡܘܪܬܐ ܗܘ ܒܠܝܐ
ܢܕܡܐ. ܒܐܠ. ܡܠܝܫܬܐ ܝܗ ܡܕܢܚܝܐ. ܐܝܟ
ܒܪܘܚܐ ܕܡܘܪ. ܒܫܘܒܚܐ ܕܠܐ ܢܠܐ. ܒܡܬܠܬܐ
ܕܡܘܫܬܐ. ܥܘܠܦ ܬܘܕܝܐ. ܒܗ̇ ܕܠܡܕܡܐ ܡܕܝܢܝܐ
ܣܓܝܐ ܢܡܘܣ. ܕܒܐ ܘܒܗ̇ ܕܒܗܐܘ ܐܝܟ ܒܢܕܕܐ
ܐܠܐ ܒܡܬܪܡܐ ܘܫܟܝܟܐ ܡܬܡܢܝܐ ܐܝܟ ܡܕܡܐ.
ܘܡܝܐ ܘܪܚܡܐ ܘܬܢܝܐ ܢܦܫ ܐܢܫܘܬ. ܚܝܝܐ.
ܠܬܪܥܝܐ ܕܒܐ ܢܪܕܐ. ܘܒܡܘܪܝܐ ܢܬܪܐ ܕܬܢܝܐ
ܡܬܦܠܫܐ. ܐܢܫܝܐ. ܘܐܠܦ ܠܐ ܡܕܝܐ ܕܟܐܘܬ
ܐܘܬܪ ܠܗ ܫܢܕܐ ܐܝܟ ܗܘܕܡ ܗܘܡܢ ܓܝܘܢܐ
ܗܘܡ: ܥܘܢܐ. ܘܠܚܡܘܪܐ ܡܬܕܡܝܢ ܗܘܡ.
ܐܘܢܟܠܝܘ. ܡܛܠ ܕܟܠ ܐܢܫ̈ ܕܡܫܦܠܝܐ ܘܡܢܛܠܬܐ
ܡܬܐܫܪ ܗܘܐ. ܒܢܛܠܬܐ ܡܬܦܪ̈ ܓܝܘܢܐ ܗܘܐ:
ܥܘܢܐ. ܘܡܫܦܠܝܐ ܡܟܦܫ ܓܝܘܢܐ ܗܘܐ: ܥܘܢܐ.
ܘܠܐ ܡܒܟܫ ܗܘܐ ܠܡܟܒܫܗ. ܥܘܠܦ ܓܝܘܢܐ. ܚܕ
ܗܘ ܢܦܫܐ ܪܬܓܫܐ ܢܒܚܗ. ܘܡܪܥܘܬ ܪܓܫܐ ܦܪܢܣ
ܒܗ ܓܝܘܢܐ. ܘܐܝܟ ܕܡܫܬܟܚܐ ܒܡܘܪܝܐ ܢܬܪܐ
ܕܬܚܬܝܐ ܢܦܠ. ܐܝܟ ܕܟܠ ܕܗܠܟܬ, ܒܐܘܪܚܬܗ
ܕܢܬܒ. ܐܬܠ ܦܫܛ ܒܐܒܢܝܟ. ܘܗܐ ܡܠܐ ܡܢ
ܥܡܝܐ ܕܐܫܟ. ܗܘܝܘ ܒܪ ܢܡܒܟܐ ܕܒܗ ܐܪܦܠܝܬ.
ܢܦܠ ܕܝܢ ܘܡܕܡ ܚܠܝܐ ܒܡܘܪܝܐ ܢܬܪܐ. ܐܝܟ ܒܗܘ

ܠܒܢܝ̈ܬ ܢܫܘܗ̈ܝ. ܘܐܝܬ ܐܘܟܐ ܕܒܠܝܐ ܢܘܦ. ܐܝܟ
ܐܪܢܒܐ ܡܫܬܠܛܐ ܕܗܘܐ ܠܟܠܐ: ܘܓܒܝܐ ܢܘܒܝܐ
ܓܦܢ̈ܐ. ܘܐܢܫܝܢ ܡܢܗܘܢ ܚܕ ܢܘܡܝܐ ܐܝܟ ܕܡܓܠܝܐ ܦܣܩܝܢ
ܚܕܗ. ܗܕܡ ܒܢܫܐ. ܠܐ ܒܪܘܫܡܐ ܦܢܐ ܒܦܘܪܥܢܐ.
ܡܬܓܠܠܢܐ. ܡܢ ܒܛܠ ܙܘܒܢܐ ܐܘܟܐ ܕܡܫܬܒܪ ܕܐܝܬ
ܘܗܘܐ ܚܕ ܠܐ ܐܝܬ ܢܫܒܩ. ܐܝܟ ܠܐ ܬܬܕܒܪ ܕܐܬܪܬ
ܠܝ ܕܦܠܐ ܠܗܘܢ ܠܡܬܒܠܥܘ ܡܢ ܕܘܟ. ܘܗܕܒܐ ܐܠܝܡܘܬ
ܙܘܒܢܐ ܡܫܬܒܪܐ. ܕܒܠܝܐ ܐܘ ܬܫܘܬܐ ܐܘ ܡܕܡ
ܐܚܪܢ. ܒܕܠܐ ܒܕܒܠ ܐܬܓܠܝ ܦܘܪܥܢܐ. ܟܠܠ ܕܡ
ܙܘܒܢܐ ܒܗܝ ܕܒܪܝܫܐ ܕܢܬܦܪ ܙܡ ܘܡܒܠܥ ܘܡܓܒܕ
ܡܢ ܫܘܕܝܐ ܕܫܢܒܪܬ ܐܫܬܒܠ ܡܬܒܗܒ. ܐܝܟ
ܙܘܚܐ ܐܬܪ ܕܢܝܚܐ ܢܥܒܕܐ ܘܥܪܒܐ. ܡܚܝܕܢܐ.
ܒܦܘ̈ܠܚܢܐ ܣܓܝ̈ܐܐ ܗܟܝܢܐ ܒܢܘܢܐ. ܘܬܪ̈ܝܢܐ
ܒܫܘܪܝܐ ܡܬܓܝܡ. ܘܕܒܗ ܚܕ ܗܘ ܢܘܡܝܐ ܒܬܪ
ܗܕܒܐ ܡܕܝܢܐ. ܘܒܗ ܡܫܬܪܟ ܒܐܚܪܢܐ.
ܘܠܗܕܐ ܙܘܦܪܐ ܦܪܐ ܠܗ ܬܐܘܡܐ ܐܝܟ ܥܘܒܝ
ܒܐܘܦܝܐ. ܢܝܠܬ ܒܒܠ. ܠܝ ܚܒܘܬܐ. ܠܝ
ܒܠܝܕܐ. ܠܝ ܡܒܬܫܠܦܢܐ. ܥܘܫܠܦ ܡܫܝܕܢܐ.
ܢܕܒܗ ܗܘ ܒܕ ܗܘ ܢܕܒܐ ܕܡܢܝܕܢܐ ܐܝܬܘ. ܘܒܪܝܢܐ
ܦܪܝܥ ܡܢܗ. ܒܐܘܟܬ ܕܒܘܢܝܐ ܬܘܒ ܐܝܟܢܐ
ܕܒܫܘܪܝܐ ܬܪܝܢ ܗܕܒܐ ܗܘ ܦܬܟܡܗ. ܐܝܟ
ܡܕܕܪܝܢ ܒܣܒܠܐ ܦܢܝܢ ܕܠܐ ܣܟܠܐ. ܟܪܘܪܐ
ܠܗܕܒܐ ܗܕܝܡܐ ܣܓܝܐܐ ܟܕ̈، ܠܢܕܕܐ ܢܘܦ. ܘܢܕܒܗ
ܠܦܘܡܕܐ ܕܟܐ ܒܐܘܟܬ ܚܕ ܢܘܡܝܐ ܡܕܡ ܐܬܘܬܐ
ܡܬܬܕܒܚܒܬܐ ܕܒܪܝܥ ܒܠ ܗܕܒܐ. ܦܘܠܘܣ. ܐܠܐ
ܒܟܠ ܡܕܡ ܢܒܝܘܐ ܢܦܥ. ܕܡܥܩ ܚܡ ܕܐܠܗܐ.

ܢܒܝܐ ܒܪܫܐ ܕܝܢ ܩܘܕܡܝܐ ܢܚܘܡ. ܘܐܝܟ
ܒܫܘܟܠܐ ܠܡܠܝܘ ܘܡܠܝܐ ܘܐܫܬܡܥܐ ܘܐܡܪܢܐ
ܘܐܡܪܐ ܢܘܦ. ܐܝܟ ܘܐܬܦܪܫܬ ܙܥܘܦܐ ܥܠ ܥܡܠܝ
ܘܐܦܪܫܬ ܠܦܪܕܐ ܬܠܝܘ ܥܒܕܐ ܫܘܐ ܕܬܐܬܐ
ܒܝܫܠܐ ܠܟܘܪܝܢ. ܘܫܦܪ ܘܐܦܪܙ ܬܠܝܐ ܐܬܪ
ܡܪܝܐ ܠܦܪܕܘ. ܡܢ ܐܝܡܟܐ ܐܢܬ. ܐܡܪܝܐ ܠܐ
ܕܒܠܬ ܠܡܫܟܠܘ ܐܝܟ ܠܡܒܠܠܘ ܠܡܥܒܕܐ ܕܡܪܝܐ.
ܐܡܪܐ ܫܒܠ ܐܣܘܟ. ܐܡܪܐ ܗܘ ܦܪܐ ܐܬܬܟ.
ܡܒܣܬܐ ܡܢ ܡܬܒܣܬܘ ܘܡܘܟܟܐ ܘܬܡܒܪܘܬ ܠܦܐ
ܢܦܒܕ. ܘܒܦܣܐ ܢܫܦܘܟ ܐܦܪ. ܕܠܐ ܡܢ ܒܠ ܘܡܪܘܟܐ
ܙܒܕܟ. ܐܠܐ ܬܬܒܝܐܒܬ ܦܠܐ ܠܦܡܪܐ ܠܬܬܟܟܐ
ܕܟܠܘܗܝ ܡܒܣܬܐ. ܘܣܝ ܗܘ ܢܒܝܐ ܟܫܬܪܐ ܒܪܥ
ܒܪܬ ܩܠܐ ܢܚܘܡ. ܘܐܝܟ ܕܒܫܘܟܠܐ ܩܕܡ ܬܫܬܐ
ܡܬܦܢܝܢ. ܐܫܟܠܐ. ܕܠܡܐ ܒܘܡܐ ܚܠܦ ܕܟܪ ܐܟܪܐ
ܠܦܪܕ. ܘܪܘܦ ܘܦܘܡ ܐܪܟܘ. ܘܠܐ ܐܬܦܐܡܪ ܠܟܘܢ
ܡܢ ܙܥܒܬܟ. ܢܡܦܢ ܕܝܢ ܡܒܣܬܐ ܘܬܣܬܟ ܐܦ
ܠܥܡܐ ܠܣܘܕܐ. ܐܝܟ ܦܪܝܢ. ܐܦܪܗ ܒܝܬܗ ܕܦܢ
ܐܢܬ ܘܥܪܟܐ. ܘܐܝܬܝܟ ܐܡܟܐ ܕܟܠܝܐ ܢܘܦ ܠܡܣܬܐ.
ܐܪܬܐ. ܒܝܐ ܡܪܝܐ ܚܠܦܘܢ ܘܒܙܘܢ. ܕܐܦܐܫܬܘܢ
ܠܙܘܢ ܟܬܒܝ ܦܪܟܘܢ ܘܟܬܒܝ ܟܦܪܘܗܝ. ܠܦܬܠ ܠܝ
ܠܣܪܟܐ ܟܐܒܪܘܗܝ ܠܡܒܣܪܝܢ. ܘܐܝܬܝ ܐܡܟܐ
ܕܦܫܘܩܐ ܢܘܦ. ܐܪܡܝܐ. ܐܫܬܦܠܘ ܘܒܝܘ. ܟ.
ܐܝܬ ܦܐܟܐ ܐܝܟ ܦܐܟܝ ܕܦܟܕ ܠܝ ܡܪܝܐ.
ܡܬܦܪܡܪܝܐ ܠܬܬܦܫܐ ܕܬܟܐ ܢܚܘܡ. ܘܟܢܘܗܝ ܕܒܪܥ
ܒܪܬ ܩܠܐ ܩܝܐ ܫܡܟܝ ܦܪܥ ܦܢܘܡ. ܐܝܟ ܐܡܪܝܐ
ܒܩܠܐ ܥܡܟܐ. ܐܡܪܝܐ ܐܦܢܝ ܡܪܝܐ ܒܪܘܟܘܗ

ܕܡܫܒܚܐ ܗܘܐ ܡܪܓܢܝܬܐ ܡܫܒܚܝܢ. ܘܗܠܝܢ ܕܒܠܝ ܒܗܘܢܐ
ܦܬܓܡܐ ܓܠܝܙܐ. ܟܠ ܡܘܕܐ ܡܫܒܚ ܠܗ. ܡܗܒ
ܛܝܒܘܬܐ. ܐܝܟ ܛܝܒܘܬܗ. ܠܟܠ ܕܐܫܬܘܕܥ ܠܗ ܓܠܗ.
ܛܝܒܘܬܗ ܠܟܠ ܕܫܐܠ ܒܗܝܡܢܘܬܐ. ܘܢܗܪܗ ܚܕ ܢܘܗܪܐ
ܡܢ ܫܘܠܛܢ ܦܢܝܬܐ. ܘܢܦܫܗ ܬܘܒ ܡܢܗܪܐ.
ܘܐܝܟ ܙܟܝ ܬܐܘܡܐ ܚܝܠܬܢܐ ܚܕ ܝܘܚܢܢ ܡܥܡܕܢܐ
ܘܢܗܒ ܛܝܒܘܬܐ ܘܢܬܬܢ. ܒܕܒܝܫܐ ܥܒܝܕ. ܘܐܦ
ܒܡܥܡܕܢܘܬܐ ܟܠܗܘܢ ܕܫܡܥܐ ܒܬܥܡܕܢܘܬܐ ܕܐܘܪܚܬ
ܡܬܓܒܝܢ ܗܘܐ ܫܡܝܐ. ܒܢܗܪ ܛܝܒܘܬܐ ܕܝܢ ܟܠ
ܦܪܨܘܦܗ ܕܟܘܪܝ ܦܬܓܡܐ. ܦܘܪܐ. ܐܝܟ ܬܘ
ܠܘܬ ܠܐܒܐ· ܘܡܬܒܝܥ ܘܐܢܐ ܐܢܫܝܢ. ܘܕܗܘܢܐ
ܬܘܒ ܢܗܒ ܚܕ ܢܘܗܪܐ ܡܢ ܒܪܬ ܩܠܐ ܦܪܘܬܐ
ܘܒܢܦܫܗ ܬܘܠܕܐ. ܡܢܝܘܢܐ. ܐܝܟ ܗܘ ܐܒܪܗ
ܕܐܠܗܐ. ܗܘ ܗܘ ܕܐܬܝܪܬ ܟܠܗܘܢ ܕܒܬܪ ܬܪܬܝܢ.
ܘܐܦ ܗܢܐ ܚܕ ܗܘ ܢܘܗܪܐ ܢܒܗ. ܘܒܪܝܫܗ ܦܪܝܫ ܡܢ
ܕܡܠܟ ܡܒܝܗ. ܡܠܝܠܐ. ܢܒܗ ܚܕ ܗܘ ܢܘܗܪܐ. ܡܢ
ܪܥܝܐ. ܘܬܪܝܢ ܒܫܬܪܐ ܟܠ ܫܘܪܝܬܐ ܬܪܝܨܐ ܒܥܘܠܡ
ܥܘܕܢܐ. ܘܟܠ ܫܘܪܒܢܐ ܕܢܦܫܗ. ܗܘ ܕܟܠܝܙܐ
ܡܬܬܫܝܡ. ܐܝܟ ܐܬܚܘ ܕܒܥܡܢܝ ܢܬܦܪܫ ܥܡܝ.
ܬܐܬܐ ܓܠܝܬܘܢ. ܢܗܘܐ ܓܠܝܢ. ܡܫܝܚܐ.
ܠܕܡܓܠܝܢܐ ܕܟܐ ܢܒܗ. ܐܝܟ ܡܪܢܝ ܛܘܠܪ ܠܝ
ܥܠܡܐ. ܘܐܪܒܥܘܬ ܥܘܕܢܐ ܬܪܬܝܢ: ܢܦܩ.
ܘܡܢܫܒܩܬ ܦܘܪܩܢܐ ܬܫܥܝܬܐ ܐܝܟ ܡܪܢܐ. ܐܝܟ
ܟܠܗ ܕܕܢܘܚܬܝ· ܬܪܬܝܢ. ܕܡܫܝܚܬ ܟܠܢ. ܬܫܥܝܬܐ.
ܢܦܩܬ ܪܘܚܝ ܘܫܒܬܝ ܡܢ ܡܢܝܢܬܝ ܐܘܪܫܠܡ
ܘܒܡ ܛܘܪܝ ܡܪ. ܡܫܐܠܢܐ. ܘܕܗܘܢܐ ܬܘܒ. ܚܕ ܗܘ

ܪܗܛܬ ܥܘܕܪܢܐ ܡܫܬܟܚ . ܘܐܦ ܐܪܒܥܐ ܢܗܘܐ
ܦܘܪܥܢܐ . ܒܒܢܝܐ ܕܝܢ ܐܝܟ . ܘܒܪܢܫܐ ܕܒܫܬܐܣܝܗ܆
ܒܬܫܬܐ ܕܝܢ ܒܗܘ ܕܒܢܝ . ܡܬܦܠܐ ܗ̱ܘܐ ܡܩܒ
ܒܢܝܬܐ ܒܝܬ ܙܪܥܐ . ܘܒܩܘܫܐ ܬܘܒ ܐܝܟ ܠܐܣܝܪܐ
ܐܣܝܪ܆ ܢܦܫܗ ܠܐ ܡܥܒܕ ܠܦܓܪܗ . ܘܡܬܠܬܠܗ̇ ܕܗܪܝܘܬ
ܪܬܝܒ . ܥܣܝܪܐ ܐܬܘܪ܆ . ܬܚܘܡܐ ܕܝܢ ܡܕܢܚܝܐ
ܡܥܒܕܢܐ ܪܒܐ ܕܬܘܪܐ . ܒܥܒܕܐ ܕܪܬܝܒ
ܕܡܥܒܕܢܐ ܗܘ ܕܒܪܐ . ܘܦܬܚ ܠܗ ܐܦ ܢܒܥܐ .
ܘܠܡܘܒܕܢܐ ܬܘܒܪܐ ܠܢܫܐ . ܘܢܕܒܪ ܬܘܪ ܢܦܫܐ ܗܘ
ܕܦܠܓܘܗܝ ܠܐܦ ܠܬܚܬ ܕܝܢ ܡܘܕܥܐ ܡܬܬܚܡܝܢ . ܠܐ
ܗ̱ܘܐ ܒܥܡܠܐ ܦܬܓܡܐ . ܐܘ ܒܥܘܪܗ ܐܘ ܒܒܝܬܗ .
ܘܗܘ ܗܢܐ ܐܘ ܒܢܝܐ ܕܡܘܐܠܐ ܡܦܪܫܢܐ
ܘܡܦܩܢܐ ܗܘܐ . ܐܝܟ ܐܡܪ ܒܪܢܐܝܬ ܕܒܝܘܬܐ
ܡܫܠܠܝܢ ܐܢܬܘܢ . ܡܫܐܠܢܐ ܕܢܦܩ ܠܗ ܡܘܦܣ ܗ̇,
ܕܗܘܐ ܒܠܒܘܢ ܫܘܠܐ ܡܫܠܠܝܢ ܐܢܬܘܢ ܒܐܪܒܥܐ .
ܘܫܪܒܐ . ܐܘ ܒܢܝܐ ܕܡܘܐܠܐ ܒܒܘܢܐ . ܐܝܟ ܕܠܒܢܐ
ܒܫܪܐܒ . ܒܠ ܕܬܒܝܢ ܡܠܝܠ . ܐܘ ܒܢܝܐ ܕܐܘܠܝܬܐ .
ܐܪܒܥܐ . ܐܡܪ ܢܐܦܠ ܢܒܝܐ ܒܐܪܡܝܐ ܒܠܘܕܐ
ܕܡܬܘܡܝܢ . ܐܡܪ ܢܬܘܠܠ ܒܦܪܥܢܘܗ ܕܡܪܝܐ܅ ܒܗܢܐ
ܘܒܢܝܐ . ܡܬܦܢܝܢ ܕܝܢ ܬܚܘܡ ܐܦ ܦܪܙ, ܬܡܥܒܕܬܐ .
ܐܝܟ ܒܪ ܕܬܝܪ ܬܚܘܡܐ . ܘܐܬܚܝܕܗ̇ ܠܐܪܒܥܐ ܠܐܒܘܢ.
ܡܦܠܫܢܐ . ܐܝܟ ܠܦܘܪܥܢܐ ܕܐܪܥܐ ܗܘܕܐ . ܘܡܢܐܝܬ
ܦܐܪܒܘܠܘܢܘܣ ܡܬܘܪܐ ܗ̄ ܕܗܘܕ ܗܘܠܐܒ
ܐܣܪܬܐ ܒܕܬܠܬܐ ܐܝܬ ܒܗ ܗܢܒܐ . ܪܬܝܒ .
ܫܒܥܐ ܘܬܠܝܬܝܐ ܐܣܪܐ . ܕܗܘܝ ܡܦܠܫܢܐ . ܗ̄
ܕܗܘܕܐ . ܗ̇ ܕܒܢܝܢܐ ܬܬܠܒܢܐ . ܘܢܦܠܢܐ ܫܠܛܘܗܝ,

ܘܢܕܡܗ ܠܬܠܬܐ ܢܩܘܫܐ ܗܘ ܐܝܟ ܕܒܝܒܠܘܢ. ܘܣܠܩ
ܦܩܕܐ ܡܬܢܣܝܢ ܒܗ. ܐܝܟܐ ܕܡܙܕܪܪܐ ܢܘܪܐ ܚܕܝܢ.
ܘܪܗܛܐ ܕܒܪܬܗ ܡܢ ܕܡܘܬܐ ܕܕܡܘܬܗ ܦܪܝܫ ܠܗ.
ܘܪܗܛܐ ܕܬܠܬܐ ܬܘܒ. ܐܝܟ ܪܫܡ ܒܠܐ ܐܠܗܐ ܀
ܐܝܟ ܕܡܬܘܬܝܢ. ܘܠܐ ܠܗܘܢ ܡܢ ܠܒܝܬܐ ܀ ܠܢܘܪܐ
ܕܠܚܡ. ܡܥܡܕܢܐ. ܘܡܬܡܪܐ ܡܩܦܠܢܐ ܬܘܒ.
ܒܕܡܫܝܚܐ ܘܪܚܡܘܬ ܢܘܪܐ ܘܡܗܪܡܢܐ ܡܬܬܦܪܫ.
ܘܠܘܬ ܬܠܝܬܝܐ ܗܘ ܢܕܡܐ. ܘܠܘܬ ܡܕܢܚܐ ܬܠܝܬܝܐ
ܕܬܠܬܐ. ܘܡܥܡܕܢܐ ܫܠܝܚܐ ܦܪܝܫ ܡܢ ܬܠܝܬܝܐ. ܘܗܘ
ܗܢܐ ܐܦ ܒܢܝܐ ܕܬܫܡܫܬܐ ܗܘܐ. ܐܦ ܒܢܝܐ ܕܐܘܠܝܬܐ.
ܘܡܕܡܢܐ ܗܘ. ܐܘܪܚܬܐ. ܘܢܛܪ ܢܦܫܗ ܘܐܡܪ.
ܐܠܗܘ ܕܐܒܐ ܐܒܪܗܡ. ܐܠܗܗ ܕܐܒܐ ܐܝܣܚܩ.
ܐܠܗܐ ܕܬܪ ܦܬܓܡܐ ܐܚܪܢܐ ܚܒܝܒܐ ܝܥܩܘܒ.
ܦܠܓ ܡܢ ܐܒܗܘܗܝ ܕܗܝܡܢ ܐܝܟ ܡܛܠ ܕܐܝܬ ܐܝܢܐ
ܡܢܗ. ܬܪܝܢܐ ܕܝܢ ܐܪܡܝܐ. ܒܗ ܬܠܡܝܕܘ ܣܦܪܝܬܐ.
ܘܒܗ ܬܬܠܡܕܘܢ ܒܬܪܥܝܬܐ ܕܕܡܘܬܐ. ܒܗ ܬܬܝܠܕܘܢ
ܒܢܕܘܐ ܒܢܝܢܘ. ܠܦܪܫܘܬܐ ܗܘ ܡܬܝܠܕܬܐ ܐܢܬܘܢ.
ܦܘܩܕܢܐ. ܣܡ ܗܘ ܢܡܘܣܐ ܕܡܠܟܘ. ܘܡܡ ܪܫ ܒܪܬ ܐܠܐ
ܦܘܩܕܢܐ. ܐܝܟ ܕܐܠ ܐܡܝܢܐ ܕܡܡܢܘܬ ܢܡܘܣܐ ܠܟ.
ܠܐ ܬܬܠܘܢ ܡܘܕܥܐ ܠܥܠܡܐ. ܘܕܝ ܕܐܝܟ ܗܢܐ
ܢܡܘܣܐ ܘܡܕܡܢܢ ܡܢ ܦܘܩܕܢܐ ܡܬܬܥܒܕ. ܘܡܢܢ
ܦܘܩܕܐ ܡܬܢܣܝܐ. ܘܡܢ ܪܘܫܡܐ ܒܫܠܘܡ ܘܠܐ
ܡܢ ܪܢܝܐ. ܦܘܠܘܣ. ܡܚܫܒܬܐ. ܣܗܕܐ. ܥܕܡܐ ܗܢܐ.
ܡܢܘܫ ܒܥܬܐ. ܢܦܩܬ ܪܚܡܐ ܕܠܐܒܘܗܘܢ ܠܐ
ܡܬܬܟܝܢ. ܥܡܝܕܐ. ܗܢܐ ܠܗ ܪܢܝܐ ܕܒܠܥܐ ܡܢܗ.
ܒܕܬܠܬܐ ܢܦܫܐ ܒܪܢܫܐ ܗܪܡ ܡܢ ܪܬܡܐ. ܡܢܬ

ܐܝܟ ܠܝ܆ ܫܘܠܛ ܚܐܪܘܬܐ. ܕܠܐ ܬܬܕܝܢ ܡܢ ܬܘܡ
ܒܥܒܕܐ ܕܬܬܠ ܚܘܒܐ ܐܚܪܢܐ. ܫܘܠܛ ܫܢ̈ܝܐ
ܒ̈ܐܪܒܥܘܬ ܙܒܢܐ ܦܪܝܫ ܡܢ ܫܢ̈ܝܐ. ܘܒܫܘܠܡ ܫܘܘܕܝܐ
ܡܬܬܚܝܡ. ܡܢܐ ܕܡܘܪܒܐ ܒܡܫܗ ܢܦܫ. ܘܠܐ ܦܓܪܐ
ܒܠܘܩܒܠ ܕܙܒܢܐ. ܘܒܠܗܕܐ ܫܪܝܐ ܡܬܦܪܣܐ.
ܐܪܘܬܐ. ܘܝܠܕ̈ܝ ܠܗܘܢ ܒܢܒܝܐ ܕܡܢ ܒܠܡ܆ ܫܘܠܛ
ܫܢ̈ܝܐ. ܒܢܒܝܐ ܕܫܟܝܢܘܬܐ. ܦܓܪܐ. ܦܘܠܚܢ. ܘܕܝܠܗ
ܘܢܦܫܗ܆ ܠܒܢ̈ܝܬܐ ܐܦ ܡܢ ܕܠܟܪܘܣܝܣ܆ ܫܘܠܛ
ܫܢ̈ܝܐ. ܕܠܗ ܬܫܒܘܚ ܘܒܘܪ̈ܟܐ ܟܝܢܐ. ܠܟܠܡ ܚܠܡܝܢ
ܐܡܝܢ. ܦܓܪܐ. ܘܗܕܐ ܬܫܒܘܚܬܐ ܦܘܠܚܢܘܬܐ ܫܢ̈ܝܐ
ܕܟܝܢܐ ܡܬܦܪܣܐ ܒܕܡܘ ܠܫܢ̈ܝܐ ܟܝܢܐ ܢܦܫ.
ܪ̈ܓܠܐ ܕܦܓܪ ܢܬܪܘܬ ܫܘܘܕܝܐ ܡܬܒܪܪ. ܘܠܚܡܘܬ
ܦܓܪܐ. ܩܝܐ. ܘܡܬܪ̈ܬܚܢܐ ܦܘܡ ܠܗ ܦܪܝܫ ܡܢܗ.
ܘܢܕܡܘ ܬܪܝܢ ܗܘ ܢܘܩܪܐ ܥܠ ܡܘܪܓܠܐ ܬܪܝܨܐ ܠܟܠ
ܠܬܚܬ. ܘܪ̈ܓܠܐ ܕܦܓܪ ܐܬܡܪ ܒܕܡܡ ܪ̈ܓܠܐ ܦܓܪܐ.
ܢܓܠܘܬ ܒܗ. ܒܪܡ ܕܝܢ ܠܐ ܡܬܒܪ. ܐܠܐ ܠܝܬܝܐ
ܢܦܫ. ܦܬܓܡܐ ܐܚܪܢܐ. ܐܪܡܝܐ ܠܐ ܠܗܘܢ ܥܠ
ܒܢ̈ܝ ܐܢܫܐ܆ ܪ̈ܓܠܐ ܕܦܓܪ ܘܦܓܪܐ ܐܫܬܡܠܝ ܘܝܕܥ.
ܘܡܬܕܡܐ ܡܢ ܢܦܫܐ ܠܗܘ ܦܓܪܐ. ܒܬܪܐ ܐܢܫܐ.
ܘܠܐ ܢܬܬܝܒ. ܘܐܢ̈ܫܝܢ ܪ̈ܓܠܐ ܕܒܬܪܗ ܦܓܪܐ ܡܕܡ
ܐܢܫܐ. ܪ̈ܓܠܐ ܕܠܐ ܦܓܪ ܪܓܝܫܐ ܐܦ ܢܕܥܝ ܐܝܟ
ܦܓܪܗ ܕܡܕܡܐ ܐܝܟ. ܦܪܝܫ ܕܝܢ ܒܗ̇ܝ ܕܗܠܝܢ ܡܢ ܦܓܪܐ
ܠܡܕܡܐ ܬܪܝܨܐ ܢܦܫ. ܐܝܟ ܠܐ ܬܬܚܫܒܘܢ ܚܕ ܚܠ
ܚܕ ܐܢ̈ܫܝ܇ ܪ̈ܓܠܐ ܕܠܐ ܦܓܪ. ܒܐܡܬܐ ܠܐ ܢܓܠܘܬ ܠܗ
ܦܓܪܐ. ܕܠܐ ܬܬܕܝܢܘܢ. ܐܘ ܢܦܫܬܐ ܪ̈ܓܠܐ ܚܠܝܠܐ.
ܡܕܢܚܝܐ ܕܝܢ ܪ̈ܓܠܐ ܐܚܪܢܐ ܬܠܝܬܝܐ ܢܕܡܝܢ.

ܘܡܘܣܦ ܐܚܝܕܐ ܠܦܘܪܩܢܐ: ܫܘܚܐ. ܒܒܪܟܐ ܕܐܠܗܘܬܐ
ܕܬܫܒܚ ܫܡܝܐ. ܬܫܒܘܚܬܐ. ܘܗܐ ܠܒܪܐ ܚܕ ܡܫܝܚܐ ܕܒܢ
ܦܪܘܩ ܐܠܗܢ: ܟܠܢܐ. ܩܒܠܝܢ ܗܘܘ ܐܢܫܐ ܐܠܝܢ
ܕܡܚܪܡ ܗܘܘ ܢܟܣܘܗܝ ܘܩܛܠܝܢ ܠܗ: ܟܠܢܐ. ܒܬܘܪܒܐ
ܕܦܘܪܩܢܐ ܕܬܫܡܫܬܐ ܢܨܒܪܐ. ܫܘܒܚܐ. ܘܐܦ ܠܐ ܦܠܓ
ܐܪܝܟ ܦܘܪܩܢܐ. ܚܕ ܒܠܚܘܕ ܟܠܢܐ ܡܬܦܪܣ ܒܗ.
ܬܐܘܠܘ. ܐܠܐ ܗܘ ܡܢܐ ܕܠܐ ܪܒܢܐ ܒܗ ܒܡܕܒܪܢܘܬܐ
ܕܫܒܝܐ ܡܬܦܩܚܢ: ܫܘܚܐ. ܗܢܐ ܠܡܬܚܡܢܐ ܠܟܠܢ.
ܬܫܒܘܚܬܐ. ܗܘ ܕܒܗ ܫܠܘ ܕܐܬܝܗܒܘܢ ܡܬܦܩܚܢ:
ܟܠܢܐ. ܐܝܟ ܙܘܥܐ ܕܒܗ ܡܬܦܩܚܢ ܘܒܢܝܐ. ܫܘܒܚܐ.
ܘܐܬܪܥܬܝܗܘܢ ܢܦܫܐ ܒܐܠܝܢ ܦܬܓܡܐ ܫܠܝܚܐ
ܘܫܠܝܚܐ ܡܬܦܢܝܢ.

ܫܘܒܚܐ ܕ ܕܟܠ ܫܢܬܐ ܦܪܝܫܐ ܫܢܝܬܐ.

ܡܕܡܬ ܫܘܠܡ ܟܠܢܐ ܒܐܪܒܥܬ ܙܒܢܝܢ ܡܢ ܟܠܢܐ
ܦܪܘܩ. ܘܡܬܬܩܝܡ ܒܬܪ ܫܘܒܚܐ ܕܢܨܦ ܫܘܒܚ
ܠܦܘܪܩܢܗ. ܡܢ ܚܠܦ ܐܢܫܐ ܟܠܗܘܢ ܕܪܚܝܩܐ.
ܢܛܘܒ ܩܠܝܢܐ. ܟܠ ܢܨܘܐ ܬܫܘܐ ܠܟܘܢ ܐܚܝ:
ܫܘܠܡ ܟܠܢܐ. ܒܗ ܬܟܠܘܢ ܠܝܡܝܢܐ ܫܟܝܢܐ
ܘܡܫܬܠܛܐ. ܫܘܒܚܐ. ܢܕܟܪܘܢ ܠܟܢ ܕܒܦܘܡܐ ܕܗܝܢ.
ܬܫܒܘܚܬܐ. ܢܫܡܥ ܠܟܘܢ ܡܫܒܚܢܘܬܐ. ܫܘܒܚܐ. ܫܘܠܡ
ܬܫܒܘܚܬܐ. ܒܫܘܪܪܗ ܡܬܪ ܦܪܘܩ ܡܢ ܬܫܒܘܚܬܐ.
ܘܟܠܗܕܐ ܡܕܢܚܝܐ ܢܘܗܪܐ ܢܬܬܪܐ ܬܠܝܬܝܬܐ ܒܗ
ܢܩܘܫܝܢ. ܘܬܫܒܘܚܬܐ ܕܬܬܠܬܐ ܠܗ ܦܪܩ. ܦܪܘܩܢ.
ܗܕܝܢ ܢܗܘܢܐ ܐܠܦ ܠܗܬܟ. ܘܫܟܚ ܟܠܗܘܢ ܐܚܕܐ
ܘܐܡܪ ܠܗ. ܫܐܘܠ ܐܝܟ. ܘܫܘܠܡ ܬܫܒܘܚܬܐ ܡܢ
ܡܫܘܕ ܢܗܪܝܢ. ܘܫܪܒܐ. ܐܘܢܓܠܝܘܢ. ܘܐܡܢ ܐܡܪ

ܒܝܡܪܢܝ. ܐܝܟ ܚܢܪ ܐܢܫ ܕܐܚܕ ܚܝܠܐ ܒܝܡܢܗ:
ܘܡܒܕܡ ܟܠܗ ܐܡܪ ܟܠ ܕܟܝܢ. ܦܫܩ̄ܗ. ܣܕܐ
ܠܚܡܐ ܕܝܢ. ܐܦ ܠܫܡܐ ܢܡܘ ܦܫܩ̄ܗ. ܒܡܟܝܢܘܬ
ܦܚܡܐ ܕܝܢ. ܒܢ ܠܗܬ ܡܪܢܐ ܗܘܬ ܗܕܐ: ܥܫܩܐ:
ܘܐܬܬܢ ܬܕܒܘܪܬܐ ܒܒܢܝܢ. ܦܫܩ̄ܗ. ܘܗܠܝܢ ܕܢ
ܦܩܘܕܐ ܢܬܬܒܐ. ܦܫܩ̄ܗ ܕܝܢ ܫܐܠܐ ܐܬܬ̄ܘ. ܦܘ
ܕܟܒܘܪ، ܦܬܚܡܐ ܢܟܠ. ܡ ܢܡܘ ܬܫܬܐ. ܘܒܬܪܗ
ܦܫܩ̄ܗ ܡܪܢܝܐ. ܐܝܟ ܦܘܠܘܣ ܫܠܝܚܐ ܕܫܦܪ
ܡܒܝܢܐ. ܦܫܩ̄ܗ. ܒܦܘܡܢܐ ܕܐܠܗܐ ܕܒܢܝܢ.
ܬܫܬܐ. ܘܕܡܒܝܢܐ ܗܒܪ. ܐܦ ܚܢܪ ܘܬܪܝܢ ܕܢ
ܣܒ. ܢܡܘܣ ܠܣܕܪܐ ܦܫܩܘܡܐ ܫܐܠܐ. ܡ ܬܫܬܐ. ܡ
ܦܫܩ̄ܗ ܢܒܝܘܬܐ. ܐܝܟ ܐܬܘܗ ܠܡܪܢܐ ܒܬܪ ܕܟܬܒܐ.
ܦܫܩ̄ܗ. ܐܬܘܗ ܠܡܪܢܐ ܫ̄ܒ ܘܐܬܦܪܐ. ܦܫܩ̄ܗ. ܗܢܐ
ܟܠܗ ܡܢ̄ܗ ܒܦܫܩܘܡܐ ܫܐܠܐ ܡܬܦܪܫ. ܘܠܣܪܬܐ
ܡܪܢܐ ܢܬܠ ܢܒܠܐ ܠܚܡܢ. ܬܫܬܐ. ܘܡܪܢܐ ܢܛܪܟ
ܠܚܡܗ. ܦܫܩ̄ܗ ܡܪܢܝܐ. ܘܐܬܐܡܪܐ ܕܣܠܩ ܬܫܬܐ
ܗܢܐ ܐܣܪܢܐ ܟܠܢܐ ܟܐܠ. ܐܝܟ ܦ̄ܗ ܒܒܪܐ ܕܫܦܪ
ܡܒܝܢܐ. ܦܫܩ̄ܗ. ܦܪܢܐ ܘܫܠܝܚܐ ܦܫܩ̄ܗ. ܕܐܬܦܪܫ
ܠܐܘܟܠ ܕܐܠܗܐ. ܕܒܢ ܡܒܝܢ ܡܠܟ ܒܢܝ ܠܒܝܬܗ،
ܒܬܘܒܐ ܩ̄ܕ: ܟܠܢܐ. ܟܠ ܒܪܗ ܦܘ ܕܐܬܦܠܫ ܒܟܡܪ
ܒܢ ܙܘܓܐ ܕܒܝܬ ܕܘܝܕ. ܦܫܩ̄ܗ. ܡܒܝܢܘܬܐ. ܒܕ
ܥܦܘܕܐ ܐܪܒܥܐ ܢܦܫܐ ܒܫܘܡܐ ܒܬܦܠܓ. ܒܬܫܬܐ
ܡܥܠܡ. ܡ ܢܡܘ ܦܘܪܩܢܐ. ܘܐܦ ܦܠܓ ܐܪܒܥ
ܬܠܬܐ ܡܬܒܒܝܢ ܒܢܝ ܗܕܡܘܗܝ، ܡ ܢܡܘ ܦܫܩ̄ܗ.
ܦܪܡܝܫܘ. ܘܗܘܦܐ ܕܒܕ ܦܠܓܝܢ ܥܒܕܗ ܒܐܦܪ

ܕܫܘܠܐ ܡܫܝܚܝܐ ܠܣܘܪܝܝܐ ܢܡܘܣܝܢ. ܡܢ ܬܫܘܬܐ ܡܢ ܦܣܩܐ.
ܐܝܟ ܐܢ ܠܗܘܢ ܐܡܪ ܐܠܗܐ: ܫܩܠܐ. ܘܠܐ
ܡܟܝܟ ܒܬܠܬܐ ܕܝܪܬܘܬܐ: ܫܩܠܐ. ܠܐܚܐ ܠܐܒܐ ܕܐܒܐ
ܦܪܫܘ ܘܝܪܬܘ ܠܒܢܒܢܐ: ܫܩܠܐ. ܐܚܘܗܝ ܐܡܪܬܘܗܝ:
ܕܡܟܪܟ ܐܚܬ: ܫܩܠܐ. ܒܠ ܕܐܡܪܬ ܠܟܘܢ:
ܬܘܩܢܐ. ܕܒܪܗ ܐܝܟܐ ܕܐܠܗܐ. ܘܐܢ ܠܐ ܚܒܪ
ܐܝܟ ܚܒܪܐ ܕܐܒܝ ܠܐ ܬܫܡܫܘܢ. ܦܣܩܐ.
ܡܪܢܝܬܐ. ܡܬܬܣܝܡܝܢ ܕܝܢ ܫܩܠܐ ܘܡܢܝܢ ܡܬܠܬܐ
ܕܡܪܝܐ. ܒܪ ܡܫܝܚܐ ܠܡܘܕܝܐ ܢܦܫܗܘܢ. ܘܡܢܐ
ܕܒܬܫܘܬܐ ܡܬܬܢܝܢ. ܒܡܦܣܩܐ ܡܬܠܬ ܦܘܪܫܢܐ.
ܬܐܘܠܝܐ. ܒܪ ܫܡܥܝܢ ܐܢ ܫܦܝܪܐ ܠܚܠܦܘܗܝ ܗܘܢ
ܐܣܪܐ: ܫܩܠܐ. ܠܒܢܬܐ: ܠܐܚܘܗܝ ܗܘ: ܫܩܠܐ.
ܠܬܪܝܢ: ܫܩܠܐ. ܠܐܢܫܐܝܬ: ܫܘܠܐ. ܠܐܚܐ: ܫܩܠܐ.
ܠܐܚܬܐ: ܫܩܠܐ. ܠܐܠܝܬܐ: ܫܩܠܐ. ܠܒܢܬܐ ܕܒܢܝܐ:
ܫܩܠܐ. ܠܐܚܝܢ: ܫܩܠܐ. ܠܐܠܝܬܐ: ܫܩܠܐ. ܠܬܪܬܝܢ
ܬܠܬܝܢܐ: ܫܩܠܐ. ܠܗܘܢ ܕܡܬܪ ܡܠܝܢ ܠܝܬܡܬܐ:
ܗܘܢ ܕܡܬܦܪܫܬܐ ܡܫܝܚܝܐ ܘܡܬܬܠܐ ܝܬܝܪܝܢ
ܠܦܘܡܦܘܬܐ ܒܪܝܬܐ ܕܝܠܗܘܢ ܚܠܝܦ ܡܫܝܚܘܢ:
ܫܩܠܐ. ܒܪ ܠܗܠܝܢ ܒܠܗܘܢ ܚܪܝܢ. ܠܗܠܝܢ ܒܠܫܢܐ
ܒܪܝܟ ܡܠܬܐ. ܦܣܩܐ. ܝܗܝܒܐ. ܦܣܩܐ. ܡܪܝܐ
ܐܝܬܝ ܒܠ ܢܡܘܣܐ ܕܡܫܠܡ ܦܘܪܫܢܐ ܡܬܬܣܝܡ.
ܒܪ ܡܬܡܪܡ ܫܡܥܬܐ. ܐܝܟ ܐܠܗܐ ܫܡܥܬܐ. ܠܐ ܝܗܒ
ܐܢܫ ܡܢ ܡܬܠܬܡ. ܦܣܩܐ. ܐܦ ܒܪ ܡܬܠܬܡ ܬܫܘܬܐ.
ܐܝܟ ܗܘ ܕܠܐ ܡܬܝܩܪ ܠܒܪܝ. ܬܫܘܬܐ. ܠܐ ܡܬܝܩܪ
ܠܐܚܐ ܕܝܪܬܘ. ܘܡܫܐ ܗܢܘܢܐ ܐܝܟ ܕܡܫܘܚܬܐ
ܡܬܬܢܝܢ. ܡܫܬܘܡܠ ܕܝܢ ܘܡܬܪ ܚܠܝܐ ܬܘܒ ܕܝܢ

ܘܠܗܘܢ ܕܡܥܢܝܢܘܬܐ ܢܝܣܢ܆ ܥܠܝܐ. ܡܩܝܡܢܐ
ܘܙܩܝܬܐ. ܦܣܘܩܐ. ܡܫܝܚܐ. ܬܚܬܝܐ ܕܝܢ ܡܬܬܣܝܡ
ܒܫܠܡ ܦܬܓܡܐ ܡܕܡܝܢܐ. ܡܢܐ ܕܬܪܝܢܐ ܒܦܣܘ̄
ܡܫܠܡ. ܐܝܟ ܘܐܦܩܘ ܒܬܪܗ ܒܢ̈ܝܐ ܡܣܟ̈ܢܐ. ܬܚܬܝܐ.
ܘܐܡܪ ܐܢܘܢ. ܦܣܘܩܐ. ܘܐܢ ܐܪܒܥܐ ܢܦ̈ܫܐ ܬܪܝܢܐ
ܒܪܘܟܐ· ܘܫܡܥܬ ܘܦܣܘ̄ ܡܫܠܡ. ܐܝܟ ܘܒܪܟܗ
ܠܬܗ ܦܪ̈ܝܫܐ. ܬܚܬܝܐ. ܘܡܟܢܫܝܢ· ܠܘܟܐ. ܗ̱ܘܘ
ܠܗ ܦܩܘܕܐ. ܘܐܡܪܝܢ. ܦܣܘ̄. ܘܐܝܬ ܐܝܟܐ ܕܬܪ̈ܝܢ
ܬܚܬ̈ܝܢ. ܡܕܡ ܦܣܘܩܐ ܒܬܓܢܘܢ. ܐܝܟ ܢܦܫ
ܒܐܦ̈ܝ. ܬܚܬܝܐ. ܐܟܢ ܠܡܕܡ ܦܪܬܬܐ ܟܕ ܓܒܝܢ.
ܬܚܬܝܐ. ܘܗܕܝܡ ܡܬܦܢܣ ܠܝ ܠܓܘܫܡܝ ܓܠܐ ܡܢ
ܚܝܠܗ ܕܐܫܟܚ. ܦܣܘ̄. ܘܐܝܬ ܐܝܟܐ ܕܬܠܬܐ. ܐܝܟ
ܘܬܚܬ ܬܚܬ̈ܝܢ ܕܐܫܟܚ ܚܠܝܢ ܐܝܟܢܐ ܡܕܡ.
ܬܚܬܝܐ. ܥܒܕܬ ܬܚܬ ܡܢܚ̈ܬܝܢ ܟܠ ܡܕܡܝܢ.
ܬܚܬܝܐ. ܘܐܦ ܠܡܕܡ ܐܦܪܥܐ ܟܕ ܐܫܟܚ.
ܬܚܬܝܐ. ܘܗܕܝܡ ܬܐ ܦܢܝ ܡܢܚ̈ܬܝܢ. ܦܣܘ̄. ܒܬܪ
ܡܢ ܬܠܬ̈ܐ ܕܝܢ ܢܩܘܫܝܢ. ܒܡܠܦܢܘܬܐ ܟܕ ܡܬܟܬܒ.
ܡܫܝܚܐ. ܥܨܝܐ ܡܬܬܣܝܡ ܒܫܠܡ ܦܬܓܡܐ
ܡܕܡܝܢܐ. ܟܕ ܢܦܩܘ ܐܪ̈ܝܢ. ܟܕ ܢܦܩ ܬܚܬܝܐ. ܟܕ
ܦܣܘ̄. ܐܝܟ ܘܐܠܦ ܣܦܪ̈ܐ ܠܐ ܡܠܟܘܬܐ ܠܒܢ̈ܝܗܘܢ:
ܥܨܝܐ. ܐܝܠܝܢ ܕܐܫܬܪ ܠܗ ܚܕܐ. ܬܚܬܝܐ. ܠܝܬ ܗ̱ܘܐ
ܠܗܘܢ ܫܠܝܛܐ. ܦܣܘ̄. ܘܐܝܬ ܐܝܟܐ ܕܚܕܐ ܬܚܬ̈ܝܢ
ܥܨܝܐ ܢܦܩ ܬܚܬ̈ܝܬܐ. ܟܕ ܦܣܘ̄. ܐܝܟ ܡܢܐ ܕܝܢ ܕܐܬܦܐ
ܦܘܠܛܐ: ܥܨܝܐ. ܗܘ ܕܐܡܪܐ ܡܫܒܕܪ ܐ̱ܢܐ ܠܟܘܢ
ܟܡ ܠܗܬ ܐܚܕ: ܥܨܝܐ. ܙܘܓܐ ܕܥܙܪܐ ܗܘ ܕܟܡ ܠܗܬ
ܐܚܕ ܢܦܫ. ܗܘ ܢܩܘܫ ܟܠ. ܦܣܘܩܐ. ܘܐܝܬ ܐܝܟܐ

ܒܐܫܐ ܪܬܡܓܐ ܣܝܡ . ܘܬܘܣܦܬ ܒܢ̈ܝܢܐ ܦܫܝܛܐ .
ܘܡܫ̈ܚܐ ܙܘܥܝܐ . ܙܪܥܐ: ܒܒܐܫܐ ܒܒܢ̈ܝܐ ܡܫ̈ܚܠܐ .
ܟܠ ܙܪܥܐ: ܘܟܠ ܒܢܝܐ: ܪܗܛܐ . ܐܦ ܓܒܪ
ܘܡܡܠܠܝܢܐ ܬܘ̈ܡ ܩܘ̈ܒܐ ܒܢܝܙ ܙܒܢܐ ܢܦܠ ܟܢܫܐ .
ܕܟܦܬܢ . ܘܡܬܢܫܡܐ ܩܘܒܬ ܕܫܡܝܐ ܫܠܡܐ ܗܘܐ .
ܚܕ ܟܕ ܗܘܐ ܡܒܥܐ ܒܠ . ܫܢܝܐ ܫܠܡܐ ܗܘܐ ܒܡܢܝܚܬܐ
ܒܫܠܡ ܗ̱ܘܐ . ܐܡܪܐ ܕܝܢ ܪܒܗ ܠܗ ܪܡ ܓܐܘܪܓܝܣ
ܦܢܠ . ܐܚܪܢܐ ܕܝܢ ܕܗܘ ܦܐܣܠ ܫܢܝܐ ܫܠܡܐ ܗܘܐ .
ܒܡܢܐܠܐ . ܐܡܪܐ ܕܝܢ ܪܒܗ ܡܬܚܫܠܛܠ ܦܢܠ .
ܘܗܡܢܐ ܟܠ ܫܦܪܐ ܐܝܟ ܕܟܦܪ ܠܗ ܦܢܝܡ .

ܦܣܘܩܐ ܬܠܝܬܝܐ . ܡܛܠ ܠܫܡܥܘܬ ܣܦܪ̈ܐ ܕܢܒܝ̈ܐ
ܐܪܒܥܐ ܪ̈ܘܪܒܐ .

ܚܠܝܐ ܟܕ ܡܬܬܣܝܡ ܒܗ ܦܬܓܡܐ ܘܕܡܝܐ
ܡܬܬܡܠܝܐ ܒܬܫܒܘܚܬܐ . ܘܢܦܩ ܠܗ ܦܬܓܡܐ
ܬܪܝܢܐ ܕܐܪܝܢ . ܒܙܓܘ ܒܢ̈ܝ ܗܕܡܘ̈ܗܝ ܕܡܬܓܠܠ .
ܐܝܟ ܘܡܐ ܕܡܓܙܠܐ ܐܢܫ . ܬܫܒܘܚܬܐ . ܠܐ ܗ̱ܘܐ ܐܝܟ
ܢܦܩ ܒܐܦܐ : ܚܠܝܐ . ܕܪܝܫܝܗ ܠܡܫܡ ܒܡܢܝܢܘܬܐ
ܘܕܘܩܬܐ ܕܫܘܩܐ ܠܡܢܓܠܝܗ : ܚܠܝܐ . ܕܢܬܣܘܢ
ܠܡܢܝܚܐ . ܦܣܘܩܐ . ܡܬܬܣܝܡ ܕܝܢ ܘܡܫܒܐܠܐ
ܐܪܒܥܐ . ܐܝܟ ܢܒܝܐ ܡܒܥܐ ܟܢܒܪܐ ܕܐܒܬ ܠܗ
ܓܙܪܐ ܚܕ : ܚܠܝܐ . ܘܐܢ ܢܓܠ ܒܢܒܝܐ ܒܢܘܡܐ
ܕܢܬܒܐ : ܚܠܝܐ . ܐܠܐ ܐܢܬ ܘܡܥܝܡ ܠܗ . ܦܣܘܩܐ .
ܡܬܬܣܝܡ ܕܝܢ ܘܡܥܒܪ ܬ̈ܓܝܐ ܗܢ̈ܓܐ ܡܫܠܡܐ .
ܬܐܘܠܘܓ̄ . ܕܐܬܕܡܘ ܕܐܡܬܝܐ ܡܓܝܪܐ ܐܡܫܝܢܐ
ܕܬܦܪܣܐ ܠܟܠ ܐܬܪܐ : ܚܠܝܐ . ܘܠܡܕܒܪܢܐ ܡܦܪܫܐ :
ܚܠܝܐ . ܘܠܫܘܢܗ ܕܫܡܥܢ ܗܘ ܕܠܐ ܒܥܡ : ܚܠܝܐ .

ܕܬ̈ܠܡܝܕܐ ܒܢܝܪܐ ܠܕܝܠܝܗܘܢ ܒܠܚܘܕ ܐܠܐ ܕܟܠ ܦܬܟܪܐ
ܢܫܐ ܙܒܝܢܐ ܕܒܢܝܢܐ ܐܣܟܡܐ. ܐܦ ܕܠܐ ܡܫܬܟܪܐ
ܢܬܬܬܐܡܪ ܠܐ ܐܘܪܚܐ. ܘܟܠܗܘܢ ܒܢ̈ܝ ܡܢ ܕܐܝܟ ܗܢܐ
ܒܪܬܐ ܫ̈ܡܫܐ ܠܫܬܢܝܘܬܐ ܡܕܝܢܬܐ ܦܫܝܫܐ: ܡܢ ܙܒܢܐ
ܒܙܘܢܐ ܘܐܡܙܘܢܐ. ܕܠܐ ܗܘܐ ܠܦܘܬ ܣܘܟܠܐ ܐܢܫܐ
ܣܒܝܢ ܦܘܪܫܢܐ ܒܟܠܬܪ ܡܢܐ. ܐܠܐ ܠܦܘܬ ܕܐܬܒܢܝܬ
ܠܙܘܥܐ ܡܢ ܕܒܗ ܦܢܝܘܬܗܘܢ ܐܬܢܓܕܘ. ܒܙܒܢܐ
ܠܗ ܠܡܦܠܓܘ ܒܟܬܪ ܡܢܐ ܐܝܟ ܡܕܝ̈ܢܬܐ ܕܠܐ ܥܘܠܝܐ.
ܡܬܬܘܕܐ ܐܡܪܢܐ ܗܢܐ ܠܢܠܘܩܘܣ. ܙܒܢܐ ܗܘ ܓܝܪ
ܗܕܐ. ܘܕܒܓܠܝܢ ܢܒܠܐ ܐܢܫܐ ܠܐ ܡܒܟܝܢ. ܐܠܐ
ܕܠܫܬܝܐ ܕܟܝ ܒܕܘ ܡܦܠܓܝܢ. ܢܬܬܘܕܝܢ ܒܗ
ܢܒܘܢ. ܘܐܡܪܢܐ ܕܡܬܡܪܐ ܡܢ ܙ̈ܒܢܝܗܘܢ. ܢܠܦܘ
ܢܦܪܘܢ ܙ̈ܒܢܝܗܘܢ. ܡܢܙܢܐ. ܒܕܘܟ ܗܢ ܦܬܓܡܐ
ܡܠܬܐ ܠܦܢܝܬܗ ܒܠܬܐ ܕܕܝܠܗܘܢ ܫܬ̈ܝܐ. ܐܡܪܢܐ
ܕܦܬܓܡܬܐ ܗܢ ܒܙܥܝܪܘ ܦܙܐ ܐܠܗܐ. ܗܘ ܥܡܪܝܢ ܘܗܘ
ܐܘܪܚܐ. ܒܗ̇ ܕܙ̈ܢܐ ܠܦܘܬ ܚ̈ܙܘܝܢ ܥܡܪܐ ܢܒܝܬ.
ܥܡ ܐܠܗܐ ܗܢ ܒܬܘܪܐ ܡܦܩܝܢ. ܥܡܪܐ ܕܥܡܪܐ
ܕܝܢ ܒܦܓܪܡܝܢ ܐܚܪܢܐ ܕܬܘܪܬܐ. ܒܣܪܬܐ ܕܝܢ ܒܬܪܬܐ
ܕܒܠܝܕܘܬܗ ܕܥܘܕܪ ܡܒܝܢܐ: ܒܙܗ ܕܗܘܐ: ܒܙܗ
ܕܐܒܪܗܡ. ܒܗ ܕܡܒܝܢܐ ܒܪܐ. ܠܐ ܕܗܘܐ ܙܒܢܐ
ܓܒܝܠ ܦܬܓܡܐ ܒܣܘܟܠܐ. ܥܡܪܐ ܕܡܒܝܢܐ ܗܢ ܒܟܠܝܐ
ܡܦܬܟܪ. ܒܗ ܒܝܬ ܕܗܘܐ ܕܝܢ ܒܙܬܓܐ ܐܚܪܢܐ
ܕܟܠܝܐ. ܒܕܘܟ ܕܝܢ ܠܬܪܝܢ ܐܕܫܝܢ ܕܫܬ̈ܝܐ ܠܣܡܟܝܢ
ܢܒܥ ܦܬܓܡܐ ܐܚܪܢܐ ܕܡܪ̈ܝܐ ܐܘܗܪܐ ܕܐܝܡܢܐ
ܢܒܝܐ. ܙܒܢܐ ܓܒܐܝܢܐ ܒܝ̈ܢܝ ܡܢܝܬܐ. ܒܠ

ܐܦ ܡܙ̈ܒܢܐ. ܘܡܫܒܛܠܐ ܡܢ ܒܥܕܢ ܘܬܡܚܢܢܐ
ܐܬܬܚܫܘܗܝ ܫܘܡܠܝ ܚܠܡܐ: ܫܘܡܠܝ ܬܫܘܒܚܬܐ.
ܫܘܡܠܝ ܫܒ̈ܐ: ܪ̈ܗܛܐ ܕܦܘܡ. ܡܓܒܝܢܐ. ܦܘܕܐ.
ܥܝܒܘܬܐ. ܬܘܡܐ ܘܡܐܙܠܝܢܐ. ܪ̈ܗܛܐ ܕܠܐ ܦܘܡ
ܘܕܦܘܡ. ܬܠܬܐ ܪ̈ܗܛܐ. ܡܦܠܫܝܢܐ. ܢܗܒ ܠܗܒܐ.
ܦܘܪܐ. ܡܢܗܘܝܢܐ. ܡܙܠܝܢܐ. ܡܥܒܕܢܐ.
ܡܐܙܠܝܢܐ: ܡܢܫܬܐ. ܡܬܕܡܪܢܐ. ܡܓܠܠܢܐ.
ܡܢܝܕܢܐ. ܫܘܡܠܝ ܡܫܝܕܢܐ. ܟܘܪܐ. ܫܘܡܠܝ
ܟܘܪܐ. ܙܘܒܐ. ܦܡܒܐ. ܫܘܡܠܝ ܦܡܒܐ. ܙܘܒܐ
ܘܦܡܒܐ. ܡܐܙܠܝܢܐ ܘܡܓܠܠܢܐ. ܘܪܘܒܐ
ܘܪ̈ܗܛܐ ܕܦܘܡ. ܙܘܒܐ ܘܪ̈ܗܛܐ ܕܠܐ ܦܘܡ
ܘܦܘܦܐ. ܦܘܡܒܐ ܕܒܠ ܐܬܘ̈ܬܐ. ܦܗܦܒܢܐ.
ܫܘܡܠܝ ܦܗܦܒܢܐ. ܬܘܡܐ ܒܡ ܫܪ̈ܝ ܬܫܒܘܬܐ.
ܡܒܣܐ. ܡܒܥܐ ܕܢܒܥܐ ܒܠܒܐ ܬܪ̈ܝܢ ܗܘ̱ ܢܘܩܕܡ. ܚܕ
ܬܚܘܬ ܫܘܠܡ ܦܬܓܡܐ. ܘܐܚܪܢܐ ܡܕܡ ܫܘܠܡܐ
ܠܐܦ̈ܝ ܠܟܠ ܡܠܬܐ: ܘܕܬܚܘܬܐ ܬܪ̈ܝܢ. ܚܕ ܬܚܘܬ ܫܘܠܡ
ܦܬܓܡܐ. ܘܐܚܪܢܐ ܡܕܡ° ܫܘܠܡܐ ܠܐܦ̈ܝ ܠܬܒܬ
ܡܠܬܐ. ܘܕܫܘ̈ܒܐ ܗܘ ܕܐܦ ܘܠܘܬܐ ܡܬܓܒܠܐ. ܬܪ̈ܝܢ
ܢܘܩ̈ܕܐ ܫܘ̈ܝ ܦܫܝܛܐ ܡܠܬܐ: ܘܕܦܘܡܐ ܚܕ ܢܘܩܕܐ
ܬܚܘܬ ܫܘܠܡ ܦܬܓܡܐ ܡܠܬܐ. ܘܐܚܪܢܐ ܡܠܝܢ ܡܒܗ
ܕܫܠܡ ܢܘܩ̈ܕܘܗܝ. ܩܒܗ ܫܘܩ̈ܠܗܐ ܢܕ̈ܬܝܗܘܢ.
ܡܬܒܪܢܘܬܐ. ܒܕ ܡܢ ܢܬ̈ܒܠ ܓ̈ܒܫܐ ܩܠܝܢ ܢܬ̈ܒܠ
ܦܬ̈ܓܡܘܗܝ ܡܬܪ̈ܒܢ. ܒܬܪ̈ܢܬܐ ܕܒܠ ܚܕܐ ܚܕܐ
ܡܢܗܝܢ ܢܬܪ̈ܐܬ ܓܬܒܕܒܢ. ܘܕܓ ܐ̄ܘ ܦܘܪܐ

" ܢܘ̄ ܐ̄ ܒܡܐܪ.

ܟܕܐ ܒܬܪܐ. ܘܡܒܠܐ ܗܘ ܕܦܢܪܐ. ܢܐܟܐ ܠܐܬܘܬܐ܆ ܕܒܗ ܚܠܝܐ ܪܥܡܗ ܬܢܓܠܐ ܠܐܠܗܝ. ܐܠܦ ܢܓܝܡ ܬܒܗܐ ܝܘܡ ܐܬܘܬܐ. ܘܬܘܬܐ ܝܘܡ ܐܠܗܝ. ܠܐ ܢܕܒ ܐܢ ܐܪܐ ܢܓܘܡ ܬܓܒܠܐ ܥܠܝܗܐ ܠܐܬܘܬܐ ܕܚܠܠܐ ܪܥܐ ܬܢܓܠܐ ܐܘ ܚܠܐ. ܒܡ ܐܘܬܢܐ ܡܫܟܐܐ ܕܓܡܦܐ ܡܠܝܡ ܒܓܝܗܘܢ ܒܬܟܐ. ܡܒܝܢܐ ܒܬܕܒܐ ܢܡ ܗܠܝܡ ܬܓܝܫܐ ܕܒܠܘܩܪܐ ܡܠܒܗܡ ܬܘܪܟܝ ܢܒܥܐ ܕܦܘܫܒܐ ܐܬܓܢܝܗ. ܒܗܝ ܕܐܒܒܐ ܕܠܒܠ ܡܠܐ ܡܠܝܠܐ ܠܗܬ ܢܒܥܐ ܫܘܥܒܐ ܦܫܒܐ ܐܝܬ ܕܝܠܝܐ ܘܒܗ ܡܬܓܕܡ. ܗܒܠܐ ܘܠܒܠ ܡܕܒܐ ܢܘܡܘܫܐ ܡܢ ܗܠܝܢ܆ ܠܗܬ ܚܠ ܡܠܐ ܡܠܝܠܐ ܕܠܗܬ ܢܒܥܐ ܫܐܪ ܫܘܥܒܝ ܦܫܒܐ ܐܝܬ ܕܝܠܝܐ ܘܒܗ ܡܬܝܕܒ. ܡܒܝܢܝ ܒܥܓܝܗܬ ܒܬܕܒܐ ܕܢܒܥ ܦܘܫܒܐ. ܗܦܪܐ ܡܢܐ ܘܕܡܠܝܡ ܗܘܪܫܐ ܕܝܠܐܝܬ ܡܬܓܕܪܡ. ܘܒܗܘܢ ܗܦܪܐ ܐܘܬܢܐ ܚܠܝܢ ܓܝܗܘܢ ܒܕ ܡܬܓܕܡ ܪܥܐ ܡܪܝܒܡ. ܘܡܛܠ ܕܡܢ ܚܢܗܐ ܕܓܝܐ ܠܒܓܬܘܢܐ ܐܝܬܘܢ ܢܒܥܐ ܗܠܝܡ. ܐܠܐ ܡܢ ܥܒܕܐ ܘܓܥܠܒܘܢܬ ܓܠܦܢܐ ܠܢܠܗܦܐ ܡܢ ܠܒܢܐ ܠܐ ܪܕܝ ܠܐ ܡܒܓܫܐ ܠܐܕܘܢܐ ܠܡܒܓܫܝ ܠܗܘܢ ܠܓܘܫܐ. ܐܦܠܐ ܠܡܕܪܟܝܬܗܘܢ ܐܝܬ ܦܘܪܫܐ.

ܦܣܘܩܐ ܬܪܝܢܐ. ܡܛܠ ܓܝܫܐ ܕܢܒܥ ܦܘܫܒܐ ܘܥܒܕܘܗܝܗܘܢ ܒܡ ܒܬܕܒܗܘܢ.

ܐܪܒܥܝܢ ܢܕܒܝܢ ܡܕܪܒܢܐ ܢܒܥ ܦܘܫܒܐ. ܐܪܒܥܐ ܓܝܫܝܢܐ. ܘܐܝܬܝܗܘܢ ܒܠܢܐ܆ ܬܘܬܝ. ܥܩܐ܆ ܦܣܘܩܐ. ܘܬܠܬܝܢ ܘܥܬܐ ܓܕܒܢܐ܆ ܕܓܝܗܘܢ ܡܣܬܪܟܝܢ. ܘܗܢܘܢ ܗܠܝܢ. ܐܘ ܦܬܓܠܐ ܐܝܟ ܐܢܘܢ

ܡܠܬܐ ܕܡܫ̈ܝܚܐ

ܡܢ

ܠܐܪܬܘܪܣ ܒܪ ܒܒܪܐ.

ܡܐܡܪܐ ܕܒܒܠܝܐ.

ܡܟܠܐܘܢ ܥܒܝܬܐ ܡܛܠ ܢܘܡܝܐ ܪܘ̈ܡܝܐ ܀ ܦܫܘܩܐ
ܡܢܗܝܐ ܡܛܠ ܐܠܝܘܬܐ ܕܢܝܫܐ ܦܘܫܩܐ.

ܡܛܠ ܒܪ ܟܠ ܠܚܫܫ ܡܢ ܥܒܕܐ ܕܫܝ ܦܬܓܡܐ
ܗܕܕܗܝܐ ܟܠܕܝ ܬܘܘܫܦ ܒܘܝܪ ܕܥܡ̈ܗܐ ܘܡ̈ܠܟܐ
ܘܐܘܫ̈ܪܐ ܕܟܗ. ܐܠܐ ܒܥܘܠܩܐ ܟܠܫܘܕ ܪ̈ܒܝܫܐ.
ܫܘܟܠܐ ܡܥ̈ܝܢܝܐ ܡܟܢ ܗܘ ܠܚܒܝܠܐ ܥܢܗܕܐ.
ܐܬܘܠܝܒܘ ܫܦ̈ܪܐ ܫܘ̈ܪܝܐ ܫܢ̈ܝܢ ܕܘ̈ܟܫܐ ܬܘ̈ܪܝܐ
ܠܝܡܠܠܗܘܢ. ܘܠܝܒ̈ܩܐ ܦܘܫ̈ܩܐ ܢ̈ܕܟܐ ܠܝܫܘ
ܢܘܩܪܝܐ. ܐܡܟܐ ܕܗܘܢ ܩ̈ܠܐ ܦܬܓ̈ܡܐ ܕܟܠܫܝ
ܝܕܗܘܢ ܢܒܥܐ ܡܢܘܕܒ ܕܝܠܝܐ. ܐܡܟܐ ܕܡܢ
ܐܦܘܪܐ ܒܝܡܟܐ ܗܟܢܐ ܐܦ ܡܢ ܦܘܪܐ ܒܝܕܬܐ ܟܕ
ܢܬܝܒܘܢ ܒܬܝܠܕܘܢ. ܡܟܝܢܐ ܕܐܬܠܝ ܗܘ ܫܢܐ
ܢܘܡܝܐ ܕܢܝܫ ܦܘܫ̈ܩܐ ܝܕܝܥܐ ܡܢ ܗܘ ܕܐܢܫܐ ܕܦܪܐ.
ܠܐ ܗܘܐ ܡܢ ܙܪܟܗ ܕܕܘܝ: ܘܡܢ ܟܠܗ ܠܫܢ ܕܢܫ
ܡܥܝܢܐ. ܐܢ ܠܐ ܢܝܫܐ ܝܕܥܐ ܕܬܦܫܐ ܝܘܡ ܠܐ
ܗܘܐ: ܘܥܩ̈ܪܐ ܝܘܡ ܕܘܝ: ܘܡܥܐܠܬܐ ܝܘܡ ܡܥܝܢܐ.
ܡܫܒܢ ܕܡܢ ܙܪܟܗ ܕܕܘܝ ܘܡܢ ܟܠܗ ܠܫܢ ܠܐ ܡܬܬܠܝ
ܡܥܝܢܐ. ܘܟܠܝܐ ܕܠܘ ܠܐ ܡܬܬܠܝ. ܐܠܐ ܕܡܬܬܠܝ

ܦܬܓܡܐ. ܀ ܥܘܫܢܐ ܕܝܢ ܠܗܘܢ ܢܐܡܪ ܒܫܬܐ.
ܠܗܘ ܕܟܠܗܘܢ، ܗܦܟ ܡܢ ܢܘܡܐ ܐܚܪܢܐ ܐܬܬܗ،
ܒܦܬܓܡܐ: ܗܘ ܕܝܢ ܗܦܟ ܡܢ ܬܫܬܐ ܐܘ ܟܠܝܐ
ܘܕܪܘܫܐ. ܀ ܬܘܒ ܕܝܢ ܪܗܛܐ ܕܦܫܩ ܘܕܠܐ ܦܫܩ.
ܘܟܠܐ ܐܢܬ ܟܟܗ ܐܟܚܢܐܝܬ. ܗܘ ܕܝܢ ܟܠ ܗܕܡܐ
ܫܘ ܕܦܪܩ ܪܗܛܐ: ܕܐܝܟ ܐܡܪ. ܫܘܪ ܡܪܥܝ̈ܬܐ ܘܣܝ،
ܥܘܟܒܝ. ܪܦܝܩ ܟܠ ܡܪܥܝܐ.. ܬܘܒ ܕܝܢ ܠܟܢ̈ܫܐ ܩܠܐ
ܕܥ̈ܘܕܟܢ ܐ̇ܘܢܐ ܐ̇ܟܪܙܬ ܐ̇ܟܒܕ ܘܟܠܗܘܢ ܕܪܘܫܐ
ܕܕܝ̈ܢ ܀ ܘܟܬܪܝܢ ܟܠ ܐܕܘܢ ܡܢ ܠܬܫܬܐܝܬ ܠܗܘܢ
ܢܩ̈ܘܡܐ. ܀ ܗܠܝܢ ܕܝܢ ܕܡܩ̈ܘܕܟܢ. ܐܡ̈ܪ ܐ̇ܟܠ
ܘܕܪܘܫܐ. ܡܢ ܠܟܠ. ܀ ܗܠܝܢ ܕܝܢ ܕܡܫ̈ܘܡܝܢ ܐܢܬ.
ܐܕܘܢ ܐܠܗܐ ܬܘ̈ܪ ܐܢܬ ܠܗܘܢ. ܗܘ ܕܝܢ ܡ̇ܚܦܛܢܐ.

ܕܐܦܪܢܐ: ܕܗܘܐ ܐܡܪܗ ܕܐܠܗܐ ܗܘ ܕܫܡܠ ܚܠܝܬܗ
ܕܠܒܟܐ. ܘܬܘܒ ܗܢܘ ܗܘ ܕܐܡܪܬ ܕܒܬܪ، ܐܬܬܐ. ܀
ܦܘܪܩܐ ܕܝܢ ܦܢܐ ܠܗ ܠܒܝܬܢ ܢܒܝܐ. ܬܘ ܟܠܟܘܢ ܠܚ̈ܝܐ.
ܬܘ ܒܢ̈ܝܟܘ ܕܐܕܡ ܀ ܦܘܩܕܐ ܕܝܢ. ܗܪܬ ܠܦܠܛ ܠܐܪܥܐ
ܕܥܕܐ ܩܝܢܐ. ܀ ܟܝܠܢܝܐ ܕܝܢ ܐܝܟ ܗܝ، ܕܡܢ ܒܚ̈ܝܠܐ
ܠܘܬ ܐܠܗܐ ܒܝܠܘܬܐ ܡܬܐܡܪܢܐ. ܣܦܩܐ ܣܘ̈ܥܪܢ
ܠܒܝ ܫܠܡܢ. ܥܒܕܘ ܩܠܝܠܘܬܢ ܘܕܥܪܐ ܀ ܗܘܒ
ܠܗܘܢܐ ܕܝܢ ܗܘ ܕܒܗ ܒܟܠܬܐ ܠܟܝ̈ܢ ܠܗܘܢܐ.
ܠܗܘܢܗ، ܠܒܝܢܐ. ܀ ܐܝܬ ܕܝܢ ܬܘܒ ܬܚܝܐ ܟܡ ܥܐ،
ܬܫܝܢܬ ܗܡ. ܟܕܠܐ ܐܬܬܐ: ܘܐܡܪܝܢܗ ܠܐܪܥܐ
ܠܐܟܕܢ. ܘܢܗܘܘܢ ܕܘܡܪܝ: ܠܟܠܟܫܪ ※ ܡܬܕܡܪܢܐ
ܕܝܢ ܬܘܒ ܡܫܝܠܦ ܡܢ ܡܢܝܬܐ ܘܡܟܠܠܢܐ. ※
ܡܬܕܡܪܢܐ ܡܢ ܒܝܬ ܟܕ ܫܐܪ ܠܘܬ ܪܟܘܬܗ ܕܝܟܘܬܐ
ܡܬܕܡܪ ܒܗ ܗܟܢܐ. ܐܡܟܢܐ ܦܘܘ ܠܬܡܢܗܐ ܡܢ
ܟܠܝܐ. ܐܡܟܢܐ ܐܬܟܝ، ܒܗܘ ܘܢܩܒܠ ܡܠܦ̈ܢܘܬܗ. ܀
ܡܢܝܬܐ ܕܝܢ ܕܠܐ ܡܢ ܥܠ ܢܝܚ ܘܪܗܡܐܝܬ ܢܦܪܐ.
ܐܠܐ ܕܡܬܢܐܝܬ ܢܦܪܘܗ، ܠܬܠܡܝܕܐ ܕܟܠܗ، ܦܝܡ
ܡܢܝܬܐ. ※ ܡܟܠܠܢܐ ܕܝܢ ܣܘܟܠܐ ܗܘ ܕܘܟܝ
ܘܟܕܠܝܢ ܟܠ ܐܝܟܐ ܕܡܬܬܟܪ ܕܘܟܐ ܗܘ ܐܟܝ
ܦܝܡ ܡܟܠܠܢܐ. ܐܘ ܠܗܘܟܠ ܡܫܐܠܢܐ ܦܝܡ ܬܘܒ.
ܐܝܟܢܐ ܕܐܦ ܢܘܩܦܐ ܬܕܪܝܢ ܗܢܘܢ ܕܣܘܟܐ
ܡܬܐܡܪܝܢ ※ ܘܠܗܘܟܠ ܙܘܟܐ ܘܣܘܟܐ ܦܝܡܝܢ:
ܗܢܘ ܕܝܢ ܕܢܦܘܩ ܟܠ ܢܫܐ ܕܬܫܡܫܬܐ: ܟܕ ܠܐ ܕܘܟܐ
ܐܦܠܐ ܕܣܘܟܐ ܐܟܪܝܢ ܠܬܠܡܝܕܐ ※ ܦܘܩܕܐ ܕܝܢ
ܘܫܡܝܢܐ ܡܫܡܠܝܢ. ܟܗ، ܕܟܠ ܟܠ ܢܘܡܘܣܐ ܐܝܬܐ
ܠܡܐܡܪ ܦܘܩܕܐ ܡܫܬܡܗ ܗܘ ܕܦܝܡ ܒܫܘܠܡ

ܕܢܣܒܘܢ ܗܢܘܢ ܦܬܟܪ̈ܐ ܒܬܪ ܫܐܕ̈ܐ.. ܚܘܠܦ
ܕ̈ܒܚܐ ܕܝܢ ܕܥܘܒܕܬ ܥܘܪܐ. ܚܕ ܠܫܘܕ ܐܫܬܘܗܝ،
ܒܬܥܒܝܕܬܐ. ܘܥܒܝܕܬܐ ܒܬܪܗ̇. ܘܠܐ ܬܘܒܬܐ. ܀
ܚܝܠܐ ܕܝܢ ܘܙܘܟܐ ܡܫܠܡ ܒܗ̇ ܕܚܝܠܐ ܠܫܘܕܝܐ
ܗܘ [β] ܒܬܫܒܘܚܬܐ. ܘܙܒܢܐ ܕܝܢ ܒܗ̇ ܫܘܒܚܐ
ܡܬܬܣܝܡ ܀ ܬܘܒ ܕܝܢ ܐܝܬ ܢܡܘܣܐ ܕܕܚܡ ܠܫ̈ܕܐ.
ܬܫܥܝܬܐ. ܡܦܫܩܢܐ. ܡܒܝܢܢܐ. ܀ ܘܬܫ̈ܥܝܬܐ [γ] ܡܢ
ܒܐܡܪܘܗ ܚܙܝܢ ܒܬܥܒܝܕܬܐ. ܀ ܀ ܡܦܫܩܢܐ ܕܝܢ ܠܗܬ
ܗ̇ܘ ܕܪܒ ܡܬܐܡܪ. ܕܐܝܟ ܐܡܪ. ܥܒܕܐ ܐܢܐ ܐܢܐ ܡܢܟ
ܡܪܝ، ܐܬܪܚܡ ܥܠ. ܥܒܕܐ ܐܢܐ ܡܫܒܚܢ ܡܪܝ
ܗܠܟ ܠܗܬ ܒܕܒܚܘܢ ܀ ܡܥܒܕܢܐ ܕܝܢ ܒܗ̇ ܡܫܘܐ
ܠܡܫܘܚܐ ܐܘ ܠܕܚܠܬܐ ܡܟܒܐ. ܐܝܟ ܗ̇ܘ ܕܐܡܕܪܐ
ܠܡܫܡܫ ܙܢܐ ܐܟܣܢܝܬܐ. ܐܠܗܗ ܕܐܒܝ ܐܒܪܗܡ.
ܐܠܗܗ ܕܐܒܝ ܐܝܣܚܩ. ܡܪܝܐ ܕܐܡܪܬ ܠܝ : ܗܦܘܟ
ܠܐܪܥܐ ܕܡܘܠܕܘܬܟ ܘܐܛܐܒ ܠܟ. ܬܘܒ ܡܥܐܠܢܐ.
ܡܫܘܚܢܐ. ܦܪܘܫܐ. ܦܘܪܕܐ. ܡܚܠܢܝܐ. ܡܫܒ
ܠܡܠܬܐ ܀ ܘܡܥܐܠܢܝܬ ܒܬܪܝܢ ܙܢܝܐ ܡܬܐܡܪ. ܐܘ
ܕܫܐܠ ܗ̇ܘ ܕܡܥܐܠ ܠܓܒܝ. ܐܘ ܡܫܐܠܢܘܬ ܡܥܐܠ.
ܘܕܫܐܠ ܡ̇ܢ ܐܝܟ ܗ̇ܘ ܕܡܢ ܬܠܡ̈ܝܕܐ ܠܗܬ ܦܪܘܩ
ܐܡܪܢܐ: ܐܡܪܬ، ܗܠܝܢ ܢܫܘܡ. ܘܐܫܟܚܗ ܠܐܚܘܗܝ،
ܕܗܘܐ ܢܘܪܐ ܘܩܫܬܐ. ܐܡܪܘ ܐܡܪܐ ܠܚܠܬܐ ܀ ܕܢܫܒܐ
ܕܝܢ ܐܝܟ ܗ̇ܘ، ܕܡܢ ܡܪܝܐ ܐܡܪܢܐ: ܐܡܪܐ ܐܝܬ ܐܝܟ ܐܕܡ.
ܘܐܡܪܗ ܡܚܒܠ ܐܝܟܢ: ܐܢܘ ܗܢܐ ܕܟܐܒܝܢ ܀
ܡܫܘܚܐ ܕܝܢ ܐܝܟ ܗ̇ܘ ܕܟܠܡܚܒܐ ܐܫܘܐ ܐܝܟ ܗ̇ܘ،

[β] ܒ. ܒܬܫܒܘܚܬܐ ܗܘ. [γ] ܒ. ܡܫܡܪ ܡܢ.

ܘܪ̈ܗܛܐ ܕܦܩܘܡ . ܐܬܟܐ ܗܝ ܕܐܝܬܘܗܝ · ܡܘ̈ܬܐ ܀
ܦܩܘܕܐ ܘܐܘܟܐ ܘܪ̈ܗܛܐ ܕܠܐ ܦܩܘܡ ܘܦܩܘܡܐ .
ܙܘ̈ܢܐ ܕܙܘܥܬܐ· ܕܢ̈ܘܢܐ ܕܐܪܥܐ . ܀ ܘܫܡܝܐ . ܘܢܗܪ̈ܐ
ܘܗܘܐ ܡܓܥܠ ܐ̈ܦ ܐܪܥܐ . ܘܟܢܘ̈ܫܐ ܕܥܠܡܐ ܐܬܬܢܝܗ .
ܕܪܫܝܡ ܕܐܢ ܘܢܦܬܠܬ ܀ ܡܗܦܟܢܐ ܐܘ ܟܝܢܬ
ܡܣܪܩܢܐ . ° ܕܬܘ̈ܢ ܥܡܝܩܐ ܘܐܡܠܠ . ܀ ܥܡܝܩܘܗ
ܟܝܢ ܐ̈ܬܘܬܐ . ܬܥܒܕ ܐܪܥܐ ܡܐܟܪܗ ܕܦܘܩܕ .
ܐܝܢܐ ܟܝܢ ܡܪ̈ܦܐ . ܢܪܡܐ ܐܝܟ ܡܠܦܐ ܘܠܦܢ .
ܟܠ ܐ̈ܬܘܬܐ ܕܝܢ ܕܗܝ ܠܬܢܝܬ ܕܟܠܢ . ܗܝ ܠܟܠ ܕܝܢ
ܕܪܫ . ܀ ܬܫܡܫܐ ܟܡ ܥܪܝ ܬܫܒܘܚܬܐ . ܟܕܠܐ ܐ̈ܬܬܐ :
ܘܐܡܟܣܢܗ ܠܐܪܥܐ ܠܐܟܝܢ ܀ ܡܫܬܟܪܐ ܗܟܝܠ
ܕܡܠܠ ܡܪܟܘܬܐ ܕܕܘܟܬܐ : ܐܘ ܡܠܠ ܠܚܟܡܬ
ܦܬ̈ܓܡܐ : ܘܕܓܒܘܬܐ ܕܢ̈ܘܪܐ ܡܟܝܐ ܕܢܒܠܘ ܐܝܟ
ܠܠܓܡܐ ܕܡܪܢܐ ܕܢ̈ܘܪܐ . ܐܠܐ ܢܬܬܘܣܦ ܦܘܪܫܢܐ
ܗܢܐ (ܒ) . . . .
. . . .
. . . .

° ܒ . ܬܘܢ.

(ܒ) ܕܚܣܝܐ ܒ . ܡܢ ܝܘܡ ܩܠܐ ܕܢܗܘܐ ܠܡܒܥܐ ܕܘܪܝܐ : ܕܟܠܢܐ
ܘܡܫܘܚܬ ܟܠܗܝܢ . ܒܪܡ ܕܝܢ ܦܘܪܫܐ ܒܠܫܢܐ ܐܚܪܢܐ . ܘܡܢ ܩܕܡ
ܕܡܫܚ ܒܪܝܐ ܕܠܐ ܦܫܛ ܡܫܚܗ ܡܫܘܚܬ ܟܠܗܝܢ . ܐܬܬܚܡܘ ܕܝܢ
ܡܢܗܘܢ ܐܢܫܘܬܐ ܕܒܠܚܘܕܝܗܝܢ ܗܘ ܕܟܠܗܘܢ ܐܬܬܚܡܘ . ܕܐܚܪ̈ܢܐ ܕܝܢ
ܡܢܗܘܢ ܕܟܠܗܝܢ ܡܢܝܢܐ ܕܡܬܚܫܒܢܘܬܐ ܘܐܚܪ̈ܢܐ ܘܐܝܟܢܐ ܟܠܗܝ ܩܕܡܝܐ .
ܗܢܐ ܡܫܘܚܬ ܟܠܗܝܢ ܕܝܢ . ܘܡܪܟܒܘܬܐ ܡܫܘܚܬܐ ܘܟܠܗܝܢ ܡܫܘܚܬܐ .
ܘܗܟܢܐ ܘܡܫܘܚܬ ܐܢܫܐ . ܡܪܟܒܘܬܐ ܡܫܘܚܬܐ ܘܟܠܗܝܢ .
ܘܟܠܗܝܢ ܥܡ ܐܟܠܗܝܢ . ܘܩܕܡܐ ܘܡܫܘܚܬ ܩܕܡܐ ܗܘܘܢ .

ܗܢܘ ܗܘ ܕܐܡܪܝܢܢ ܕܟܠܗܝ ܐܬܪܐ ܀ ܡܢ ܠܠܝܐ. ܠܝܒܫ
ܬܠܬܝܢ ܥܒܕܘ ܟܘܠܗ ܡܕܝܢܐ. ܀ ܡܦܫܩܢܐ. ܟܪܟܐ
ܐܢܐ ܡܢܝܢ ܡܪܝ. ܀ ܡܫܐܠܢܐ. ܐܬܒܘ ܗܟܢܠ
ܐܫܘܢ ܀ ܡܢܫܬܐ. ܒܝ ܐܢܬ ܒܐܒܐ ܐܝܟ ܒܐܒܐ
ܕܒܝܒ ܠܗ ܡܕܝܢܐ. ܀ ܡܬܕܡܪܢܐ. ܒܡܒܥܐ ܐܬܒܝ
ܒܥܘ ܘܢܒܥ ܬܠܬܝܢ. ܒܡܒܥܐ ܗܘܘ ܠܬܒܥܐ ܡܢ
ܥܠܝܐ ܀ ܡܒܠܠܢܐ. ܒܬܘܗܝ ܒܝܪ ܐܠܗܐ ܥܙܝܙܐ. ܀
ܡܣܓܕܢܐ. ܓܘܐ ܒܐܘܫܢܐ ܫܒܠܬ ܒܒܠ ܠܐ
ܟܘܬܐ. ܀ ܥܘܠܒ ܡܣܓܕܢܐ. ܗ̄ ܡܕܕܟܝܢ ܒܣܒܠܐ
ܦܢܒܝܢ ܕܠܐ ܣܒܠܐ ܀ ܚܙܘܪܐ. ܟܥܘܪܐ. ܟܝܘܡܐ.
ܟܠܐܘܬܐ. ܒܐܫܘܪܐ ܀ ܥܘܠܒ ܚܙܘܪܐ. ܡܩܡܐ
ܘܡܝܢܐ ܘܩܒܝܢܐ ܘܥܒܝܢ ܕܠܢܡ ܐܝܬܘܗܝ ܀ ܟܝܢܐ.
ܒܗܘ ܡܘܡܐ ܬܕܒܘܢ ܕܐܢܐ ܒܐܒܝ ܘܐܝܬܘܗܝ ܒܝ
ܐܝܬܘܗܝ ܀ ܡܢܫܬܐ ܘܟܝܢܐ. ܕܒܬܐܡܪ ܡܘܡܢܐ
ܒܠܦܘܪܐ ܗܢܐ ܡܕܝܢܐ ܢܒܝܐ ܀ ܘܒܥܐ. ܘܡܕܘܠܐ
ܘܡܫܠܐ ܀ ܡܡܒܥܐ. ܘܕܢܡܝ ܟܡܝܪܡ ܒܐܪܒܐ.
ܘܬܠܝܢ ܕܬܒܡܪܡ ܡܢܗ. ܀ ܥܘܠܒ ܡܡܒܥܐ. ܠܝ
ܡܒܘܬܐ. ܘܠܝ ܚܢܝ. ܀ ܘܒܥܐ ܘܡܫܘܡܐ. ܕܕܒܐ
ܡܒܐܥܐ· ܩܢܝܐ ܡܣܒܠܐ. ܀ ܡܡܒܥܐ ܘܟܒܠܠܢܐ.
ܒܪܥܝܬ ܐܢܬܘ ܗܘܐ ܡܠܬܐ. ܀ ܡܥܐܠܝܢ ܘܒܥܐ

ܘܫܘܒܚܐ. ܘܗܕܐ ܕܟܠ ܐܬܘ̈ܬܐ. ܘܡܫܒܚܢܐ ܐ̄ܘ ܟܝܬ
ܘܡܙܪܘܙܘ̈ܬܐ. ܫܘܠܚܗ ܟܢܝ ܐ̈ܬܘܬܐ ܐ̄ܘ ܟܢܝ
ܦ̈ܪܝܫܬܐ. ܬܫܡܫܬܐ ܕܡܢ ܫܪܝ، ܬܫܒܘܚܬܐ ܀ ܐܬܬܚܡܘܗܝ
ܕܡ ܫܘܠܛ ܫܡ̈ܗܐ ܕܒܢܝܐ ܕܡ ܦܬܓ̈ܡܐ ܗܢܝܐ ܀
ܚܠܝܢ. ܚܬܝܐ ܕܠܝܠܘܬܗ ܕܫܘܒ ܡܫܝܚܐ. ※
ܬܫܘ̈ܚܝ. ܚܬܝܐ ܡܕܡܝܐ ܓܢ̈ܘܚܬ ܐܘ ܬ̈ܐܘܓܢ̈ܝܬܐ. ※
ܫܘܒܚܐ: ܘܒܪܐ ܡܢܝܐ ܕܗܓܝܬ ܒܢܝܬܐ ܕܐܢܫܐ
ܒܐܪܒܥܐ: ※ ܫܘܠܛ ܫܘ̈ܒܚܐ: ܓܒܪ̈ܐ ܕܡܢ ܚܠܡ:
ܗܢܐ ܐܬܘ ܫܪܝܐ ܕܬܫܒܘܚܬܐ. ※ ܦܫܘܛܐ. ܟܠ ܢܘܡܝܐ
ܕܫܘܠܡ ܦܬܓܡܐ ܐܬܘܗ. ܦܫܘܛܐ ܗܘ ܫܡܗ.
ܗܠܝ ܡܢ ܫܒܝܚܐ ※ ܕܗܠܝܐ ܕܦܫܡ.. ܠܐ ܠܟܘܢ ܟܠ
ܚܒܪ̈ܝ ܐܘܪܚܐ.. ※ ܡܓܒܝܢܐ ܐ̄ܘܟܝܬ ܡܫܘܒܚܢܐ.
ܐܠܗܗ ܕܐܒܐ ܐܒܪܗܡ. ܐܠܗܗ ܕܐܒܐ ܐܝܣܚܩ. ※
ܫܘܠܛ ܚܠܝܐ. ܟܠ ܣܓܘܐ ܬܘܕܝܐ ܠܟܘܢ ܐ̈ܚܝ: ※
ܫܘܠܛ ܬܫܘ̈ܚܝܐ. ܫܒܘܩ ܐܢܚ. ※ ܦܫܘܛܐ. ܢܦܘܩ
ܣܓܝܐ ܡܢ ܡܛܠܘܗܝ. ※ ܫܒܝܚܐ ܘܓܠܝܬܐ ܡܢ ܟܝܬ
ܟܠܘܗܝ. ※ ܬܓܡܪܐ. ܐܡܪ ܒܬܘܡܠܠ ܟܡܙܪܢܗ ܕܡܪܢܐ
ܓܡܪܐ ܘܢܓܝܪ. ※ ܬܫܡܫܬܐ ܘܫܘܒܚܐ. ܟܠ ܗܠܝܢ ܠܐ
ܐܦܡܘܬ ܐܡܪܢ " ܡܢܝܐ: ※ ܬܫܡܫܬܐ ܘܡܫܐܠܢܐ. ܠܐ
ܐܡܪܢܬ ܠܟܘܢ ܠܐ ܬܬܐܠܘܢ. ܀ ܬܫܡܫܬܐ ܘܬܫܘܬܐ.
ܐܠܗܢ ܗܕܢܐ ܢܠܟܫ. ※ (ܐ) ܡܫܒܚܢܐ . . . .

. . . .

. . . .

" ܒܟܠ . ܘܒܟܬܒܐ ܕܗܠܝܢ · ܠܐ ܐܝܬܝܗ ܢܣܒ.

(ܐ) ܚܣܝܪ ܒ. ܫܪܟܐ ܕܠܐ ܦܫܩ. ܠܐ ܐܝܬܝܗ ܗܢܐ ܒܟܠ ܗܢܐ.

ܒܦܬܓܡܐ ܫܒܝܚܝܢ: ܐܝܬܝܐ ܠܓܐܡܪܝ. ܥܠܝܐ
ܠܫܡܗ. ܐܘ ܙܘܓܐ ܘܥܙܪܐ. ܡ̈ܙܘܓܐ ܕܝܢ
ܐܡܬܝ̣ ܕܗ̈ܘܝܢ ܢܩܦܝܢ ܡܢ ܫܡ̈ܗܐ ܕܓܫܡܬܢܝܢ
ܥܠܝܗܘܢ ܒܬܘܠܕܐ ܕܠܗܘܢ ܥܡܠܝܢ. ܐܝܟ ܐܝܬܝܐ
ܠܓܐܡܪܝ ܦܘܣܝܐ. ܐܘ ܬܘܬܝܬܐ. ܐܘ ܙܘܓܐ
ܘܡܟܠܐ ܘܥܙܪܐ. ܡܚܝܠܐ ܗܝ ܕܝܢ ܕܢܩܫܐ
ܕܥܠܝܗܘܢ ܐܘ ܡܓܐܡܘܢ ܡܬܦܪܫܝܢ ܒܗ ܫ̈ܡܗܐ.
ܐܦ ܠܐ ܥܠܝܗܘܢ. ܒܗܢ ܕܝܢ ܙܢܝܐ ܐܬܝܢ ܘܡܬܪ.
ܐܬܬܢܝܗܘܢ ܕܝܢ ܢܩܦܝܢ ܒ̈ܫܡܗܝܗܘܢ ܡܚܝܐ. ܥܠܝܐ.
ܬܘܬܝܬܐ. ܬ̈ܡܢܝܐ: ܥܡܠܝܢ ܬ̈ܡܢܝܐ: ܐܘܟܝܬ ܙܪܥܐ
ܕܡ̈ܥܠܝܬܐ. ܪ̈ܘܚܝܐ ܕܦܣܘܩ.. ܦܣܘܩܐ. ܡ̈ܦܪܫܢܝܐ.
ܐܘܟܝܬ ܡ̈ܣܘܡܢܝܐ. ܥܡܠܝܢ ܥܠܝܐ. ܥܡܠܝܢ
ܬܘܬܝܬܐ. ܦܘܣܝܐ. ܥܒܝܕܐ. ܬܟܦܐ. ܡ̈ܐܐܠܝܐ.
ܪ̈ܘܚܝܐ ܕܦܣܘܩ ܘܙܠܐ ܦܣܘܩ. ܬܠܬܐ ܪ̈ܘܚܝܐ.
ܡܠܦܢܝܐ ܐܘܟܝܬ ܗܘ ܕܓܬܐܡܪ ܡܢܐܝܬ
ܦ̈ܐܪܐܓܘܓܐܦܘܣ. ܗ ܕܙܒܢ ܣܘܠܐܓܝ ܐܢܕܪܘܬܐ.
ܡܢܟ ܓܘܦܐ. ܦܪܘܫܐ. ܡܣܘܡܢܐ. ܡܩܠܝܢܝܐ.
ܡܦܝܣܢܐ. ܡܐܐܠܝܐ. ܡܢܣܝܬܐ. ܓܬܪܡܪܢܐ.
ܡܓܠܠܝܐ. ܡܣܝܒܪܐ. ܥܡܠܝܢ ܡܣܝܒܪܐ ܗܘ ܕܡܢ
ܠܥܠܐ ܡܣܝܐ ܢܦܩ. ܟܢܘܪܐ. ܥܡܠܝܢ ܟܢܘܪܐ.
ܚܝܘܬܐ. ܙܘܓܐ. ܫܓܝܐܐ. ܥܡܠܝܢ ܫܓܝܐܐ. ܙܘܓܐ
ܘܫܓܝܐܐ. ܫܓܝܐܐ ܘܡܓܠܠܝܐ. ܡܐܐܠܝܐ ܘܙܘܓܐ.
ܪ̈ܘܚܝܐ ܕܦܣܘܩ.. ܙܘܓܐ ܘܪ̈ܘܚܝܐ ܕܠܐ ܦܣܘܩ

ᵖ ܒ. ܐܝܟ ܐܡܬܝ ܡ̈ܠܬܐ ܐܘܚ̈ܕܢܐ. ˣ ܒ. ܕܥܙܪܐ.
ᵠ ܒ. ܗ̅ ܢܝܡ ܡ̈ܠܬܐ ܗ̅.

ܕܠܝܠ. ܐܬܦܬܚ ܐܬܕܒܪ ܘܕܐܝܟ ܗܠܝܢ. ܗܠܝܢ ܕܐܬܝܢ
ܕܡܚܘܬܐ ܕܦܬܓܡܐ ܘܚܬܡܐ ܘܬܒܥܐ ܐܚܪܢܐ. ܡܢ ܠܒܠ
ܡܢ ܥܒܕܝܢܐ. ܚܒܪܐ ܚܒܪܐ ܚܒܪܐ. ܡܠܟܐ ܡܠܟܐ. ܡܢ
ܠܬܘܬ ܕܝܢ ܥܒܕܝܢܐ ܚܒܪܐ ܡܠܟܐ. ܬܘܒ ܕܝܢ ܐܬܡܪ.
ܐܬܒܪ ܐܬܡܪ ܐܬܒܪ: ܐܬܐ. ܐܬܐ. ܐܬܐ. ܐܬܐ.
ܐܒܠ. ܐܒܠ: ܐܒܠ. ܒܪܐ ܒܪܐ ܒܪܐ. [a]ܒܐܪܐ.
ܒܐܪܐ. ܒܪܐ. ܒܪܐ ܒܪܐ. ܦܓܪܐ. ܦܓܪܐ. ܦܢܝܐ.
ܦܢܝܐ. ܦܢܝܐ. ܬܘܒ ܕܝܢ ܘܫܒܝܩܬܐ ܡܬܐܡܪܝܢ
ܗܠܝܢ ܘܡܬܚܫܒܢܬܐ. ܡܬܦܪܫܝܢ ܕܝܢ ܒܚܕ ܢܘܩܙܐ ܐܘ
ܒܚܕ ܐܬܘܬܐ. [b]ܕܐܝܟ ܐܡܪ. ܐܠܗܐ ܐܠܗܐ.
ܒܪܬܐ ܒܪܬܐ ܒܪܬܐ. ܒܪܬܐ ܒܪܬܐ. ܕܝܢܐ.
ܕܝܢܐ. ܫܡܝܢ. ܫܡܝܢ. ܬܡܝܢ ܬܡܝܢ. ܘܕܐܝܟ
ܗܠܝܢ.

ܩܦܐܠܠܐܘܢ ܕܬܫܥܐ ܡܛܠ ܫܡܗܐ ܕܫܡܐ.

ܐܣܟܡܐ ܕܝܢ ܕܫܡܗܐ ܐܬܝܗܘܢ ܗܠܝܢ. ܕܐܝܬ
ܡܬܚܙܝܢܐ ܒܗܘܢ ܣܘܓܦܬܐ ܕܡܠܬܐ. ܡܛܠ
ܕܐܝܬ ܐܢܫܝܢ ܗܝܠܐ ܘܡܪܡܘܬܐ: ܕܡܠܝܢ ܗܢܐ
ܕܩܪܝܢ ܐܬܐܡܪ. ܐܣܟܡܐ ܕܝܢ ܕܫܡܗܐ ܘܡܪܟܒܐ.
ܘܫܒܝܩܐ ܐܝܟ ܐܡܪ ܕܚܕ ܢܘܩܙܐ ܡܢ ܡܦܣܩܢܘܬܐ
ܫܡܝܢ. ܫܡܝܢ ܡܢ ܦܪܘܣܐ [c]ܐܣܟܡܐ ܕܗܘ

[a] C. ܒܪܐ ܣܛܟ ܒܪܐ. ܒܪܐ. [b] A. ܠܐܠܗ.
[c] C. ܐܣܟܡܐ.

ܕܐܬܡܢܪܝܢ ܦܬܝܚܐ܆ ܐܘ ܕܡܬܬܘܣܒ ܢܡܬܩܢܘܬܐ܆
ܚܪܝܪܝܢ ܚܘܪܝܢ. ܐܪܝܬܝܢ. ܟܡ ܫܘܚܠܐ ° ܕܦܬܝܚܐ.
ܬܘܒ ܕܝܢ ܐܣܝܪܐ ܕܥܘܦܝܢ܆ ܘܕܡܟܝܢ ܘܡܚܡܘܪܟܝܢ ܡܘܡܟܐ
ܟܕܡ ܕܐܣܝܪܐܝܬ ܘܡܚܝܠܐܝܬ. ܗ̄ ܚܪܝܪܝܢ ܚܘܪܝܢ.
ܐܪܝܬܝܢ. ܐܝܟ ܐܢܫ ܢܐܡܪ. ܚܪܝܪܐ ܕܠܝ. ܚܘܪܐ
ܕܠܝ. ܐܪܝܬܐ ܕܠܝ. ܘܗܠܝܢ ܡܢ ܥܘܦܝܢ ܟܬܝܒܬܐ.
ܦܫܝܩ ܕܝܢ ܒܟܬܒܬ ܡܠܟ ܡܛܠ ܢܩܘܫܐ ״ܕܒܠܝܫܘܢ܆
ܗܠܝܢ ܕܝܢ ܦܫܝܩ ܒܟܬܝܒܬܐ. ܘܢܦܩܝܢ ܒܟܬܒܬ ܡܠܟܐ: ܐܘ
ܒܡܡܠܠܐ ܦܪܝܫ ܠܗܘܢ ܗܘ ܕܢܛܥܐ: ܐܘ ܚܫܝܘܬܐ
ܗܘ ܕܦܪܬܐ... ܐܬܬܘܣܘܢ ܕܝܢ ܕ״ܐܝܟܢ ܗܟܢ. ܡܘܡ.
ܐܝܡܬܝ. ܡܘܡܢ ܐܝܡܬܝ. ܡܘܡܢ ܐܝܡܬܘ. ܠܐ ܟܡ ܦܠܝ.
ܠܐ ܚܡܐ. ܠܘ ܠܗܠ. ܠܐ ܠܟܐ.

ܩܦܐܠܐܘܢ ܕܬܠܬܐ ܡܛܠ ܙܢܝܐ.

ܙܢܝܐ ܕܝܢ ܕܐܝܟ ܐܝܟܢ. ܕܟܪܒ ܗܘ ܡܢ ܠܬܚܬ. ܐܝܟ
ܕܒܫܘܠܡܐ. ܕܐܝܟ ܐܝܟܢ. ܟܪܒ ܦܘܪ ܐܒܪ. ܘܕܐܝܟ
ܗܠܝܢ. ܕܡܐܡ ܕܝܢ ܡܢ ܠܟܠ. ܟܪܐ. ܦܐܪ. ܐܒܪ.
° ܘܕܐܝܟ ܗܠܝܢ. ܕܟܬܒܐ ܕܝܢ. ܟܪܐ ܦܐܪ ܐܒܪ.

ܩܦܐܠܐܘܢ ܕܐܪܒܥܐ ܡܛܠ ܒܢܬ ܩܠܐ.

ܒܢܬ ܩܠܐ ״ ܕܝܢ ܕܡܬܚܡܝܢ ܗܟܢ܆ ܡܫܬܘܕܥܢ ܡܢܬܚܠܠ

° ܒ. ܕܢܩܦܐ ܦܫܝܩܐ ܡܠܟ ܕܦܫܝܩܐ. ״ ܒ ܀ ܟܬܒ ܕܒܠܝܫܘܢ.
ᵖ ܒ. ܘܠܝܢ ܡܠܟ ܕܐܝܟ ܗܟܢ. ° ܒ. ܡܣܬܡܟ ܘܕܐܝܟ ܘܫܪ̄.
ᵗ ܒ. ܡܣܬܡܟ ܕܝܢ.

ܗܟܢܐ ܕܒܙܢ، ܡܥܡܕ ܡܛܠ ܦܬ̈ܓܡܐ ܘܥܪ̈ ܗܘ

ܐܬܗܘܐ ܕܝܢ ܕܒܢܝܐ : ܫܡܥܐ ܕܠܒܢܝ̈ܢ ܐܝܬ ܠܚܠܡ.
ܡܥܢܘܢ [א] ܟܡ ܕܢܩܡܝܐ ܘܡܫܒܚܐ ܐܝܬ ܠܗܘܢ.

ܡܠܐܘܢ ܡܕܡܝܐ ܡܛܠ ܦܬ̈ܓܡܐ.

ܦܬ̈ܓܡܐ ܕܝܢ ܬܠܬܐ. [ב] ܕܐܡܝܢ ܐܝܟ ܡܕܡܝܐ. ܐܘܪܐ. ܬܪܝܢܐ ܐܘܪܐ. ܬܠܝܬܝܐ ܕܝܢ ܐܘܪܐ ܕܒܗܪܐ. ܗܢܐ ܕܝܢ ܐܘܪܐ ܡܦ̈ܩܕܢܐ ܐܝܬ ܠܗ ܠܡܫ̈ܠܐ.

ܡܐܦܐܠ̈ܐܘܢ ܕܬܪ̈ܝܢ ܡܛܠ ܟܬ̈ܡܐ.

ܟܬ̈ܡܐ ܕܝܢ ܬܪ̈ܝܢ. ܕܒܢ̈ܝܐ ܘܡܫܒ̈ܩܢܐ ܀ ܕܒܢܝܐ ܕܝܢ ܟܒܪܬ ܟܒܠܬ ܐܒܠܬ. ܡܫܒܩܢܐ [ג] ܕܝܢ ܟܒܪܬ ܟܒܠܬ ܐܒܠܬ. ܡܬܚܠܦܝܢ ܕܝܢ ܟܬ̈ܡܐ ܘܦܬ̈ܓܡܐ : ܡܛܠ ܫܘܚܠܦ ܬܘܒܬܐ ܡܬܦܪܫܝܢ ܒܢܩܡܝܐ ܗܢܢܐ. ܦܪܚܬ. ܦܪܚܬ. ܦܪܚܬ. ܦܪܚܬ. ܦܪܚܬ ܦܪܚܬ. ܀ ܬܘܒ [ד] ܕܝܢ ܗܘܝܬ ܢܗܒ ܕܐܦ ܦܘܪܫܐ ܐܚܪܢܐ ܐܝܬ ܒܟܬ̈ܡܐ ܕܒܢܝܐ ܘܡܫܒܩܢܐ : ܐܡܬܝ، ܕܢܦܩܝܢ ܒܬܘܟ̈ܬܐ ܐܘ ܒܟܢܬ ܩܠܐ. ܘܠܬܘܟ̈ܬܐ ܟܡ ܫ̈ܘܬܐ ܡܦܪܫܝܢ. ܢܩܡܝܐ. ܐܡܟܢܐ ܕܒܗ ܢܦܘܠ ܕܒܢܝܬ : ܟܒܪܬ ܟܬܟܬ. ܐܟܬܟܬ : [ה] ܕܠܐ ܫܘܡܠܐ ܕܬܪ̈ܝܢ ܢܩܡܝܐ :

[א] ܒ ܣܟܘܡ ܥܠ.
[ב] ܒ ܣܟܘܡ ܕܐܡܘ ܐܡܪ.
[ג] ܒ ܦܠܓ ܣܟܘܡ ܕܡܢ.
[ד] ܒ ܣܟܘܡ ܕܡܢ.
[ה] ܒ ܕܠܐ ܟܠܗ ܣܟܘܡ ܕܠܐ.

ܕܐܠܗܗ ܟܕ ܕܐܠܗܗ ܕܡܟܪ ܢܦܩܘܢ ܡܛܠ
ܦܬܘܪܐ ܘܡܢܪܬܐ.

ܗܠܝܢ [α] ܗܟܝܠ ܕܐܡܪ ܠܗ ܠܡܘܫܐ ܕܢܬܒܢܝܢ ܒܬܫܡܫܬܐ
ܕܝܠ ܡܫܟܢ [β] ܗܠܝܢ ܦܬܘܪܐ ܕܠܚܡܐ [γ] ܘܡܢܪܬܐ. ܒܬܪܗ
ܕܝܢ ܥܠܡܐ ܕܢܦܫܐ. ܡܛܠ ܕܥܠܡܐ ܕܢܦܫܐ ܦܢܝܢ ܗܘܐ
ܠܢܡܘܣܐ: ܐܡܪܬ ܕܝܠ ܦܬܘܪܐ ܗܢܝܢ. [δ] ܘܕܝܠ
ܦܠܚܐ ܘܡܬܬܒܥܐ ܫܦܝܪ. ܐܬܪܐ ܘܡܥܒܕܐ ܕܚܘܠܦ
ܢܦܫܐ [ε] ܗܢܘܢ. ⁘. ܘܦܬܘܪܐ ܗܘ ܬܠܝܬܝܐ. ܡܕܒܪܢܐ
ܘܬܪܝܢܐ ܘܬܠܝܬܝܐ. ⁘ ܚܘܫܒܐ ܕܝܢ ܬܪܝܢ. ܕܟܝܢܐ
ܘܡܬܒܪܝܢܐ ⁘ ܡܢܝܢܐ ܕܝܢ ܬܠܝܬܝܐ. ܕܒܝܬ ܘܕܦܢܝܢ
ܘܕܒܝܬܝ: ܘܒܬܪܗ ܩܠܐ ܕܟܒܢܝܢ [ζ] ܘܕܢܡܘܣܐ. ⁘ ܬܘܒ ܕܝܢ
ܥܠ ܦܬܘܪܐ ܐܘ ܒܝܬ ܗܕܝܐ. ܐܝܟܐ ܗܘ ܕܟܒܝ
ܐܘ ܦܬܐ ܒܒܪܬ ܡܠܝ. [η] ܬܘܒ ܗܘ ܠܟܠ ܥܡܠ ܢܡܘܣܐ.⁜
ܐܝܟܐ ܕܝܢ ܕܡܠܝ ܐܘ ܢܦܩ ܗܘ ܠܬܚܬ. ⁜ [θ] ܐܟ ܡܕܒܪܢܐ
ܐܝܬܘ ܕܡܠܝܢܐ ܘܒܢܝܢܐ: ܘܐܝܬ ܬܪܝܢ ܐܚܪܢܐ ܕܥܒܕܝܢ
ܠܗ ܒܬܫܡܫܬܐ ܬܪܝܢ ܢܡܘܣܐ ܥܡܠ ܚܕ ܗܘ ܠܟܠ ܘܚܕ ܗܘ
ܠܬܚܬ. ܘܡܬܚܫܒܐ ܗܘ ܗܘܝܐ ܕܦܪܢܝܐ. [ι] ܢܦܫܐ. ܒܪܐ ⁘

[α] ܒ ܥܠ ܗܟܝܠ.
[β] ܒ ⁘ ܒܬܪ ܗܠܝܢ.
[γ] ܒ ܡܫܟܢ ܘܡܢܪܬܐ.
[δ] ܒ ܘܟܠ.
[ε] ܒ ܡܫܟܢ ܗܢܘܢ.
[ζ] ܒ ܘܕܦܠܚܘܬܐ ܘܕܢܡܘܣܐ.
[η] ܒ ܡܫܟܢ ܠܟܠ.
[θ] ܒ ܐܝܟ ܡܕܒܪܢܐ.
[ι] ܒ ܐܝܟ ܓܒܐ.

ܐܓܪܬܐ ܕܡܪܝ ܝܥܩܘܒ ܡܛܠ ܗܪܛܩܐ ܣܘܪܝܢܐ ܠ

ܕܠܘܬܟ. ܘܡܬܪܟܢ ܡܦܣ ܢܦܫܐ ܠܐܚܝܘܬܟ ܠܓܒܝܢܘܗܝ
ܟܪܝܗܘܬܟ: ܘܡܢ ܐܓܪܬܐ ܕܠܗ ܒܗ ܟܬܒ ܐܢܬ ܠܘܬ
ܐܟܣܢܝܐ ܡܢܝ. ܡܠܦܢܐ ܘܫܪܝܪܐ ܐܢܬ ܫܠܝܚܘ ܡܢ
ܡܫܝܚܘܬܟ. ܫܪܪܗ ܠܗ ܘܠܐܓܪܬܐ ܘܠܗ ܠܓܒܝܢܘܬܐ
ܗܝ ܡܢ ܒܢܝܬܐ: ܐܝܟܢܐ ܕܗܘܐ ܡܢܝܢܐ ܒܓܘܡܝܗ.
ܘܒܬܪܡܐ ܐܦ ܡܫܝܚܐ ܕܗܠܝܢ ܢܘܡܝܐ: ܘܐܦ
ܒܗܠܝܢ ܕܗܦܝܟܝܢ ܘܐܦ ܒܗܠܝܢ ܕܫܠܝܚܘܗܝ ܘܬܘܒ
ܐܦ. ܒܗܠܝܢ ܢܦܘܩܐ ܕܠܐ ܡܢ ܠܓܒܝܢܘܬܗ ܗܘ ܒܬܘܒܐ
ܐܝܠܝܢ ܕܡܫܝܚܝܢ ܗܘܘ ܠܗ: ܘܐܦܠܐ ܒܓܘܫܡܘܬܐ ܕܠܫܡܝܐ.
ܟܠܐ ܐܢܐ ܕܐܦ ܐܚܝܬܘܢ ܦܘܫܩܗ ܠܗ ܣܘܟܠܐ
ܠܡܫܝܚܐ ܓܒܝܐ ܗܘ ܕܐܡܪ: ܘܕܐܦ ܠܟܢܫܐ ܕܠܐ
ܢܐܠܦ: ܕܟܠܐ ܐܢܐ ܕܢܦܩ ܘܢܬܘܒ ܐܝܟ ܢܦܫܗ.
ܘܐܘܪܚܬܐ ܕܗܘܐ ܐܝܬܘܗܝ ܬܘܒ ܕܢܦܩ ܡܢ ܗܘܐ: ܡܢܗ
ܡܢ ܐܘܪܚܐ ܕܦܬܟܝܢ ܒܗܠܝܢ ܕܐܬܬܝܕܥ. ܘܠܝܠܝܐ ܬܘܒܠܐ
ܒܡܢܝ ܐܘܚܕܐ ܫܘܝܐ. ܒܗ ܚܝܠܐ ܐܢܬ ܫܠܘ
ܡܫܝܚܘܬܟ: ܘܚܠܡܐ ܐܢܬ ܠܗ ܬܒܥܐ ܡܢ ܐܠܗܝ
ܐܡܝܢ ܀

ܫܠܡܬ ܐܓܪܬܐ ܕܡܪܝ ܝܥܩܘܒ
ܕܠܘܬ ܟܘܪܝܐ.

ܒ. ܣܣܣܝ ܠܗ.   [a] ܒ. ܣܣܣܝ ܐܦ.
[b] ܒ. ܒܗܠܝܢ ܕܠܐ ܗܘܐ.   [c] ܒ. ܣܣܣܝ ܕܡܠܟܐ.

ܡܢ ܐܓܪܬܐ ܕܡܪܝ ܝܥܩܘܒ ܕܥܠ ܣܗܕܐ ܚܡܝܪܝܐ

ܚܠܦ ܗܠܝܢ ܕܗܠܝܢ: ܕܗܘܝܢ ܫܠܝܛ ܠܗ ܘܡܫܬܠܛ: ܠܘܬ
ܗܘ ܕܐܡܪ ܕܠܘܩܒܠ ܐܡܪܐ ܐܬܬܘܬܐ ܘܠܟܠ ܡܢܗ ܐܬܐ ܘ
ܠܬܘܬ ܡܢܗ: ܐܡܪܬ ܐܢܐ ܠܦܩܕܬܐ ܕܢܡܘܣܐ. ܗܠܝܢ
ܢܦܩܘ ܕܥܒܕܬܐ: ܠܘܬ ܡܠܟܘܬܐ ܕܟܬܒܘܬܐ ܐܢܫܝ
ܐܠܗܐ: ܗܢܘܢ ܕܐܫܬܡܥܘ ܥܒܕܝ ܬܪܥܝܬܐ:
ܒܬܘܬܒܢܝܬܐ ܘܡܟܠܠ ܬܘܪܓܡܐ: ܠܘܬ ܕܝܢ ܐܘܪܚܬܐ
ܕܠܝܟ ܫܒܝܩܬܐ. ܗܕܐ ܟܕ ܡܦܣܩ ܝܕܥܐ ܐܢܐ ܝܕܥܐ.
ܠܬܘܠܡܬܐ ܕܠܐ ܗܕܐ ܕܠܘܬ ܫܒܝܩܘܬܟ: ܦܩܘܕ
ܠܬܘܕܝܬܐ ܬܘܒ ܠܗ: ܡܕܡ ܦܘܩܕܢܐ ܗܘ ܡܥܝܢܘܬܐ
ܕܬܘܕܝܬܐ ܗܢܐ ܕܐܡܕܝܢܬܐ ܐܦܘܪܘܣܐ. ܘܠܢܡܘܣܐ
ܗܢܘܢ ܕܫܠܝܚܝܢ ܕܝܠܝܦܘܬܐ ܗܘ ܕܐܬܒܪܬ. ܗܘ ܐܡܪܐ
ܕܠܡܣܒܪܗ ܐܢܫܐ ܡܢܗܘܢ ܦܘܩܕܢܐ ܘܫܠܝܚܐ ܐܢܘܢ
ܚܕܐ ܓܝܪ ܡܠܠ ܚܘܒܗ ܕܠܡܗܘܢ ܕܐܬܪܬܐ ܕܝܢ ܡܠܠ
ܕܝܬܝܪ ܢܦܫܐ ܕܠܐ. ܥܒܕܘ ܐܢܘܢ ܒܗ ܐܝܟ
ܕܐܬܚܫܒܘܢ ܘܠܐ ܕܒܪܢܫܐ ܡܢܗ ܚܕ ܡܢܗܘܢ.
ܒܥܒܕܐ ܕܒܬܘܠܘܬܐ ܢܦܫܐ ܢܝܚ ܗܘ ܕܗܘ. ܐܡܝܢܐ
ܕܒܕ ܡܢܐ ܠܗܘܢ ܟܘܠܟܐ: ܠܗܘܢ ܒܠܥܕ ܕܫܠܝܚܝܢ
ܘܠܗܘܢ ܕܐܠܝܨܘܢ ܐܬܬܦܝܣܘ. ܢܦܩܘܢ ܠܢܝܚܐ
ܕܠܐ ܕܟܠ ܢܦܫܐ ܗܠܝܢ: ܕܒܐܓܪܬܐ ܕܠܐ ܗܕܐ

---

[v] ܒ. ܡܬܬܒܢܝܢ ܣܥܪ̈ܐ. [φ] ܒ. ܢܦܠܘܢ ܣܥܪ̈ܐ.

[χ] ܒ. ܣܥܪ ܗܢܐ. [ψ] ܒ. ܣܥܪ ܡܠܟܐ.

[ω] ܒ. ܬܘܪܓܡܐ. [a] ܒ. ܢܦܫ.

[β] ܒ. ܣܥܪ ܟܠܗ.

ܐܠܗܘܬܐ ܕܟܪܝ، ܝܥܩܘܒ ܡܛܠ ܦܘܪܓܠܐ ܣܘܪܝܝܐ ܠܐ

ܕܐܬܬܣܝܡܢ ܒܟܬܒܐ ܗܢܐ ܢܘܗܪܐ: ܐܘܟܝܬ
ܐܘܗܪܢܐ: ܐܘ ܬܘܪ ܡܫܘܕܥܢܘܬ ܠܡܐܡܪ ܦܘܪܫܢܐ.
ܠܐ ܡܬܩܢܝܢܘܬܐ ܘܡܫܘܕܥܢܘܬܐ: ܘܐܝܟܢܐ ܕܠܐ ܐܝܬ ܣܝܡ
ܗܕܡܐ ܕܒܬܪܬܝܢ ܡܢ ܐܢܫܝܢ ܕܕܟܪܐ ܠܗ ܒܐܬܪܘܬܐ:
ܘܗܝ ܕܒܬܫܡܫܬܗ ܢܦܘܩ ܐܘ ܕܢܣܒܘܢ ܒܒܠܠܝܢ
ܘܒܬܪܗ ܠܐܢܫܐ ܘܠܬܓܠܝܐ ܕܐܝܟ ܒܗܝܢ ܣܒ ܣܒ
ܢܚܡܬܐ: ܘܐܬܚܠܐ ܕܢܣܒܘܢ ܫܘܢܝܐ ܘܒܢܝܢܐ ܡܢ
ܡܢܬܐ: ܠܗܬ ܗܝ ܕܒܬܦܩܕ ܗܕܡܐ ܡܢ ܗܠܝܢ ܐܢܫܝܢ
ܕܕܟܪܢ ܠܗ ܐܝܟ ܒܢܝܐ. ܡܛܠ ܕܐܝܟܢܐ ܕܐܬܬܚܝܒ
ܬܘܪܬܐ ܕܠܐ ܥܒܝܕ. ܗܟܢܐ ܐܦ ܒܢܘܪܬܐ.
ܒܢ ܗܕܐ ܘܗܝ ܕܐܦ ܒܕܘܟܬܐ ܕܠܫܡܫ ܠܗܘܢ
ܒܬܫܡܫܬܗ. ܘܠܐ ܐܝܟܢܐ ܕܐܝܬ ܐܬܪܐ ܣܦܝܩܐ:
ܐܢ ܐܠܐ ܠܐ ܐܦ ܠܐ ܐܠܐ. ܘܐܝܟ ܕܠܬܫܡܫܬܐ
ܗܘ ܡܢܝܢܐ ܝܠܐ ܕܐܝܟܢ ܟܕܡ ܟܕܡ: ܠܘ ܥܒܕܐ
ܕܗܘ ܡܢܐ ܕܢܟܪܐ ܐܢܫܐ ܕܐܠܗ. ܚܕܪܐ ܐܬܬܢܐ
ܡܕܪܬܐ ܒܚܕܪܐ ܚܕ ܘܬܪܝܢ ܘܗܟܢܐ ܦܘܪܐ ܠܚܕܪܐ
ܘܠܡܟܢܫܬܐ ܠܡܚܕܐ ܚܕܪܐ ܦܩܝܢܐ. ܚܕ ܐܢܫ
ܕܠܐ ܟܠܐ ܥܡܐ ܕܒܒܬܐ. ܐ. ܟܢܫܝܢ. ܡܛܠ
ܕܠܥܕܬܐ ܕܠܐ ܠܐ ܡܥܒܕܐ ܐܬܬܕܝܪ ܗܕܐ. ܡܛܠ
ܕܠܘ ܡܠܘܐ ܐܢܫܝ، ܡܟܢܫ ܐܠܐ ܡܠܘܐ ܕܡܟܢܫܬܐ
ܡܫܡܫܢܐ ܐܢܫܐ ܟܠ ܢܦܫ ܕܐܢܫ، ܟܡ، ܕܐܢܫ، ܠܐ ܥܒܕܐ

ܒ . ܣܒܪܗ .　　　ܒ . ܠܐ ܐܢ .
ܒ . ܘܣܡܘܢ ܣܠܩ ܐܘ ܢܣܡܘܢ .

ܐܚܪܬܐ ܕܡܪܝ ܡܚܫܒ ܡܛܠ ܗܪܟܐ ܦܘܪܫܢܐ

ܕܐܝܟ ܐܡܪ: ܕܒܗܘܢ ܕܫܪܝܐ ܚܝܠܘܗܝ: ܐܘ ܕܫܪܝܐ
ܐܕܢܐ: ܐܘ ܕܫܪܝܐ ܥܝܢܐ: ܐܘ ܐܝܕܐ ܐܘ ܪܓܠܐ
ܕܐܬܪܟܒ ܬܪܟܒܬܐ ܠܢܦܫ. ܗܟܢܐ ܡܕܡ ܥܒܝܕܐ ܘܠܐ
ܦܫܝܛܐ ܐܝܬܘܗܝ: ܕܢܬܚܫܒ ܦܪܨܘܦܐ ܐܘ ܪܫܐ
ܕܒܪܢܫܐ ܐܘ ܕܫܘܬܦܘܬܐ ܐܣܪܐ ܕܝܠܗ: ܕܐܝܬ ܒܗ ܬܠܬ
ܐܕܢܐ ܐܘ ܬܠܬ ܥܝܢܐ ܐܘ ܡܕܡ ܐܚܪܢ ܝܬܝܪܐ: ܠܒܪ
ܡܢ ܗܠܝܢ ܕܢܦܩܝܢ ܒܟܝܢܐ ܗܘ ܟܝܢܐ. ܠܐ ܓܝܪ ܥܒܝܕܐ
ܐܝܟܢܐ ܕܐܝܬ ܒܗ ܥܠ ܬܘܩܢܬܐ ܐܝܕܐ ܪܓܠܐ. ܐܝܕܐ
ܦܘܡܐ ܕܐܝܬ ܒܗ ܥܝܢܐ ܡܬܚܙܝܢܬܐ. ܘܫܢܝܐ ܕܢܦܩ
ܘܢܦܩ ܠܒܪ ܡܢܗ. ܐܘ ܩܘܡܬܐ ܕܐܪܝܟ ܘܡܬܬܪܝܡ
ܠܬܚܬ. ܗܟܢܐ *ܬܘܒ ܐܦ ܗܕܐ ܥܒܝܕܐ: ܕܠܒܪ
ܡܢ ܕܪܟܫܬܐ ܗܠܝܢ ܕܐܬܬܚܝܡ ܡܢ ܟܝܢܐ: ܢܬܬܠܝܡܘܢ
ܒܬܬܚܡܘܢ ܗܕܡܐ. ܠܐ ܦܐܝܐ ܕܬܬܩܢ ܟܝܢܐ
ܒܓܠܝܘܬܐ. ܘܐܦܠܐ ܐܕܢܐ ܒܥܝܢܬ ܚܝܘܬܐ ܕܒܪܢܫܐ.
ܘܐܦܠܐ ܬܪܟܒܬܐ ܒܫܘܪܟܐ ܐܘ ܟܐܦܘܝܐ. ܘܐܦܠܐ
ܠܚܘܪܐ ܒܫܘܡܐ ܘܒܓܘܫܡܘܬܐ ܘܒܓܒܝܠܘܬܐ. ܐܠܐ ܗܘ
ܥܘܩܒܗ ܕܟܝܢܐ. ܕܠܐ ܢܗܘܐ ܒܗ ܡܬܪܬܝܐ
ܘܒܝܪܘܬܐ. ܕܢܗܘܘܢ ܡܠܘܚܝܢ ܠܢܦܫ ܡܢ ܗܕܡܐ:
ܕܥܘܒܕܐ ܗܘ ܕܐܬܬܓܒܠ ܘܐܬܠܒܫܬ ܠܗ ܡܢ ܟܝܢܐ
ܗܘ ܡܟܒܪܐ: ܕܐܝܟ ܐܠܗܐ ܡܟܒܪܐ. ܟܠ ܒܕܡܘܬܐ
ܐܝܬ ܠܓܝܣܐ ܐܦ ܡܛܠ ܗܕܡܘܗܝ ܕܒܦܪܐ: ܗܠܝܢ
ܕܐܝܬܝܗܘܢ ܦܪܨܘܦܐ ܘܡܫܡܫܢܐ: ܕܢܗܘܐ ܡܕܡ:

* ܒ. ܘܗܕܐ ܡܛܠ ܬܘܒ ܐܦ ܗܕܐ.

ܐܚܪܬܐ ܕܒܪ ܡܚܡܕ ܡܛܠ ܣܘܪܬܐ ܦܘܪܩܢܐ ܠ

ܗܘ ܕܐܡܘܣܝ ܐܘ ܦܠܓܐ ܦܘܪܩܢ ܗܘܘ ܐܘ ܐܢܫܘܬܐ. ܐܘ
ܐܝܟ ܕܡܫܡܠܝܐ ܐܢܫܘܬܐ ܐܚܝܕܝܢ ܗܘܘ. ܠܐ ܢܬܚܒܠܘܢ
ܒܗ ܗܘ ܠܚܠܡܝܢ: [a]ܠܗܘ ܐܚܝܕܝܢ ܕܐܝܬ ܒܡܠܟܘܬܐ
[b]ܕܫܡܝܐ. ܒܗ ܗܠܝܢ ܓܝܪ ܐܦ ܐܢܫܘܬܐ ܡܫܡܫܢܘܬܐ
ܐܝܬ ܗܘܐ ܠܗ ܠܡܓܪܫ ܒܡܬܒܥܬܐ ܗܕܐ. ܐܠܐ ܢܠܒܫ
ܗܘ، ܗܟܢܐ ܒܡܗܝܪܘܬܐ: ܡܛܠ ܕܡܕܪܫܗܘܢ ܕܟܬܒܐ.
ܫܠܘ ܕܟܬܒܝܢ ܒܡܫܠܡܢܘܬܐ ܕܡܢ ܡܠܬ [c]ܢܦܫܐ ܒܠܚܘܕ
ܕܫܦܪ ܠܗܘܢ: ܒܗ ܦܓܪܝܢ ܕܠܐ ܐܢܫ ܡܬܕܠܐ ܒܠ
ܗܕܐ. ܒܠ ܕܡܫܟܚܐ ܕܝܢ ܗܠܝܢ ܕܟܬܒܝܢ ܒܠ ܫܘܕܥܐ
ܕܡܬܒܥܐ ܐܘ ܕܡܬܐܡܪܐ ܐܝܟ ܕܟܬܝܒ: ܘܒܠ ܫܘܠܡܐ
ܟܠܗ ܒܥܒܘܕܘܬܐ: ܘܒܠ ܫܘܠܛܢܐ ܘܒܠ ܬܫܒܘܚܬܐ ܘܒܠ
ܦܘܪܢܝ. ܡܛܠ ܐܝܬ ܠܗ ܠܡܐܡܪ. ܡܛܠ ܕܝܢ ܕܐܦ
ܒܫܡܝܐ ܕܢܗܘܪܐ ܐܘܬܝܘܬܐ ܢܦܠ ܒܠܒܟ ܠܒܨܘܗ
ܕܐܝܟ ܕܫܦܪ ܠܗ ܢܦܫ ܐܢܐ: ܘܟܕܪܝܬܐ ܡܠܠ ܩܠܐ
ܕܢܬܒ ܕܐܘܡܦ ܐܡܪ [d]ܗܪܟܐ: ܐܢ ܐܡܪܐ ܕܒܬܘܠܬܐ
ܕܢܫܬܠܡ ܘܢܬܡܠܟܘܢ. ܒܗܢ ܕܝܢ ܗܠܝܢ ܐܡܪ ܐܢܐ
ܬܫܒܘܚܬܐ ܡܢܗܘܢ ܒܢܘܗܪܐ. ܐܟܢܐ ܗܟܢ ܕܠܗ ܢܦܫܘܬܐ
ܐܬܬܗ: ܐܝܟ ܫܘܒܚܘܬܐ ܡܢܗܘܢ ܘܡܫܝܚܘܬܐ ܘܠܐ
ܟܐܢܘܬܐ: ܗܘ ܕܝܗܘܐ ܒܪܢܫܐ ܟܡܫܝܚܐ ܡܢܗܘܢ ܒܢܝܐ
ܘܢܒܠܐ: ܗܢ ܫܘܪܝܐ ܗܠܝܢ ܕܐܬܡܠܟܘ ܠܗ ܡܢ ܒܢܝܐ:

---

[a] ܒ. ܡܫܡܗ ܠܗܘ ܐܝܟܢ.
[b] ܒ. ܕܢܚܡܝ ܡܬܥܒܪܐ ܡܠܟܐ ܕܡܬܥܒܪܐ.
[c] ܒ. ܢܫܡܥܘܢ. [d] ܒ. ܘܟܒܠ.

ܡܒܝܢ. ܠܐ ܢܒܪܘܢ ܡܢ ܐܬܘ̈ܬܐ ܗܠܝܢ ܕܡܬܩܪ̈ܝܢ ܠܗ
ܒܫܡ̈ܗܐ ܗܠܝܢ ܡ̈ܢܝܢܐ ܘܡܒ̈ܪܝܢܐ: ܘܠܐ ܢܦܩܘܢ
ܒܠܚܘܕ. ܡܐܛܐܣܛܐܣܝܣ: ܦܐܢܛܐܣܝܐ:
ܦܐܘܠܘܟܣܝܐ: ܦܠܝܪܘܦܘܪܝܐ: ܦܝܠܘܣܘܦܝܐ:
ܘܐܣܛܝܢܐ[ܒ] ܣܟܝܢܐܐ: ܡܘܢܐܣܛܐܝܢܘܣ.
ܐܦܐܟܣܝܘܣ. ܐܦܝܠܘܩܘܣ: ܐܘܪܝܟܐܠܐ:
ܘܐܘܐܢܓܠܝܣܛܐ: ܐܘ ܕܐܝܦܛܡܘܣ: ܐܘ ܐܣܛܪܢܐ ܕܐܝܟ
ܗܢ. ܕܠܐ ܦܓܥܐ ܒܐܝܕܐ ܗܒܐ ܕܐܬܦܓܗܕ ܐܘܠܦ
ܠܐ ܢܦܠܘܢ ܠܥܘܩܐ ܗܘ ܕܡܦܓܥܢܘܬܐ. ܒܕ
ܢܫܬܠܡܘܢ: ܡܛܠ ܕܠܐ ܢܗܘܘܢ ܡܫܢܐ ܐܬܘܬܗ:
ܕܒܫܘܚܠܦ ܠܗ̇ ܕܗ̇ܝ ܒܗ̇ ܕܡܫܩܠ. ܘܐܦܠܐ ܠܗ̇ܘ
ܕܐܬܪܬܐ: ܕܫܘܚܠܦ ܠܚܒܪܬܐ ܕܬܪܬܝܢ. ܐܦܠܐ
[ܓ]ܒܬܪ ܗ̇ܘ ܕܫܠܝܛܘܬܐ ܐܘ ܕܕܠܝܫܘܬܐ ܒܝܕ ܗܘܐ ܦܣܩ
ܡܟܐ ܥܕܡ ܠܗܘܬ ܠܥܠܐ ܣܘܪܝܝܐ. ܘܠܐ ܡܫܬܟܚ ܠܗܘܬ
ܡܠܦܢܐ ܣܘܪܝܝܐ ܗܘ: ܠܗܘܬ ܡܢܝ ܐܦܪܝܡ. ܐܟܙܢ
ܐܢܫ ܐܘ ܠܗܘܬ ܡܢܝ ܐܢܛܝܘܟܝ. ܘܡܢܝ ܐܘܣܛܝܣ
ܐܘ ܡܢܝ ܐܚܪܝܬܐ: ܐܘ ܒܟܕܘܩ ܡܢ ܗܠܝܢ ܕܢܦܩ. ܡܢ
ܡܢܐ ܒܥܒܝܐ ܗܠܝܢ: ܐܘ ܐܦܝܠܘܬܐ: ܐܘ ܥܒܕܐ
ܕܐܘܡܢܐ: ܐܠܐ ܚܠܦ ܗ̇ܘ ܕܕܠܝܬܘܬܐ ܐܚܪܢܝܬܐ ܗܘܘ:
ܡܫܬܕܪܬܐ. ܚܠܦ ܕܝܢ ܗ̇ܘ ܕܐܝܟܢܝܘܬܐ ܕܢܐ. ܚܠܦ ܕܝܢ

ܐ ܒ. ܡܫܡܫ ܠܠܡܕܢܚ. ܒ ܒ. ܡܫܡܫ ܘܐܣܬܪܝ ܫܪܝܐ.
ܓ ܒ. ܠܗܘ ܡܠܟ ܕܝܢ ܗܘ.

ܡܢ ܐܝܟ ܘܦܠܓܬ ܦܫܝܛܘܬܗ. ܘܐܬܬܓܫܡܬ ܕܐܬܚܕ
ܠܗ ܦܘܪܫܐ: ܕܐܝܢܐ ܐܝܬܘܗܝ. ܟܡ[1] ܦܫܝܛܘܬܐ ܐܘ ܚܕܘܬ
ܡܬܡܢܝܢܘܬܐ. ܘܠܐ ܡܬܬܚܫܒܐ ܒܗ̇. ܐ̄. ܠܐ
ܢܬܡܢܐ ܒܡܢܝܢܐ ܐܘ ܚܕܬ ܒܚܕܘܬ ܡܠܐ ܕܡܢܝܢܐ ܗܘ
ܕܐܬܟܢܫ ܐܬܦܠܓ ܐܘ ܡܬܦܠܓ ܗܘ. ܐܠܐ ܢܬܝܕܥ
ܕܡܠܬܐ ܗܝ. ܡܢܝܢܘܬܐ ܕܐܬܟܢܫܐ ܐܬܦܠܓ ܡܬܦܠܓܢܐ
ܗܘ. ܐܘ ܟܗ̇ ܕܐܬܟܢܫ ܐܬܦܠܓ ܐܘ ܚܕܘܬ ܐܬܦܠܓܢܐ.
ܢܬܝܕܥ ܐܡܪܐ[2] ܕܡܢܝܢ ܠܬܚܘܬܐ[3] ܗܘܝܢ ܙܘܓܝܘܬܐ
ܘܦܪܝܕܘܬܐ ܠܐ ܙܘܓܝܘܬܐ. ܘܢܬܝܕܥ ܕܐܡܪܐ ܘܠܐ ܠܗܘܢ
ܕܡܫܡܥܝܢ ܠܗܘܢ ܢܩܦܢܐ: ܘܢܬܕܥܘܢ ܥܕܡܐ
ܙܘܓܝܘܬܐ: ܘܦܪܝܕܘܬܐ ܗܠܝܢ ܕܟܝܢ: ܘܙܘܓܝܘܬܐ ܬܘܒ ܡܢ
ܦܪܝܕܘܬܐ. ܢܬܝܕܥ ܕܡܢ ܗܠܝܢ ܐܝܟ ܕܠܡܬܠ ܦܪܝܫ ܚܕ
ܙܘܓܝܘܬܐ. ܠܐ ܢܬܦܠܓܘܢ ܠܚܡ ܚܕ ܚܕܟܐܝܬ: ܐܘ
ܦܪܝܫ ܚܕ ܐܘ ܚܡܫ ܚܕ. ܐܘ ܬܠܬ ܚܕ. ܐܘ ܦܫܥ ܚܕ:
ܐܘ ܗܠܝܢ ܐܚܪܢܝܬܐ ܕܐܝܟ ܗܟܢ. ܐܡܪܐ ܕܒܗܘܢ
ܦܪܝܫ: ܡܢ ܫܘܚܠܦܐ ܗܠܝܢ ܕܐܬܟܢܫܝܢ: ܬܪܝܢ. ܬܠܬܐ.
ܐܪܒܥܐ. ܚܡܫܐ. ܫܬܐ. ܘܡܢ ܟܠܗܘܢ ܗܠܝܢ ܕܙܘܓܐ ܘܦܪܕܐ:
ܢܗܘܐ ܦܪܝܫ ܒܬܘܟܡܐ[4] ܥܕܡܐ ܠܡܬܚܫܒܢܘܬܐ: ܡܢ
ܡܠܬܐ ܗܝ ܕܐܡܪܐ ܡܬܚܫܒܢܐ ܐܝܟܢܐ: ܘܗܠܝܢ ܐܚܪܢܝܬܐ
ܕܐܦܝ ܠܗ ܒܡܢܝܢ ܡܠܐ. ܬܪܝܢ. ܬܠܬܐ. ܐܪܒܥܐ. ܚܡܫܐ.

---

[1] ܒ. ܡܢܝܢ ܦܠܓ.
[2] ܒ. ܐܡܪܐ.
[3] ܒ. ܘܠܗܘܢ.
[4] ܒ. ܒܡܬܚܫܒܢܘܬܐ.

ܗ ܐܬܪܘܬܐ ܕܟܬܒ̇ ܘܡܫܡܫ ܡܛܠ ܣܪܓܠܐ ܫܘܪܝܐ

ܘܪ̈ܘܡܝܐ. ܠܐ ܢܬܬܟܝܢ ܥܠܝܡ̈ܝܢ ܐܝܟ ܒܢܝܫܘܥ.
ܣܠܩ ܥܘܠܡܝܢ ܕܠܝ. ܡܬܒܪ ܢܣܒ ܐܝܢܐ ܟܢܝܗ
ܕܚܬܡܬܐ. ܠܐ ܢܗܘܝܢ [β] ܠ ܒܪܝܬܐ ܕܠܐ ܐܝܬ ܒܗ
ܗܘ ܕܠܝ ܒܪܝܬܐ ܗܘ ܕܡܦܬܟ ܐܢܫܐ. ܘܐܦܠܐ ܚܙܝܐ
ܕܪܥܝܐ ܐܘ ܕܪܥܝܢܘܬܐ: ܐܘ ܕܡܠܟܘܬ ܒܢܬܐ ܩܠܐ ܕܡܢ
ܚܙܝܐ ܗܝܢܐ ܕܪܥܝܐ ܥܩܝܠ: ܢܬܬܟܝܢ ܕܠܐ ܗܘܕ. ܠܐ
ܢܬܠܘܢ ܒܝܫܬܝܢ ܠܝ ܡܢ ܒܚܙܝܐ ܗܘ ܕܪ̈ܘܡܝܐ: ܐܘ
ܒܗܘ ܕܪܘܡܢ ܡܬܢܣܒܐ ܕܠܐܗܘܢ. ܐܘ ܒܗܘ ܕܗܘܐ ܕܗܘܦ
ܐܘ ܒܗܘ ܕܦܐܪ̈ܪܝܬܐ: ܐܘ ܒܐܘܪ̈ܝܐ ܕܐܝܟ
ܗܡ: ܡܛܠ ܡܬܚܫܒܢܘܬܐ ܒܬܘܟܬܐ ܀ ܠܐ ܢܬܬܟܝܢ
ܗܘ ܕܡܢ ܕܦܪܝܫ ܘܐܝܟܢܐ ܡܢܗܝܢܝܢܐ ܕܪܘܚܐ ܡܢܗܘܢ:
ܐܢܫܝܐ ܒܪܚܡܬܐ ܗܘ ܗܝܕܝܢ ܕܐܝܟ ܘܡܬܚܫܒ
ܒܬܪ ܡܠܐ ܘܐܝܟܢܐ ܘܢܬܚܘܢ ܕܗܘ ܦܪܝܫ ܟܠܐ ܢܗܘܝܢ
ܠܟܠ ܡܢܗ. ܗܘ ܕܝܢ ܕܐܝܟܝܢ [γ] ܘܡܫܘܚܬ ܘܐܝܟܐ ܘܠܐ
ܟܠ ܟܠܗ. ܠܐ ܢܬܚܫܒܢ ܒܟܠ ܕܗܘܝܢ ܠܒܪܬ ܡܠܐ ܗܘ
ܕܐܢܫܝܐ. ܐܠܐ ܢܬܚܘܢ ܐܢܫܐ ܦܬܓܡܢ ܐܢܫܝܐ
ܕܐܝܟܝܢ: ܘܐܢܫܐ ܦܬܓܡܢ ܐܝܟ ܚܙܐ ܕܦܪܝܫ.
ܢܬܚܘܢ ܐܢܫܐ ܦܬܓܡܢ ܐܚܪܢܐ ܕܐܝܟܝܢ: ܘܐܢܫܐ
ܦܬܓܡܢ ܐܦ: ܘܠܐ ܢܬܚܘܢ ܠܗ ܒܗ ܗܘ ܕܒܬܪܬܢܝܬܐ
ܦܬܓܡܗ. ܠܐ ܢܬܚܫܒܢ. ܟܠ. ܡܫܬܪܬܪܦܐ: ܘܡܬܚܠܦ
ܕܡܫܢܝܢ ܒܗ ܡܫܢܝܢ [δ] ܕܡܠܠܬܐ. ܡܛܠ ܕܐܬܪܬܦܣܐ ܐܝܟܢܐ

[β] ܒ. ܡܫܡܫܢ ܠܗ. [γ] ܒ. ܡܟܦܘܪܝܐ.
[δ] ܒ. ܕܗܘܐ ܡܠܠܬܐ.

ܒܡܬܒܘܬܐ ܛܘܒܢܐܝܬ ܠܗܘܢ ܕܦܪܝܩܝܢ. ܐܦ [ω] ܝܗܘܒܐ
ܕܢܛܘܪܘܣ ܗܘܡܝܐ ܕܥܠܡ ܡܘܬܪܬܐ: ܠܒܪ ܡܢ
ܢܦܫܗܘܢ ܕܡܬܘܬܒܐ. ܠܗܝ ܕܝܠܗ ܕܗܘܝܘܢ ܡܦܩܢ ܗܘ ܘܠܐ
ܡܟܝܡ ܠܗ. ܡܛܠ ܕܡܢ ܕܢܬܝܗܒ ܠܗܘܢ ܢܩܫܐ ܕܥܠܡ
ܕܐܬܓܪܝ: ܗܐ ܦܩܚܡ ܝܗܒܐ ܠܗܘܢ ܥܠܠ ܘܡܘܗܪܐ:
ܠܘܬ ܗܝ ܕܝܐܬܝܐܘܢ ܕܢܫܐ ܗܘ ܕܥܠܡ ܡܬܬܪܐܡܬ ܐܦ
ܬܘܩܦܐ ܕܢܦܫܗܘܢ ܗܢܘ ܕܥܠܡܘܢ ܒܗ ܢܦܩܝܢ ܕܦܓܪܐ
ܗܝ ܦܘܪܫ ܕܢܣܒܐ ܢܩܫ ܗܘܪܬܐ ܒܬܪܐܝܬ ܐܘ ܣܓܝܐܝܬ.
ܐܘ ܕܢܗܘܐ ܡܢܢ ܕܡܬܚܢܢ ܠܗܘܢܐ ܘܦܪܣ ܠܗܘܢܥܠܐ.
ܘܡܬܡܠܝܐܬ ܡܦܪܢܣ ܝܗܒ ܠܗܘܢ ܠܥܠܡܘܢ ܐܝܠܝܢ
ܕܒܘܟܝܢ ܒܬܪܬܐ ܗܠܝܢ ܕܦܪܫܢܝܬ ܘܡܝܬܝܬ: ܕܠܐ ܢܦܠܓܘܢ
ܡܢ ܚܢܝܢܘܬܗܘܢ ܒܟܡܐ ܡܟܡܐ ܡܢ ܐܝܠܝܢ ܕܡܬܟܢܫܝܢ [α] ܗܘܘ
ܠܦܘܬܓܒ. ܠܐ ܒܦܘܪܫܢܝܬ ܘܠܐ ܒܢܘܡܘܣܐ. ܒܟܡܐ
ܕܦܘܪܫܢܝܢ ܝܗܒܝܢ [β] ܕܠܡܟܐ ܦܘܪܐ ܡܪܝܫܐ ܢܬܒܥܘܢ: ܡܛܠ
ܕܥܠ ܒܪ ܐܢܫܐ ܦܓܪܐ: ܐܘ ܕܥܠ ܐܘ ܕܒܬܘܠܬܐ. ܗܘ
ܕܦܘܠܓ ܡܢܝܢ: ܐܘ ܕܗܘܢܐ ܕܦܪܘܫܘ: ܐܘ ܕܒܝܫܐ
ܕܦܪܘܫܐ ܕܬܪܝܨܬ ܘܦܪܝܫܬ ܡܢ ܣܘܓܐܐ ܛܘܒܢܐ: ܒܬܪܝܨ
ܕܠܐ ܢܦܘܫܘܢ ܢܦܠܘܢ ܚܝܝܢ ܠܫܘܬܦܘܬܐ ܗܠܝܢ
ܕܡܫܡܫܝܢ ܡܢ ܥܡܘܕܐ ܘܡܢ ܟܠܗܝܢ ܘܠܐ ܡܢ ܩܘܪܒܢܐ
ܐܣܝܘܬܐ ܕܡܠܠܬܐ: ܐܠܐ ܐܝܟ ܡܢ ܠܘܬ ܒܝܬܐ
ܐܬܘܗܝ ܥܡܗܘܢ ܥܕܡܐ. ܘܐܒܠܐ ܐܝܟ ܡܢ ܠܘܬ ܡܠܟܐ

[ω] ܒ. ܠܗܘܐ. [α] ܒ. ܗܘܘ ܗܘܝܢ ܡܛܠ ܗܘܘ.
[β] ܒ. ܐܠܐ ܐܢ ܡܛܠ ܐܢ.

ܕ. ܐܓܪܬܐ ܕܡܪܝ ܝܥܩܘܒ ܡܛܠ ܣܘܪܛܐ ܣܘܪܝܝܐ

ܒܡܘܠܐ ܐܠܦ ܡܢ ܣܦܪ̈ܐ: ܘܐܦ ܗܘܐ ܕܢܗܘܘܢ
ܐܬܬܣܝܡܘܢ ܗܘܘ: ܘܠܐ ܡܢ ܗܢܘܢ ܕܐܝܟ ܕܗܘ
ܐܬܬܣܝܡܘܢ. ܐܠܐ ܫܪܐ ܐܢܫܐ ܕܒܗ ܡܬܬܠܡܕܢܐ ܬܘܒ
ܦܠܓ ܐܦ ܗܪܟܐ. ܗܢܘܢ ܕܦܠܓ ܚܝܢܢ ܡܢ ܐܣܝܢܐ.
ܦܫܝܩܐܝܬ ܐܝܟ ܕܒܡܫܟܚܐ ܒܗܘܠܐ ܘܡܣܪܗܒܘܬܐ
ܚܝܠܬܐ: ܡܫܠܡ ܘܡܠܦ ܠܗ ܘܡܠܝܢ ܡܢܗ ܘܡܨܛܪܝܢ
ܠܬܒܐ: ܒܗ ܠܐ ܢܬܒܥܐ ܠܐ ܡܢܫܐ ܫܪܝܪ ܘܠܐ ܡܢܫܐ
ܬܬܒܥ. ܠܗܠܝܢ ܡܠܐ ܒܗ ܦܪܩ ܬܬܒܥܐ. ܠܐ ܗܘܐ
ܠܘܬ ܗܘ ܕܗܘܘ ܢܣܒܠܘܢ ܢܬܬܠܘܢ. ܐܠܐ ܠܘܬ ܗܘ
ܕܢܣܒܠܘܢ ܣܘܣܝܐܬ ܘܢܬܠܘܢ. ܘܢܬܬܪܝܘܢ:
ܢܬܦܪܣܘܢ ܠܒܝܬܐ ܣܘܟܠܐܝܬ ܘܦܪܘܫܐܝܬ.
ܘܢܪܒܘܢ ܕܡܫܟܚܢܘܬܐ ܢܕܒܪܝܢ ܒܐܘܡܢܘܬܐ ܗܕܐ
ܕܟܬܒܘܬܐ: ܣܝܡ ܗܢܘܢ ܕܦܪܫܢ: ܡܠܝܢ ܡܢ ܗܢܘܢ
ܕܬܒܥܝܢ. ܗܢܘܢ ܟܡ ܚܝܢ: ܢܦܩܝܢ ܕܢܬܠܘܢ ܡܫܝܚܐ
ܕܡܦܪܫܐ ܐܝܟ ܦܘܪܫܢ ܒܗ ܐܘ ܡܬܠܠܝܢ ܠܗܘܢ
ܠܦܘܪܫܢ ܐܘ ܡܡܟܝܢ ܠܗܝܢ ܠܬܘܬܒܘܬܐ ܕܬܒܥܬܐ.
ܐܘ ܡܦܪܫܝܢ ܐܘ ܡܒܪܝܢ. ܐܘ ܢܒܥܝܢ ܡܛܠ ܦܘܫܩܐ:
ܐܘ ܡܦܣܩܝܢ ܠܬܒܥܬܐ ܘܡܒܝܢܝܢ ܐܘ ܦܣܩܝܢ ܦܘܫܩܐ
ܠܒܪܝܢ. ܘܡܫܠܡܝܢ ܠܗ ܐܦܝܐ ܕܠܐ ܘܠܐ: ܐܘ ܢܒܥܝܢ ܬܪܝܢ
ܠܚܕ ܠܐ ܠܡܬܟܣܝܘ. ܣܝܡ ܕܝܢ ܗܢܘܢ ܕܦܪܫܢ ܢܣܒܝܢ
ܕܗܘܝܐ ܘܫܘܚܠܦܐ ܕܗܠܝܢ ܕܬܒܥܝܢ ܒܬܪܬܝܢ: ܘܒܫܘܬܦ

φ ܒ. ܡܫܡܗ ܠܐ. x ܒ. ܢܬܬܠܘܢ:

ψ ܒ. ܐܘ ܡܢ ܡܫܟܚ ܡܢ ܐܘ.

ܐܚܪܬܐ ܕܒܪܝ ܡܫܡܫ ܟܠܠ ܦܪܨܘܦܐ ܦܘܪܫܢܐ ܠ
ܠܦܘܡܐ ܘܠܦܠܚܘܬܐ ܘܠܡܕܪܐ : ܘܠܐܣܝܘܬܐ ܡ̈ܫܚܐ
ܕܣܝܦܐ: ܗܟܢ ܡܢ ܗ݁ܘ ܒܒܢܝܢܐ ܕܒܪܢܫܐ ܕܐܬܒܢܝ
ܘܐܬܒܣܣܡ ܒܗܘܢ ܟܠ ܟܒܝܫܘܬܐ ܐܝܟ ܠܒܢܝܢܐ:
ܐܦ ܟܠ ܟܠܗܘܢ ܐܘ̈ܡܢܘܬܐ. ܟܬ̈ܒܐ ܡܫܘ̈ܚܬܐ ܗܟܢ
ܡܢ ܦܓܪܐ. ܐܪ̈ܓܠܝܢ ܗܟܢ ܡܢ ܟܪ̈ܥܬܐ. ܦܩ̈ܠܐ
ܐܠܩ̈ܒܝ ܗܟܢ ܡܢ ܢܩ̈ܦܬܐ. ܐܨ̈ܒܥܬܐ ܗܟܢ ܡܢ ܗ݁ܘ
ܕܦܐܬ̈ܐ ܠܗܘܢ ܠܦܐ̈ܘܢܐ. ܘܪ̈ܓܠܝ ܗܟܢ ܡܢ ܗ݁ܘ
ܕܠܓܡܝܢ. ܠܐܘܡܢܘܬܐ [ܗ]ܕܝܢ ܙܟܝܬܐ ܘܡܠܝܠܬܐ
ܕܡܬܩܢܐ ܒܗܘܢܐ ܘܒܬܘܩܢܐ ܒܬܘܩܢܬܗ̇ ܗ݁ܘ
ܕܐܬܬܣܝܡ ܒܡܡܠܠܗ̇. ܗ̇ܘ ܕܝܢ ܡܬ̈ܩܢܐ ܗ݁ܘ
ܕܦܐܪ [ܘ]ܒܗܘܢ ܒܬܠܬܐ ܗ݁ܘ ܕܐܬܬܩܢܝ ܡܢܗ:
ܦܓܡ ܠܗ̇. ܣܘܬܐܝܬ. ܘܠܗܠܝܢ ܕܣܥ̈ܪܢ ܠܗ̇.
[ܙ]ܘܡܫ̈ܘܚܬܐ ܕܦܘܡ ܠܗ̇ ܘܠܬܘܪ̈ܓܡܝܗܘܢ : ܗܟܢ ܡܢܝܢܗܘܢ
ܕܠܗܘܢ ܕܒܬܘ̈ܟܐ ܗ݁ܘ ܕܡܫܬܟܠܝܢ ܠܗ̇ . ܠܐ
ܒܠܚܘܕܝܗ̇ ܕܩܝܡܝܢ ܒܟܠܗܘܢ ܐܘ̈ܡܢܘܬܐ: ܐܝܟ ܐܘܡܢܘܬܐ
ܗܕܐ. ܠܐ ܐܚܪܢܐ ܕܬ̈ܪܝܢ ܐܢܫ ܕܐܬܬܩܢܘܗܝ. ܘܐܦܠܐ
ܕܣܘܦܪܢܐ [ܚ]ܐܚܪܢܐ ܚܕܐ. ܕܗܘ ܗܘܐ ܒܪ ܕܐܢܫܐ
ܕܗ̇ܝ ܐܘܡܢܘܬܐ ܪܒܬܐ ܘܡܫܡܠܝܢܘܬܐ ܘܡܫܟܚܢܘܬܐ ܕܟܠܗܘܢ
ܐܘ̈ܡܢܘܬܐ ܐܝܬܝܗ̇: [ܛ]ܐܦ ܫܘܡܠܝܗ̇ ܗܟܢ ܡܢܝܢܗ̇
ܙܢܐ ܡܢ ܟܠܗܘܢ ܫܥ̈ܝܬܐ. [ܝ]ܗܟܢܐ ܐܦ ܗ݁ܘ ܕܢܠܩܝܡ
ܠܗ̇ ܘܓܠܣ̈ܡ ܟܠܗ̇: ܡܢ ܗ݁ܘ ܕܙܕܩ ܘܣܓܝ ܘܡܬܚܪܝܡ

[ܗ] ܒ. ܕܝܢ ܗܘܐ ܣܠܩ ܕܝܢ. [ܘ] ܒ. ܡܫܡܫ ܒܗܘܢ.
[ܙ] ܒ. ܘܠܡܫܘܚܬܐ. [ܚ] ܒ. ܓܒܪܐ.
[ܛ] ܒ. ܘܐܦ. [ܝ] ܒ. ܕܐܦ ܣܠܩ ܗܘܐ ܐܦ.

ܒ ܐܓܪܬܐ ܕܡܪܝ ܝܥܩܘܒ ܕܒܛܢܢ ܣܪܘܓܝܐ ܣܘܪܝܝܐ

ܕܠܡܓܠܐ ܠܗܠܝܢ ܡܪ̈ܒܝܬ ܠܗ̇ ܠܐ ܠܡܫܝܚܐܝܬ : ܕܗ̇ܠܝܢ
ܕܓܬܥܣܝܢ ܒܥܘܡܠܢܝܗ̇ : ܗ̇ܠܝܢ ܢܣܒܢ ܠܗ̇ ܚܘܬܡܝܗ̇ .
ܘܡܥܡܠܢܝܬܗ̇ : ܘܠܬܫܒ̈ܚܬܗ̇ ܘܠܬܘܪ̈ܓܡܐ ܕܗܠܝܢ .
ܘܠܙܟܘܬܐ ܕܟܠܗܘܢ ܕܣܒܥܝܢ ܠܦܘܩ̈ܕܢܝܗ̇ . ܡܛܠ ܕܝܢ ܐܘܢܓܠܝܐ
ܕܝܠܗ̇ : ܗܠܝܢ ܕܡܫܬܠܡܢ ܘܡܩܒܠܢ ܠܗ̇ . ܕܐܝܟ ܐܡܪ .
ܐܚܪܢ ܐܝܬ . ܡܢ ܗܠܝܢ ܕܚܙܝܢ ܐܝܬܝܗ̇ ܕܐܚܪܢ
ܐܫܬܘܕܝܘ . ܒܠܚܘܕ ܗܠܝܢ ܕܠܗܠܝܢ ܦܪܝܫ ܐܝܬܝܗܝܢ .
ܠܐܘܡܢܘܬܗ̇ ܗ̇ܝ ܕܢܟܪܘܬܐ ܬܓܪ̈ܐ ܗܠܝܢ ܕܡܫܬܠܡܢ ܠܗ̇ :
ܢܣܒܢ ܠܗ̇ ܘܡܚܦܝܢ ܒܟ̈ܘܪܐ ܘܒܟܘܡܪ̈ܐ ܗ̇ܠܝܢ ܕܗܘܘ
ܟܗ̇ ܘܫܓܝܫܝܢ ܠܟܬܒ̈ܝܗ ܐܝܟ . ܡܛܠ ܕܝܢ ܗ̇ܠܝܢ
ܕܓܬܥܣܝܢ ܒܥܘܡܠܢܐ ܕܠܗ̇ . ܒܓܙܪ̈ܬܐ ܐܚܪܢ ܐܝܠܝܢ
ܐܘ ܒܓܒܘܪܬܐ ܐܘ ܒܡܣܟܢܘܬܐ ܐܘ ܒܡܘܪܢܐ : ܐܘ
ܒܐܣܝܪ̈ܘܬܐ ܫܥܒܕܐ ܡܢ ܗܠܝܢ ܕܡ̈ܢܗܘܢ ܬܫܬܘܡܫ . ܘܗ
ܡܛܠ ܕܐܦ ܥܠ ܡ̈ܣܟܢܘܬܐ ܐܝܬ ܠܓܝܣܐ : ܘܐܦ ܥܠ
ܡܘܡܝܬܐ . ܗ̇ܠܝܢ ܡ̈ܠܝܐ ܫܓܝܫܝܢ ܠܒܝܬܐ ܐܝܠܝܢ
ܠܡܝ̈ܬܐ ܕܦܪܘܩܐ : ܠܡܥܒܕ ܦܘܪܫܢܐ ܐܚܪܢ ܐܝܬ ܘܠܡܪܢܐ
ܘܠܢܓܪܐ ܘܠܡܛܠܬܐ : ܡܛܠ ܕܝܢ ܗ̇ܠܝܢ ܕܓܬܥܣܝܢ
ܒܗܘܢ . ܘܐܦ ܡܩܝܡܐ ܐܘܡܢܘܬ ܦܘܪ̈ܫܢܐ ܢܣܒܢ
ܠܟܘܪ̈ܗܢܐ ܐܝܟ ܠܡܫܝܚܐܝܬ . ܘܦܓܥ ܥܒܕ ܫܟܝܢܘܬ :

ܒ. ܘܟܪ̈ܝܗܐ ܕܚܠܝܢ ܠܡܠܟܐ. ܒ. ܕܝܢ.
ܒ. ܕܝܢ. ܒ. ܐܝܬ ܐܦ ܥܠ ܡܣܟܢܘܬܐ.
ܒ. ܡܘܡܝܬܐ. ܒ. ܫܓܝܫ ܐܢܘܢ.
ܒ. ܘܡܛܠܬܐ. ܒ. ܫܟܝܢܘܬ.

ܐܓܪܬܐ ܕܡܪܝ ܝܥܩܘܒ ܡܛܠ ܣܪܛܐ ܣܘܪܝܝܐ.

ܐܓܪܬܐ ܕܫܕܪ ܘܟܬܒ ܒܐܠܗܘܬܐ ܡܪܝ، ܝܥܩܘܒ
ܐܦܝܣܩܘܦܐ ܕܐܘܪܗܝ، ܠܘܬ ܩܕܝܫܐ ܘܡܫܒܚܐ ܡܪܝ،
ܓܘܪܓܝ ܐܦܝܣܩܘܦܐ ܕܣܪܘܓ ܘܒܐܬܪܘܬܗ؛ ܠܟܠܗܘܢ
ܟܬܘܒܐ: ܐܝܠܝܢ ܕܒܟܬܒܐ ܗܢܐ ܟܬܝܒܢ ܠܩܦܠܐ.
ܠܚܒܝܒܐ ܘܡܚܒܒܐ ܡܢ ܐܠܗܐ ܐܚܘܢ ܪܘܚܢܐ: ܫܠܡܐ
ܒܡܫܝܚܐ ܘܡܬܒܣܡܬܐ ܐܪܚܡܬ ܡܪܝ، ܓܘܪܓܝ
ܐܢܐ ܒܥܘܬ ܡܟܬܒܢܘܬܐ ܒܫܘܪܝܐ ܠܟܬܒܐ ܀ ܠܐ ܒܠܚܘܕܝܢ
ܘܒܝܪܐ ܫܡܥܬ ܕܐܝܬܘܗܝ، ܗܢܐ ܐܘ ܐܢܫ ܐܠܗܐ:
ܕܬܗ ܒܝܢܐ ܒܪ ܕܐܢܫܘܗ ܠܝ: [β] ܠܗ، ܕܫܡܥܬ: ܘܒܐܝܕܝܟ
ܐܦ ܠܡܟܬܒܢܐ ܐܚܪܢܐ ܕܟܬܒܝܢ ܒܟܬܒܬܐ ܗܕܐ:
ܕܟܠܗܘܢ ܗܢ ܐܘܪܚܬܐ ܗܠܝܢ ܕܐܝܬ ܠܡܫܘܚܬܐ ܕܟܠ
ܐܢܫ ܒܫܢܝܐ ܗܠܝܢ: ܐܘܪܚܬܐ ܕܠܗܘܢ ܗܢܘ ܒܝܬ
ܟܬܒܝܗܘܢ [γ] ܘܡܫܠܡܢܘܬܗܘܢ: ܗܢܘ ܕܝܢ ܠܗܘܢ: ܐܠܐ
ܡܢ ܗܠܝܢ ܕܡܬܚܫܒܝܢ [δ] ܒܗܘܢ ܒܡܘܠܦܢܘܬܗܘܢ.
ܐܘܡܢܘܬܐ ܕܝܢ ܗܕܐ [ε] ܪܒܬܐ ܘܡܝܬܪܬܐ: ܘܡܠܦܢܘܬܐ
ܐܝܟ [ζ] ܕܡܦܪ ܐܢܐ ܠܟܠ ܡܢ ܟܠܗܘܢ ܐܘܡܢܘܬܐ: ܗܝ

[α] ܢܘܣܚܐ ܒ. ܓܘܪܓܝܣ.
[β] ܢܘܣܚܐ ܒ. ܗܘܝ.
[γ] ܒ. ܘܡܬܟܬܒܢܝܢ.
[δ] ܒܗܘܢ.
[ε] ܒ. ܪܒܬܐ ܒܗܕܐ ܡܝܬܪܬܐ.
[ζ] ܒ. ܕܐܢܐ ܡܦܪ ܐܢܐ.

B

LONDON:
PRINTED BY W. M. WATTS, GRAY'S-INN ROAD;
AND WHITEFRIARS STREET, CITY.

ܐܓܪܬܐ

ܕܡܪܝ ܝܥܩܘܒ ܐܦܝܣܩܘܦܐ ܕܐܘܪܗܝ

ܡܛܠ ܣܪܛܐ ܣܘܪܝܝܐ:

ܐܦ

ܣܝܡܐ ܕܝܠܗ ܚܕ ܕܝܠܗ

ܘܡܐܡܪܐ ܕܓܪܝܓܘܪܝܘܣ ܒܪ ܥܒܪܝܐ

ܡܛܠ ܢܘ̈ܩܙܐ ܣܘܪܝܝܐ.

www.ingramcontent.com/pod-product-compliance
Lightning Source LLC
Chambersburg PA
CBHW030338170426
43202CB00010B/1166
* 9 7 8 3 3 3 7 0 1 8 9 6 2 *